COLLINS GEM
DICTIONARY OF
ENGLISH
USAGE

English Usage

Margot Butt
BA Hons (London)

Collins

London and Glasgow

General Editor
W. T. McLeod

First Published 1970
Latest Reprint 1976

ISBN 0 00 458750 2

© **William Collins Sons & Co. Ltd. 1970**

Printed in Great Britain by
Collins Clear-Type Press

INDEX OF USEFUL POINTS
OF REFERENCE

APPENDICES:

FOREWORD

Every language is in a continuous state of change and enlargement, and any dictionary is likely to be in some respects out of date by the time it is published. This was never more true than at the moment, when easier travel and technical advances in communication make people in areas where radio and television are available aware of what other people all over the world are doing, and conscious of at least some of the terms used to describe these activities. Nevertheless, we are far from achieving a world language, and even find difficulty sometimes in conveying what we want to say to our own fellow-countrymen. Words can form barriers as well as promote understanding.

There are many group languages in modern English. Apart from local dialects, there are the specialized vocabularies of scientists, administrators and teenagers, for example, which are often incomprehensible to others. This book does not attempt to throw light on these group words, but to help writers of books, articles, reports and letters to express themselves clearly and according to current practice, to use words as they are generally understood amongst those who will be reading them. Sometimes this involves reference to their origin or former meaning.

We have thus tried to indicate that where usage is changing it is advisable to use the older sense in formal writing, while the newer, looser meaning may be acceptable in conversation. Where we regard a particular use as incorrect and inexact, it is put inside square brackets. This marking does not necessarily recommend instant banishment from the whole domain of the English language. Meaning depends to a large extent upon its context and much that defies the rules of grammar and takes a cavalier approach to vocabulary will nonetheless be understood by a number of people. However, a language is used most efficiently when it is understood by the greatest number of its users. The words which we place inside [ ] are thus stigmatized and not recommended for use in formal writing. If they are used elsewhere, it should be with care and comprehension.

Grammatical rules and definitions have been kept to a minimum, for we regard grammatical correctness as an expression of logical thinking rather than as an end in itself.

Among the words and expressions included in this book are many which cause difficulty and confusion. Where there are grammatical idiosyncrasies, it has been our aim to explain and demonstrate the correct usage with reference to other words which operate in the language in a similar way. It is for this purpose that cf. has been used throughout: for example in the entry for **else** (where it is shown as being followed by *than* and not *but*) an analogy is made with *other* and *more*, both of which could be substituted for *else* in the example given.

Cross-references are used extensively in order to keep most of the entries short. The larger entries (see Index), written in the form of small essays or as clusters of information arranged under sub-headings, serve as focal points for cross-references and should be consulted for a wide view of some aspects of the English language, or for basic rules and definitions.

Malapropisms, resulting from similarities of either spelling or pronunciation, are dealt with in pairs or trios. This method, whilst running the risk of infecting the reader's mind with a blight from which he was previously immune, is the only practicable way of showing confusing words operating in distinctive contexts. In addition, differences of pronunciation may be highlighted by placing the transcriptions side by side and saying them out loud.

The pronunciation guides, or transcriptions,

are in the alphabet of the International Phonetic Association, commonly known as I.P.A. (see p. xiv). They are used either to elucidate and distinguish similarities in the pronunciation of two or more words or to give guidance on how to say words which are commonly mispronounced. They also give guidance on words which, often due to their fairly recent adoption from another language, are more frequently read than spoken.

We hope that the Appendices will be of use to readers as well as writers. The list of abbreviations and foreign words and phrases is intended as a basic coverage of what is an ever-expanding category. Though we generally fight shy of including innumerable professional associations and clubs, we hope to have included the abbreviations and foreign borrowings which are most commonly found in non-specialist reading-matter. The list of American words and phrases has been compiled mainly to assist anyone reading American magazines or novels. The other appendices cover language uses which are often employed solely to impress, but, since they are sometimes used, it is as well that they should be used accurately.

BIBLIOGRAPHY

The following are among the books which have been consulted whilst compiling this work and they will be found useful for further reference:

All the Oxford English Dictionaries, of which the most recently revised is *The Pocket Oxford Dictionary* (1969);

The Penguin English Dictionary (1965);

The Advanced Learner's Dictionary of Current English (1958);

The Encyclopaedia Britannica (1960);

A Dictionary of Modern English Usage by H. W. Fowler (revised 1965 by Sir Ernest Gowers);

Modern American Usage by Wilson Follett (1966);

The Complete Plain Words by Sir Ernest Gowers 1962);

Modern Business Correspondence by L. Gartside (1963);

Hart's Rules for Compositors and Readers at The University Press, Oxford (1967).

THE INTERNATIONAL PHONETIC ALPHABET

A simplified version of I.P.A. is used in this book in order to give a broad idea of a word's pronunciation without having to take into account regional variations in speech. The reader should be able to make himself quickly acquainted with this method of transcribing pronunciation if he realises that each symbol represents one sound only. The consonant symbols p, b, t, d, k, m, n, l, r, f, v, s, z, h, w, represent the sounds they usually elicit from a reader when placed first in an English word, i.e. *p*ie, *b*uy, *t*ie, *d*ie, *k*ite, *m*y, *n*igh, *l*ie, *r*ye, *f*ly, *v*ie, *s*igh, *Z*ion, *h*igh, *w*hy.

The following consonant symbols may be unfamiliar, although the sounds they represent are almost as common in Standard English as those listed above:

g	*g*ay	ð	*th*is
tʃ	*ch*ain	ʃ	*sh*ame
dʒ	*j*ail	ʒ	plea*s*ure
ŋ	ri*ng*		*y*earn
θ	*th*ick		

Vowels and diphthongs are represented by the following symbols. The sign : distinguishes a long vowel sound from a short one, representing a change in sound quality as well as quantity.

i:	seat	ə:	nerve
i	sit	ə	butter
e	get	ei	say
æ	cat	ou	so
ɑ:	farm	ai	fry
ɔ	cot	au	cow
ɔ:	caught	ɔi	toy
u	soot	iə	fear
u:	suit	ɛə	fair
ʌ	cup	uə	gourd

Each word of more than one syllable has a stress mark (') denoting that the main stress in the word falls on the syllable following this mark. In monosyllabic words no stress is marked, e.g. bluebell ('blu:bel) but blue bell (blu: bel).

ABBREVIATIONS USED
IN THIS DICTIONARY

Note: The grammatical labels attached to headwords of entries refer only to the part of speech which is discussed in the entry. For example, **advance** is followed only by the label *n.* and not by *v.* or *adj.*, since the entry treats of *advance* only in its noun function.

adj.	adjective
adv.	adverb
cf.	compare
comp.	comparative (of adjective or adverb)
conj.	conjunction
e.g.	for example
interj.	interjection
n.	noun
past part.	past participle (of verb)
past t.	past tense (of verb)
phr.	phrase
prep.	preposition
pres. part.	present participle (of verb)
pro.	pronoun
q.v.	see also
v.	verb

(see also the LIST OF ABBREVIATIONS)

A

a, an *indefinite article*

An is used instead of *a* before nouns and
adjectives beginning with a vowel or silent *h*,
e.g. *an egg*: *an hour*, except where the vowel
is sounded as if it had a consonant before it,
e.g. *a one*: *a utility*. *An hotel* is old-fashioned and
survives from the days when hotel was pronounced in the French way with a silent *h*.
Hors d'œuvre, still pronounced as in French,
has *an*. Where the indefinite article is followed
by an abbreviation in the form of letters, the
form follows the sound of the letter rather
than the word it represents, e.g. *an FBA*, but
where the full word is usually spoken *a* is
used, e.g. *a MS* (a 'mænjuskript) rather than
[*an MS*]. Though *a* and *an* usually come
before the adjective in a sentence, they come
after it in cases like *such a one*; *too hot a fire*;
how cold a night it is!; *many a game we had
together*. Where there is a sense of comparison
the article is either put before the adjective or
omitted, e.g. *I never saw a more vivid sunset*.

a-, an- *prefix*

This prefix means 'not' or 'without', e.g.
amoral.

1

abbreviations see PUNCTUATION, FULL STOPS;
  APPENDIX
abide *v.*
  When it means 'stay', 'remain', *abide* has the
  past tense and past participle *abode*. *Abide by*,
  meaning 'remain true to', has the past tense
  abided, e.g. *He abided by his word.* Its negative
  form sometimes means 'endure', 'tolerate',
  e.g. *I cannot abide the place* (cf. *I cannot abide in
  the place*).
abjure, adjure *v.*
  These verbs are sometimes confused. To *abjure* is to 'renounce an oath' or 'recant an
  opinion', e.g. *They will have to abjure Com-
  munism before they can join our party.* To *adjure* is
  to 'make a solemn appeal', e.g. *His friends
  adjured him to think carefully before taking this
  step.*
-able, -eable, -ible see SPELLING, ADJECTIVES
abolishment, abolition, abolitionist *n.*
  The first two nouns describe the 'bringing to
  an end' of something especially a law or a
  state of affairs, e.g. *He did not live to see the
  abolition of capital punishment.* The second of
  these is more commonly used than the first.
  An *abolitionist* was a person who believed in
  or worked for the abolition of slavery.
aboriginal *adj. n.*
  The adjective means 'native to a country' and

is used of its inhabitants, plants or animals. The noun denotes 'an original, pre-colonial inhabitant', e.g. *an Australian aboriginal*, and has the plural *aborigines*.

about see AROUND

absolutes

A term used to describe words like *almighty, unique, best, maximum, minimum*, which should not be qualified by an adverb. (see SO)

abstract *adj. n. v.*

As an adjective pronounced ('æbstrækt), it means 'separated from practical reality', the opposite of *concrete*, e.g. *His plans were too abstract to be put into operation.* As a noun, it has the same pronunciation and means 'a summary' of a document or a situation, e.g. *He read through the papers and made an abstract of their contents.* The verb is pronounced (æb'strækt), and means 'withdraw', 'separate from', 'take out', e.g. *One can abstract iron filings from sand by passing a powerful magnet over the mixture,* or *His mind was wholly abstracted by thoughts of other things.*

academic, academical *adj.* **academical, —s, academician** *n.*

The adjective *academic*, meaning 'scholarly' or 'pertaining to a learned institution', can apply to learning (*an academic discipline*), the nature of an argument, or treatment of a subject (*an academic approach to pop music*). It is also used in a derogatory sense to mean 'unpractical' or 'remote', e.g. *The question of freedom of speech is only an academic one under a dictatorship.*

In Scotland an *academical* is a past pupil at an *academy* or secondary school, whereas in England the term *academician* is used to denote a member of an elected body of distinguished practitioners of a certain art or science. The noun *academicals* means 'academic dress'.

access, accession *n.*

Access means 'the act or means of approach', 'the coming on or attack' of illness or rage; *Accession* means 'coming into office or power', 'increase or addition'. *Access to the throne* means 'a possibility of approaching the sovereign'; *Accession to the throne* means 'the act of becoming sovereign'. (see EXCESS with which *access* is sometimes confused)

accessary, accessory, *adj. n.*

As adjectives they mean 'contributing' or 'subsidiary'. *Accessory* is now the more general spelling; as a noun it means 'a person participating in a crime (usually in a minor capacity)' or 'a helper' in any act.

accompany *v.*

Meaning 'be with' or 'go with', this verb is used with *by* for persons, *with* for things, e.g.

He was accompanied by his wife but *He accompanied his words with a bow.* In music it means 'play an instrument in support of a singer or solo player'. The noun is *accompanist*, formerly *accompanyist*.

accord *n.*

Confusion arises between *of one's own accord*, i.e. 'voluntarily', and *on one's own account*, i.e. 'independently'. *In accord* means 'in agreement', *in accordance* means 'following', e.g. *in accordance with instructions. With one accord* means 'unanimously'.

account *n. v.*

The noun is used in many ways with various meanings, e.g. *a bank account, give an account of* ('description or explanation'), *on no account* ('for no reason'), *on his account* ('for his sake') *turn to account* ('make use of'), *take no account of* ('no notice'). (see ACCORD). When the verb is followed by *for* it means 'explain satisfactorily', e.g. *He could not account for his absence from school.* In sport, *to account for* is to 'defeat' or 'overcome', e.g. *The British team accounted for their opponents by two goals to one.* When it means 'consider', the verb has no preposition after it, e.g. *He is accounted a promising politician.*

accountable *adj.*

In the sense of 'responsible', this word is only

5

used after a verb with a person as its subject, e.g. *He was not accountable for his actions* not [*His actions are accountable to his past*]. It would be better to say *His past is the cause of his present behaviour.*

acknowledge *v.*

Sometimes used for 'give proof of', e.g. *By his presence at the discussion he acknowledged his interest in the subject.*

acknowledg(e)ment see JUDG(E)MENT

acquaint *v.*

Usually followed by *with*, this verb is a formal substitute for 'tell' or 'inform', e.g. *I will acquaint you with the facts.* The use of *that* or *of* following the verb, or of the verb alone, is archaic.

acquiesce *v.*

This verb, which means 'agree', can be used alone or followed by *in*, e.g. *When I put the suggestion to him he acquiesced; He acquiesced in our plans.*

activate, actuate *v.*

Activate is a term used in physics and chemistry which has been taken into ordinary speech to mean 'inspire', 'cause to act'. *Actuate* is used in much the same way, but also has the more abstract meaning of 'motivate', e.g. *He was actuated by the highest motives.*

active voice see VERB

actual *adj.* **actually** *adv.*

Both these words are frequently used to little purpose in phrases such as *the actual fact is, is it actually true?* They are useful, especially in speech, as synonyms of *real, true, in fact, really,* e.g. *The actual course of events was very different from the story I was told at first; He did not actually witness the accident, but was on the scene a minute after it.*

acute see CHRONIC

adapt *v.* **adaptation** *n.*

The verb means 'make fit or suitable for a special purpose', e.g. *The house has been adapted to make flats; He has not yet adapted to the climate. Adaptation* is most commonly used for 'an altered version', e.g. *an adaptation for radio of the play by Ibsen.* It is sometimes confused with ADOPTION (q.v.)

adhere *v.*

This verb has the literal meaning of 'stick to', and figurative one of 'remain with, give allegiance to'. The noun *adhesion* is used for the literal meaning, especially in surgery and pathology. *Adhesiveness* is the quality of 'stickiness', *adherence* is figurative and means 'loyalty' or 'allegiance', often to an idea or a cause. An *adhesive* is 'something used to stick two things together', an *adherent* a 'follower' or 'supporter'.

7

adjacent, contiguous (kən'tigjuəs) *adj.*

Adjacent means 'lying near', not necessarily touching. *Contiguous* has a narrower meaning of 'touching', 'being next to'. Spain is both *contiguous* and *adjacent* to Portugal, but *contiguous* would not be used in a sentence like *A loud crash was heard in an adjacent room.*

adjective

'A word which enlarges the meaning of a noun or pronoun', especially as to quality or quantity, e.g. *a red rose, a difficult journey, many people, his third attempt, the longest one, poor you!* It can also be used to demonstrate something (*this way to the beach,* those *people who came late*), or to ask questions (Which *day is he coming?*) and to indicate possession (*It is his coat*). The possessive adjectives are *my, his, her, one's, its* (not *it's*), *our, your, their.* Unlike the *possessive pronouns* (*mine, his, hers, ours, yours, theirs*), they cannot stand alone without a noun, e.g. *It is our only hope* (adjective) *The pleasure is ours!* (pronoun).

Nouns are often made from adjectives and have a plural form which the adjective does not have, e.g. *Two female puppies* (adjective); *The two puppies are females* (noun).

Adjectives can be used as nouns in abstract words like *the unknown, the open, the obvious,* but where the sense is more specific or concrete

8

it is necessary to use *thing* or some equivalent after the adjectives, e.g. *He knows the best when he sees it* but *He always knows the best thing to do.* To avoid AMBIGUITY (q.v.) it is important to place adjectives next to the nouns to which they refer, e.g. to write *the architect's beautiful plans* rather than [*the beautiful architect's plans*]; *the doctor's empty house* rather than [*the empty doctor's house*]. (see SPELLING, ADJECTIVES for comparative forms; PREPOSITION)

adjure see ABJURE

admission, admittance *n.*

Admittance is now used only in a few phrases like *No admittance except on business. Admission* is used as a noun in all senses of ADMIT (q.v.)

admit *v.*

'Allow to enter', 'leave room for', 'allow'. Like *allow of, admit of* is only used with an impersonal or abstract subject, with the meaning 'leave room for', e.g. *The regulations admit of no exception. Admit to* is now becoming used for the answer to an accusation, but it adds nothing to *admit*: *He admitted his guilt* or *He admitted to having taken the money.*

adopt *v.* **adoption** *n.*

To *adopt* is to 'take over a child and bring it up as one's own,' or to 'use an idea or method or fashion', e.g. *He decided to adopt a new way of*

9

keeping the firm's accounts. Adoption has the same meanings, e.g. *the baby's adoption; his adoption of the Roman Catholic religion.* It is sometimes confused with ADAPTATION (q.v.)

adopted, adoptive *adj.*

A child can be *adopted* by his new parents, but parents are not *adopted* by the child, so the adjective *adoptive* is used for the meaning 'who adopt', where the new parent or parents, not the adopted child, are referred to, e.g. *She is the child's adoptive mother.*

advance, advancement *n.*

Advance means 'progress', 'forward motion', whereas *advancement* is 'action to forward advance, or personal promotion'. The *advance* of learning, science, progress, etc. is a general process, but one man's work can be for the *advancement of his subject.*

advantage, vantage *n.*

Both these nouns have the meaning of 'a superior position', but *advantage* is used more figuratively, e.g. *Age and experience gave him the advantage,* and *vantage* more in the physical sense, as in *vantage ground, point of vantage.* Either can be used in tennis for the point scored after deuce. (see USE)

adventurous, venturesome (adventuresome, venturous) *adj.*

The first two of these forms are more commonly used. *Adventurous*, which means 'daring, bold' or 'perilous', can be applied to a course of action as well as to a person; *venturesome* can only be applied to people.

adverb

'A word which expands the meaning of a verb, an adjective, or another adverb', e.g. *The boy ran* fast, *The day was* extremely *fine*; *The boy ran* fairly *fast*. Adverbs are often formed by adding -*ly* to an adjective (see SPELLING). There are others such as *after, in, up, since*, which can also be used as CONJUNCTIONS or PREPOSITIONS. In *I woke up early, up* is an adverb; in *He climbed up the ladder* it is a preposition. In *We had an argument last week, and I have not seen him since*, *since* is an adverb; in *Since our argument I have not seen him* it is a preposition, while in *I have not seen him since we had the argument* it is a conjunction.

There are adjectives which end in -*ly* such as *cowardly, leisurely, slovenly*. To avoid adding another -*ly* and producing a form like [*slovenlily*] it is usual to say *She dressed in a slovenly way*; *He acted in a cowardly manner*. In some cases there is a choice between using an adjectival or an adverbial form, especially when a participle follows. This can sometimes be decided by the sense, as in *I did not look at it close*, i.e. 'I was not close to it when I looked

11

at it', or *I did not look at it closely*, i.e. 'I did not give it a careful inspection'. Otherwise, the choice is governed by idiom, as in *a new-laid egg*, *a new-born child*, but a *newly-wed couple*; *hard-pressed* but *hardly-treated*. Adverbs should be placed as near as possible to the verb to avoid ambiguity (see SENTENCE). Some adverbs apply to the whole sentence, in which case they are marked off by commas, e.g. *He decided, nevertheless, to ignore the warning*; *It seemed better, however, to stay where we were*.

adverse ('ædvə:s), **averse** [ə'və:s] *adj.*
   Adverse means 'contrary' or 'unfavourable', and is used of conditions, circumstances, opinions, but not of people, e.g. *The expedition encountered adverse weather conditions. Averse* means 'opposed' or 'disinclined'. It is followed by *to* plus a noun or present participle, and is used of people, e.g. *I am not averse to hard work, but this is too much.*

advert (əd'və:t), **avert** (ə'və:t) *v.*
   Advert means 'turn to, refer to', e.g. *In his speech he continually adverted to the greatly increased birth rate throughout the world. Avert* means 'turn something away', e.g. *The danger was at last averted.*

advise see LICENSE

advocate *n. v.*
   As a noun this word means 'one who pleads a

12

case in a court of justice'. It is a technical title
in courts retaining Roman Law, for example
France and Scotland; but it is not generally
used in ordinary English law courts, the exceptions being Admiralty courts and special
tribunals. *Barrister* is the term in general use.

As a verb *advocate* means 'praise or recommend, often publicly'. It is followed by a noun
object rather than a noun clause, i.e. *He
advocated the use of force* rather than *He advocated that they should use force*.

aeroplane, aircraft *n.*

Plane is a recognized abbreviation of *aeroplane*, so there is no need to write it with an
apostrophe; *aircraft*, which is singular and
plural in meaning, is the term more generally
used in the RAF and civil airlines.

affect *v.* **affect, affectation, affection** *n.*
affected *adj.*

This verb has two sets of meanings:

1. to 'influence, have an effect on (*The new
railway timetable will not affect the Sunday train
services*), stir the emotions (*The news of her
sister's elopement affected her deeply*), attack with
disease.' The noun *affect* is used only in
psychology. *Affection* has two quite distinct
meanings: one as in *She had a great affection for
the town where she grew up*, the other, rarer use
as in *a throat affection*.

13

2. to 'assume, adopt, make a pretence of' (*He affected ignorance of the whole affair*). From these meanings come the adjective *affected* (*When she spoke of the Count, her son-in-law, she would adopt a very affected manner*) and the noun *affectation* (*He cultivated a slight lisp as an affectation*).

affinity *n.*

This noun is used for 'a similarity, an inclination or attraction, which is mutual, between two substances or persons', so it can only be followed by *between* or *with*. Sometimes it is loosely used with *to* or *for*, e.g. *She had an affinity for the colour red*, where *liking* would be a better word. In scientific language *affinity for* is recognised when one substance has a tendency to unite with another.

afflict *v.*

To 'torment; cause suffering'. This verb is most frequently used in the passive, followed by *with*, e.g. *He was afflicted with rheumatism.* (see INFLICT, with which it is confused)

African, Africander, Afrikaner *adj. n.*
Afrikaans *n.*

African refers to a native of Africa, but *Africander* (or *Afrikaner*) refers to a European settler in South Africa. *Afrikaans* is the language of the Africanders and is derived from Dutch.

after *prep.*

As well as having the usual sense of 'following in place or time', *after* can mean 'according to' or 'in imitation of', and is used in this way of painters and paintings. It is generally understood in this sense from statements like *This is a painting after Vermeer.* If the passing of time is to be indicated, the statement should be *This was painted after Vermeer's time.* (see BETWEEN)

aged *adj.*

This is pronounced ('eidʒid) in *an aged man*, but in *a boy aged five* it is (eidʒd).

agenda *n.*

A list of subjects to be discussed at a meeting. This is a Latin plural, used as a singular in English. Plural *agenda* or *agendas.*

aggravate *v.*

'Increase', 'make worse', the opposite of *alleviate.* Colloquially used, especially in the participle *aggravating*, to mean 'irritate, annoy', but this is not yet generally accepted.

agnostic, atheist *n.*

These terms are often confused, and loosely applied to any religious unbeliever. An *agnostic* is a person who believes that nothing can be known or proved as to the existence of God, whereas an *atheist* denies God's existence. (see SCEPTIC)

15

ago *adv.*

'In the past'. If a clause follows, it is introduced by *that*, e.g. *It was long ago that I first
saw her.* The use of *since* after *ago* is common
but repetitive, as they have parallel meanings.
It is five years ago since he died could be simplified to either *He died five years ago* or *It is five
years since he died.*

agrarian *n. adj.* **agriculturalist, agricultur-
ist** *n.* **agricultural** *adj.*

An *agrarian* is 'a person who is in favour of the
redistribution of land', and is quite distinct in
meaning from the other two nouns, the
second of which is becoming more popular.
An *agricultur(al)ist* is 'an expert in agriculture'; the word is often pedantically used
for 'farmer'. The adjective *agrarian* means
'having to do with land and its ownership'
(*agrarian laws, agrarian disputes*) and is also
used in Botany for 'plants which grow wild in
fields'. *Agricultural* means 'concerned with
agriculture' (*agricultural implements, agricultural labourers*).

agree *v.*

'Concur', 'consent', 'hold the same opinion'.
Followed by *with* in questions of opinion, by
to in cases of contract, e.g. *I agree with your
views on the subject* but *He agreed to the price that
was being asked.*

16

agricultural, agriculturalist see AGRARIAN

aim v.

In the transitive form, this verb means 'point' 'or direct', e.g. *to aim a weapon at a target*. In the intransitive form, it means 'attempt', 'plan to', often in a figurative sense, and is used with *at* and a present participle, e.g. *She aims at finishing her book next year*. In America it is followed by *to* with the infinitive, but this is colloquial in Britain.

ain't v.

Dialectal and colloquial abbreviation for *isn't, is not, are not, has not, haven't, have not*.

aircraft see AEROPLANE

akin adv.

A form of *of-kin*, meaning 'related', 'of the same type'. Followed by *to* rather than *with*.

alarm, alarum n.

The first form is the one generally used, the second appears only in poetry, in phrases such as 'alarums and excursions' and when describing a ringing mechanism on a clock, which can be pre-set.

ale n.

This drink is distinguished from beer in the brewer's trade, but not in common speech.

alias ('eiliəs) adv. n.

'Otherwise'. Used only of names, e.g. *Jack Dawkins, alias the Dodger*. As a noun, it means

'an assumed or false name'. Plural *aliases*.
(see PSEUDONYM)

alibi *n.*

In Law this word means 'a proof of absence
from the scene of a crime at the time it was
committed', but it is sometimes colloquially,
though inaccurately, used for 'an excuse for
not doing something'.

alien ('eiliən) *adj. n.* **alienable** *adj.* **alienation**
n. **alienist** *n.*

The adjective *alien* means 'foreign', 'strange'
or 'repugnant'. It is sometimes followed by
from, more often by *to*. As a noun, it means
'a foreigner, one not naturalized'. The
adjective *alienable* is used of property,
meaning that it is 'capable of being trans-
ferred to another owner'. *Alienation* can mean
either 'a form of mental disorder', 'estrange-
ment', or 'transference of property to another'.
An *alienist* is a specialist in mental illness.

all *adj. adv. n.*

This word is combined with others in three
different ways:

　　1. by using a single *l* and making one
word, e.g. *almighty, almost, already, altogether,
always.*

　　2. by keeping the double letter *ll* and using
a hyphen, e.g. *all-clear, All-Hallows, all-in, all-
night, all-round, all-star, all-time, all-white.*

3. by keeping the words separate with no hyphen, e.g. *all alone, all fours, all right, All Saints, all up. Altogether* has a different meaning from *all together*; it means 'entirely' or 'quite', e.g. *It was an altogether cloudless sky; Altogether they collected three hundred pounds* but *The family was sitting all together in one room.* Similarly *already* differs from *all ready*, e.g. *The equipment has already been collected* but *The equipment was all ready for their departure. All* is sometimes followed by *of*, e.g. *all of the eggs were speckled*, but this is unnecessary except where a pronoun follows, e.g. *all of us.*

-all *suffix*

Some compounds made with the suffix are: *be-all, end-all, holdall, know-all, overall.* Plurals are made by adding *s* at the end of the word, e.g. *know-alls* etc.

allegory ('æligəri) *n.* **allegorical** (ælə'gɔrikəl) *adj.* **parable** *n.*

An *allegory* is a story told in symbolical language, a kind of extended metaphor, whose object is to exemplify and enforce some moral truth. Very often it takes the form of a lengthy piece of personification, e.g. Bunyan's *Pilgrim's Progress.* The term can also be used of poetry and painting, e.g. Spenser's *Faerie Queene* and *The Scapegoat*, by Holman Hunt. A *parable* is a shorter form of allegory.

19

allergic (ə'lə:dʒik) *adj.* **allergy** ('ælədʒi) *n.*

These are medical terms used with reference to someone who is abnormally sensitive to a specified substance. They are colloquially used with the very much weaker meaning of 'having a dislike of something', e.g. *I am allergic to brass bands*. The term is used more formally in *She has an allergy to certain plants and develops a rash if she goes near them*.

alliteration

Repetition of the same sound or letter at the beginning of two or more words in the same sentence or line, e.g. *The wicked war-lord wound his weary way* or *A load of learning lumbering in his head*.

allow see ADMIT; ATTEMPT

all-powerful *adj.*

This is an adjective which cannot have a comparative, because it describes an absolute quality. (see ABSOLUTES)

allure, lure *v.*

To *allure* is to 'attract, entice, charm' a person. It is not necessarily deliberate, whereas to *lure* is to 'attract a person to his disadvantage, into danger or sin', 'lay a trap for'.

ally ('ælai) *n.* (ə'lai) *v.*

almost *adv.*

'Very nearly, virtually'. This word is some-

20

times loosely used as an adjective, e.g. *It was an almost certainty that he would be the winner.* This is a colloquial use of *almost a certainty.*

alone *adv. adj.*

Used as an adverb, usually with *not,* it is archaic and can be replaced by *only,* e.g. *He was not the only person to see such an opportunity.* rather than *He was not alone in seeing . . .* As an adjective, it is used only after the noun, whereas *only* is used before the noun.

along *prep.*

This word often appears unnecessarily in informal speech, in phrases like *along with, along about the year 1900.* The colloquial phrase *Do you go along with me?* can mean either 'Are you following my reasoning?' or 'Do you agree with me?'

also *adv.*

'As well as, besides, too'. It is sometimes loosely used as a conjunction, e.g. *They were cheering, also singing, as they set out.* Sometimes the use of *also* results in ambiguity, e.g. *He also hoped to see the building completed in his lifetime,* where *also* could belong to either *He* or *hoped.* (In such cases it is better to use *too* or *as well,* e.g. *He too hoped to see . . .* or *He hoped, as well, to see . . .*)

also-ran

Plural *also-rans.*

alternate *adj. v.* **alternately** *adv.*

The adjective *alternate* (əːlˈtəːnit) describes 'two things following on continuously by turns', and is used thus in Botany, Mathematics and Biology. It also means 'every other', e.g. *Meetings are held on alternate Thursdays.* The verb is pronounced ('əːltəneit) and means 'follow each other by turns', e.g. *Blue and green stripes alternated in the pattern. Alternately* means 'one after another, by turns', e.g. *She wore her red jumper and her blue cardigan alternately.* These forms are not used in connection with numbers other than two.

(see ALTERNATIVE with which these words are sometimes confused)

alternative *adj. n.*

The adjective means 'other, different, opposed, offering a choice', e.g. *There was no alternative route open to her.* Strictly speaking, the noun should not be used where there are more than two possibilities, so that *other* (before it) is redundant. *There is no alternative* is clearer than *There are no other alternatives.* In official language, *fresh* or *other* could often be substituted for the adjective, and *choice* for the noun, as in *Other* (or *alternative*) *arrangements are being made for those who do not wish to travel today.*

although *conj.*

Although is slightly weightier than *though*, and is more often used at the beginning of a sentence. [*Tho'*] and [*altho'*] are not recognized abbreviations.

altogether see ALL

a.m., p.m.

a.m. means 'before noon', *p.m.* means 'after noon and up till midnight'. Sometimes these abbreviations are used superfluously, e.g. [*at six p.m. in the evening.*] Their use in time-tables etc. is being superseded by the use of the 24 hour clock, in which *six p.m.* becomes *1800* (*eighteen hundred*) *hours*.

amatory, amorous *adj.*

Amatory means 'pertaining to love or a lover'; *amorous* means 'given to falling in love', e.g. *He wrote a book of amatory verses; She did not like his amorous behaviour.*

ambiguity

Careless writing may produce sentences which can be read in two ways. Often there is no doubt about which meaning is intended, but in some cases there can be real obscurity. Some of the main causes of ambiguity are given below:—

1. The use of words with more than one meaning, e.g. *When he entered the office a young man appeared to answer his questions; The master*

23

has overlooked my work; *She was appointed secretary to the director and worked in the office under him.* Headlines in newspapers produce many examples of this kind of ambiguity because they omit the less important words and so fail to distinguish between parts of speech, e.g. *Moves To Cement Gulf Grouping*; *Giant Waves Down Ship's Funnel.*

2. Words or groups of words misplaced in the sentence, e.g. *It is even not certain that he will come tomorrow,* (where *even* could apply to *certain,* or *tomorrow*); *There are thousands of old people in this town alone*; *He needs more competent help.*

3. Pronouns are sometimes used without making it clear to whom or what they refer, e.g. *I asked the hall-porter whether he had seen my friend and he said he had seen him as he was going out and he had asked him the time.*

4. Words are often omitted which would make the meaning clear, e.g. *My third attempt was the least successful.* (of my attempts, or those of others?) (see ADJECTIVE; ADVERB; NEGATIVES; PARTICIPLE; PUNCTUATION, HYPHENS; SENTENCE)

amend *v.* **amendment** *n.* **emend** *v.* **emendation** *n.*

To *amend* is to 'make right, make better', and can be used of a situation, character etc.

Emend meaning to 'correct an error' is used only for manuscripts or texts.

AMERICAN USAGE

There are now so many channels of communication between Britain and the United States that a great number of the words and expressions used in America which are not part of British English are already familiar, and it is increasingly difficult to decide which can be labelled as Americanisms and which are being absorbed into our language. Films, pop songs, television programmes, newspapers and magazines, scholarly works, politics and industrial firms all help to make different sections of the public familiar with American usage in their particular fields. On the other hand there are many differences in everyday words which come as a shock to the traveller in either direction, such as *pitcher = jug; sidewalk = pavement; call = telephone, ring up; thumb tack = drawing-pin*. A separate dictionary is required to deal with the differences between the two branches of the language, and the most useful one available is *A Dictionary of Modern American Usage* by H. W. Horwill (Oxford, 1944).

To deny admission to our language of some of the expressions of a lively, inventive and practical society is to adopt a futile and negative attitude, examples of which are frequently found in the correspondence columns of the newspapers. We have only to look at some of the words which Horwill described as Americanisms in the nineteen-thirties to wonder how we could ever have managed without them—such words as *blizzard, bogus, disgruntled, hitch-hike.* On the other hand we may perhaps hope to be spared some of the more impish tricks played by advertisers, witty and compelling as a good many of them are. In particular the use of simplified spelling must be confusing for those aiming at correctness. A few of the differences between American and British usage can be classified and are given below:—

spelling (a) Words which end in *re* in British often have *er* in American (*center, meter, theater*). (b) Words ending in *-our* in British English have *or* in American (*labor, valor,* with a few exceptions such as *glamour.* (see SQUALOR). (c) The ending *ise* is more often *yze* in the U.S. (*analyze, paralyze*). This spelling is becoming more general in Britain too, but some words have *ise* in both countries (*advertise, advise, comprise, surprise* etc.). see SPELLING, verbs. (d) In many cases where a final consonant is doubled before a suffix in

Britain it is left single in the U.S. (*traveling, counselor*). (e) While many simplified or shortened spellings are only used in advertising and commercial jargon (*his 'n hers, kwik-dri, thru*), others are recognized and used in formal writing (*program, catalog*).

idiomatic use of verbs, adverbs and prepositions The following are a few examples of cases which differ from British usage:

AMERICAN	BRITISH
come by	*call on*
figure out	*understand*
be named for	*be named after*
name him President	*name him as President*
rest up	*rest*
teach school	*teach in a school*
stay home	*stay at home*
visit with	*visit*
the worst in years	*the worst for years*
a quarter of six	*quarter to six*
ten after seven	*ten past seven*
live on Potter Street	*in Potter Street*

vocabulary As the institutions of the two countries have developed separately there are many different terms which can cause confusion. The *Administration* in the U.S. corresponds to the *Government* in Britain, a *judge* can be the equivalent of our *magistrate*, a *lawyer* might do the work of either a *solicitor* or a *barrister*. A list of common American words and phrases with their British equivalends may be found in the Appendix. (see GOT; HAVE; LOAN; METER; MOST; MOTIVATE; -OR; PATENT; PROGRAMME; RAISE; SCHEDULE; SKILFUL; STERILE; THROUGH; WOOL; Z)

amiable, amicable *adj.*
Both these words mean 'friendly', but *amiable* is used of people, *amicable* of situations or agreements, e.g. *I found her a most amiable colleague*; *We came to an amicable agreement*.

amid, amidst, among, amongst *prep.*
Amid and *amidst* are followed by a collective noun (*Amid the thunder of the waves*); *among* and *amongst* are followed by a plural (*There was a cat among the pigeons.*) The first pair is used less than the second; *amid* chiefly appears in poetry. There is no very clear distinction between *among* and *amongst*, though there is a tendency to use *amongst* before a word beginning with a vowel, and where the sense is 'out of' rather than 'in the middle of', e.g. *He found himself among friends*; *Amongst his friends there was only one who shared his opinion*.

among see BETWEEN

amorous see AMATORY

ample *adj.*
'More than enough', 'abundant', although

used colloquially for 'large'. It can be used with both abstract and collective nouns (cf. *some*), e.g. *There is ample food for all*; *Your stay abroad will give you ample opportunities to learn a new language*.

anachronism (ə'nækrənizəm) *n.* **anachronistic** (ə'nækrə'nistik) *adj.*

This noun means 'an error in placing the time or date of an event or custom', and can also be used of 'something surviving into the present day which does not belong there', e.g. *To describe Queen Anne as using a fountain pen is an anachronism; It is an anachronism to put a thatched roof on a twentieth-century house.* Sometimes confused with *anomaly* (ə'nɔməli) which means 'an irregularity', e.g. *A bird which cannot fly is an anomaly in nature.* The adjective is *anomalous* (ə'nɔmələs).

analogy (ə'nælədʒi) *n.* **analogous** (ə'næləgəs) *adj.*

An *analogy* is 'a partial likeness between two things which are otherwise unlike', such as *sleep* and *death*. This is the basis of *metaphor*; in literature sleep is often used to mean death. (see STYLE). *To draw a false analogy* is to 'assume that because one thing resembles another in certain respects it resembles it in others', to say for instance that *because a dog looks like a wolf it must be a dangerous animal.*

29

Many spelling mistakes are made on this principle, e.g. [*immitate*] on the analogy of *imminent*.

analyst, annalist *n.*

The first is 'a person skilled in analysis', which may be chemical or psycho-analysis. An *annalist*, pronounced the same way, is 'one who writes annals or books of each year's events'.

and *conj.*

This word is used to link parts of a sentence, and lists of objects. It is often used redundantly with *etc.*, which itself means 'and other things' and with *which* and *who*, e.g. [*It was a town of 10,000 inhabitants, and which had an inadequate water supply*]. *And* can be used with *which* or *who* if there is a preceding equivalent clause, e.g. *He was a man who had plenty of money, and who spent it freely*. *And* sometimes begins a sentence to provide emphasis, e.g. *It was a cold, snowy night. And I had no money left for food*. (see PUNCTUATION, COMMAS)

angle see VIEW

angler *n.*

The distinction between an *angler*, who fishes with a rod, hook and line, and a *fisherman*, who uses nets, is disappearing, and *fisherman* is often used for both. Anglers themselves, however, like to retain the distinction.

anglo- *prefix*

This term gives rise to many compounds, some of which describe people, and others language, e.g. *Anglo-American* 'an American of English stock'; *Anglo-Catholic* 'an Anglican inclining to Roman Catholic views' or 'High Church'; *Anglo-French* 'a dialect of French in Medieval England'; *Anglo-Indian* 'an Englishman who has spent most of his life in India' 'a person of mixed descent' (see MULATTO); *Anglo-Irish* 'an Englishman resident in Ireland'; *Anglo-Saxon* 'the Old English people, and their language, before the Norman Conquest' (Now used as a very wide term to cover all those of Teutonic descent, especially in the U.S.). All these words can be used adjectivally.

angry *adj.*

Followed by *at* for things and events, *with* for persons, e.g. *He was angry at finding that nothing had been done*; *He was angry with me for not having done anything*.

annex *v.* **annexe** *n.*

The verb is pronounced (ə'neks) and means 'take over, take possession of'. The noun ('æneks) means 'an addition to a building'.

anomaly see ANACHRONISM

another *adj.*

'Once more', 'a different (one)'. Sometimes

loosely used for *other*, e.g. *one way or another*, and often unnecessarily reinforced by *also*, e.g. [*There is also another way of looking at the question*].

answer *v.*

To *answer for* is to 'take responsibility for', e.g. *I cannot answer for the consequences*, but it is sometimes loosely used instead of *answer to*, e.g. [*He could not give me an answer for what I asked him*].

antecedent

The grammatical term for a word related to another word that generally follows it in the sentence; for example an adjective is usually the antecedent of the noun it describes. The term is most commonly used of a noun followed by an adjective clause, for example the word *pipe* in *This is the pipe that I like smoking best*.

anticipate *v.*

The Latin prefix *ante-* meaning 'before' has become *anti* in this word, but should not be confused with the prefix *anti-* meaning 'against'. The strict meaning of *anticipate* is 'forestall', 'take action in the expectation of something happening', as in *He was shocked to hear that his discovery had been anticipated by one made many years before*; *It is an excellent hotel where the waiters anticipate your every need*. It is now commonly used for 'expect, foresee', as in *I do not anticipate any trouble.*

antimony ('æntiməni), **antinomy** (æn'tinəmi) *n.*

Confusion arises between these two words which have no connection. *Antimony* is 'a silvery-white metal', *antinomy* is a philosophical term for 'a contradiction between two laws or principles.'

antonym

'A word of opposite meaning', 'the negative form of a positive word'. One word can have several antonyms according to its different senses, e.g. the words *coarse*, *rough* and *rainy* are all antonyms of *fine*.

any *adj. adv. pron.*

Compounds of this word are all written as one, e.g. *anybody, anyhow, anyone, anything, anyway, anywhere*. Where separate words are used the meaning is different, e.g. *Anyone can see that he is ill*, but although he has so many friends he has not told any one of them; *It may rain, but we shall go anyway*; *We shall go any way you like*. The following compounds are used generally in the U.S., but only colloquially here:—*anyplace, anytime, anyways, anywheres, anywise*. The same applies to the use of *any* for 'at all', e.g. *This does not help me any*. *Anyone* is followed by a verb or pronoun

33

in the singular, e.g. *Anyone who is over sixteen is allowed in.* (see EITHER)

aphorism ('æfərizəm)

'A short neat statement of a universal truth', 'a pithy saying', such as *Virtue is its own reward.* Maxims, proverbs and PARADOXES are aphorisms.

apocope (ə'pɔkəpi)

'The shortening of a word by omitting the final letter or syllable', e.g. the use of *my* where formerly *mine* was used, *cinema* for *cinematograph* and *tram* for *tramcar.*

apology, apologetics, apologia (æpə'loudʒiə) *n.*

An *apology* is 'an expression of regret for an injury', but it is also used in the same sense as the other two words for 'a defence or vindication by argument'.

apostrophe

1. A sign (') used to indicate the possessive case or the omission of one or some letters from the word, e.g. *The bird's beak*; *That isn't my son.*

2. In rhetoric or poetry it is used to refer to the act of addressing a person, thing, or idea, e.g. *Milton! thou should'st be living at this hour* (Wordsworth). (see POSSESSIVE FORMS)

apparatus (æpə'reitəs)

Plural *apparatuses* or *apparatus*

apposite ('æpouzait) *adj.*

Apposite means 'appropriate', 'well adapted', e.g. *His remarks were brief and apposite*. The noun form is *appositeness*.

apposition

In grammar this means 'the addition of a word or words, usually a noun or noun phrase, for further description', e.g. *Bournemouth, town of sunshine, is on the South Coast*, where *town of sunshine* is in apposition to *Bournemouth*.

appraise, apprise, apprize *v.*

To *appraise* is to 'evaluate'. To *apprise* is to 'tell, inform', e.g. *I have not been apprised of his arrival*. *Apprize* is an alternative spelling.

appreciate *v.*

Used transitively, this word means 'realize the value of something, be grateful for it', e.g. *I appreciate his generosity*. Intransitively, it means 'increase in value', e.g. *Copper shares have recently appreciated*. It is sometimes used with the meaning of 'understand', e.g. *I appreciate the difficulty*. The adjective is *appreciable* and means 'considerable'. The noun *appreciation* can mean 'a summary or assessment of a document, situation or piece of work'; it can also mean 'an increase in value'.

apprehend *v.*

As well as meaning 'fear' and 'arrest', this verb has the sense of 'understand', but it is not synonymous with *comprehend*. To *apprehend* means to 'get hold of' or 'grasp', while to *comprehend* is to 'have understanding of something', e.g. *The audience were unable to apprehend the ideas he was trying to explain. The instructor comprehends spoken German. It is apprehended that* is used in official jargon for 'I suppose'.

appropriate (ə'proupriət) *adj.* (ə'prouprieit) *v.*

The adjective means 'fitting or suitable to a person, situation or object', e.g. *She wore appropriate clothes for the journey.* The verb means to 'take possession of something' e.g. *His land was appropriated by the Army for use as a training ground.*

apt, liable *adj.*

In many uses these words overlap in sense, but whereas *apt* conveys a straightforward sense of probability (*The telephone is apt to ring more in the afternoon*), *liable* contains an element of danger or suffering (*Eggs are liable to break if not handled carefully*). (see also LIABLE)

arbiter, arbitrator *n.*

An *arbiter* is 'someone who has absolute control', 'a decision-maker'; an *arbitrator* is 'someone appointed by opposing parties to settle a dispute'.

arch-, arche-, archi- *prefix*
'Chief' or 'leading'. It makes many compounds, only a few of which have hyphens, e.g. *arch-fiend*, *arch-enemy*. Unhyphenated *arch* is followed by a consonant and is pronounced (aːtʃ), e.g. *archbishop*, *archduchess*; where a vowel follows, it is (aːk), e.g. *archangel*, *archimandrite*.

archaic (aːˈkeiik) *adj.* **archaism** (ˈɑːkeiizm) *n.*
A term used to describe a word, spelling or construction which is 'out of date and belongs to the past'. *Archaisms* are often used in the attempt to add dignity or formality to speech and writing, or to give it a popular quaintness, e.g. *Christmas Fayre*, *Ye Old Tea Shoppe*. In historical novels they are used in an attempt to imitate the speech and customs of a past age, e.g. *albeit*, *anent*, *derring-do*, *erstwhile*, *haply*, *save* (in the sense of 'except'), *to-wit* and so on. They are not acceptable in normal prose writing.

archipelago
Plural *archipelagos*

aren't *v.*
aren't I? This is the recognized negative interrogative form of *I am*, a shorter form of *am I not?*, used in familiar speech. This form has come by analogy from *aren't you? aren't they?* and has replaced *an't*, now obsolete.

arise, rise *v.*

The verb arise has been replaced by *rise* when it is used in the physical sense of 'getting up, going up, or coming in', e.g. *I rise at 8 a.m.; The temperature rises; The tide is rising.* Arise is used in a more abstract sense, e.g. *The question arose; A situation has arisen.*

around, round *adv.*

Round is the more usual form of this word, but *around* is still used to imply diffuseness, e.g. *The lamp shed its light around.* It has many colloquial uses, when it takes the place of *about* e.g. *It was around 4 o'clock; He gets around; There seems to be plenty of money around.*

arouse see ROUSE

artist ('a:tist), **artiste** (a:'ti:st) *n.*

An *artist* is 'someone engaged in the creative arts, especially painting, or 'a person showing great skill in any occupation'. The word *artiste* is only applied to 'a professional or amateur theatrical or musical performer, or a dancer.' It can be used of either sex.

as *conj. adv. pro.*

As is often misused and can cause ambiguity:–

    1. It can be used as a conjunction to mean either *because, since, when,* or *while,* e.g. *I saw her today as I was working late in the office; He felt tired as he walked home.* The meaning is clearer in *I saw her today while I was working late* or

I saw her today because I was working late; *He felt tired because he walked home* or *He felt tired while he was walking home.*

2. *I saw him as well as you*; *She likes me as well as you.* Here the ambiguity can be removed by restoring a verb which was understood, e.g. *I saw him as well as you did* or *I saw him as well as seeing you*; *She likes me as well as you do* or *She likes me as well as she likes you* or *She likes me as well as liking you.*

3. *As an expert on electricity you will understand me when I say that this is impossible.* Here a different order of words can make clear which is 'the expert': *You, as an expert on electricity, will understand me . . .* or *You will understand me when I, speaking as an expert, say . . .*

As is omitted or unnecessarily inserted in the following instances:

1. [*I am equally as sure.*] *As* is unnecessary here, and so is the first of the pair in [*as much as I should like to*]. Many official phrases are formed with *as* and used instead of simpler words, e.g. *consider as to the question of increasing output* ('consider increasing'); *during such time as* ('while'). *As from last April wages will be increased* is useful for the implication 'as if it had happened last April', but there is no need for *as* with *from next June*. *As and when* is occasionally necessary, but is often written

39

where *when* would be enough. *As to whether* can usually be cut down to *whether*.

2. [*It annoyed me that I was so foolish to lose my way*]; [*He is mad as a hatter*]. These sentences need an *as* which has been omitted, and should read . . . *so foolish as to lose my way*; . . . *as mad as a hatter*.

3. [*He said as he was hungry.*] This is generally unacceptable, even in speech. *That* could be used instead of *as*, or both could be left out.

4. *It looks as if the venture will succeed* is quite acceptable, though some people still hold that the correct form is . . . *the venture would succeed* (cf. *He behaved as if he were drunk*; *It seemed as if we should never get there*).

5. When phrases like *as much as, as long as* are in the negative, and when they open a sentence, *so* can be used instead of the first *as*, e.g. *He did not enjoy it so much as he expected*; *So long as we keep together it will be safe to go on*. *I am not as tall as she is* is now generally regarded as pedantic, and it is more usual to write *I am not as tall as her* or *I am not as tall as she is*.

as follows see FOLLOWS

ascendancy, ascendency *n.* **ascendant** *adj.*
The nouns denote 'influence, power, control'; the first spelling is commoner. In astronomy, *ascendant* means 'rising towards the zenith'; in astrology, it refers to 'a sign of the Zodiac

rising on the eastern horizon'. Figuratively, *in the ascendant* means 'rising in power or importance'.

aspirate ('æspirət) *adj. n.* ('æspireit) *v.*

Used of a consonant, meaning 'pronounced with breathing', as the letter *h*, in, e.g. *happy, hopeful, hoard.*

assay, essay *v. n.*

Assay is an archaic form meaning to 'try', 'test', now mostly confined to the testing of metals. The verb *essay* pronounced (e'sei) means to 'attempt'. The noun, pronounced the same way, means 'an attempt'; pronounced ('esei) it means 'a prose composition'.

asset *n.*

This word means 'an advantage' or 'a valuable possession', e.g. *His height was a great asset to him as a policeman.* In the plural it denotes property, especially that which can be used to pay debts, e.g. *Though doing badly at the moment, the firm has most valuable assets.*

assignation (æsig'neiʃən), **assignment** (ə'sainmənt) *n.*

An *assignation* is 'an arrangement to meet, often furtively or for amorous purposes'. In law, it means 'the transference of a property'. An *assignment* is something allotted, often a task.

assimilate see SIMULATE

associate see DISSOCIATE

assonance

In poetry, a device like rhyme, where the vowel sounds correspond, e.g. *pigeon, kitchen*; Used in proverbs to make them more easily memorized, e.g. *A stitch in time saves nine.* This term is also used for an accidental repetition in prose of a sound, syllable, or word which is awkward or ugly in effect, e.g. *The actual fact is that he has no tact*; *The ultimate step was the signing of an ultimatum*; *He told his father that he could go no farther.*

assume *v.*

This verb can mean either 'take on', 'adopt', or 'take for granted'. Where it is used as an alternative to *presume*, in the sense of 'suppose', it implies a greater shade of doubt, e.g. *I assume that he will be there*; *I presume that you know this already.*

assure *v.* **assurance** *n.*

The verb has a wide range of meanings: to 'make sure, insure, promise confidently, be convincing'. The noun and past participle have taken the sense further, so that *assured* can mean not only 'made safe', but also 'showing the signs of safety', and *assurance* means the 'aggressive bearing of confidence' e.g. *I was assured that it was a good investment*; *I was struck by the assurance of his manner.* The use of *assurance* in the sense of *Marine Assurance* etc. is giving way to *insurance*.

astrology, astronomy *n.*

Astronomy is 'a science, the study of heavenly bodies'. *Astrology* is 'a system of predicting the future by observing the planets, moon and stars.' It includes the casting of horoscopes.

atheist see AGNOSTIC

attempt *v.*

This verb should not be followed by *to be*, as in [*It is time that the task was attempted to be done again*]. This construction is probably based on the analogy of *allow*, where it is quite acceptable. *It is time (that) the task was attempted again* is a better version.

aural ('ɔːrəl) or ('aurəl), **oral** ('ɔːrəl) *adj.*

The first means 'of the ear', 'concerning hearing' and is sometimes confused with *oral* 'belonging to the mouth', 'verbal', 'vocal'. For this reason, amongst teachers, a distinction in pronunciation is sometimes observed, as shown above.

authentic *adj.*

This word is used mostly of works of art, and means 'genuine', 'proceeding from its reputed source'. It is loosely used in phrases such as *The play had captured the authentic atmosphere of a boarding house*.

autobiography see BIOGRAPHY

autocracy (ɔ:'tɔkrəsi), **autonomy** (ɔ:'tɔnəmi) *n.*
Autocracy is 'absolute government by a single ruler or power'; *autonomy* is 'the right or state of self-government'.

automation (,ɔ:tə'meiʃən), **automaton** (ɔ:'tɔmətən) *n.*
Automation is a new word which describes 'the mechanisation of industrial processes which formerly required human labour', in particular the introduction of computers. An *automaton* (plural *automata* or *automatons*) is 'a mechanical imitation of a human figure' or 'a person acting mechanically'.

auxiliary verb see VERB

averse *adj.*
This adjective is followed by *to* plus a noun or present participle, e.g. *I am averse to the idea of seeing him; They were averse to spending more on the project*. *Averse from* is correct but pedantic. (see ADVERSE)

await see WAIT

award, reward *n. v.*
Award as a noun has a strictly judicial use meaning 'the recorded decision of an arbitrator in a court of law', although its use has been extended in *the Queen's Award to Industry* etc. to overlap with *reward*, which means 'something given in return for a voluntary act or for merit'. *Reward* is also used by the

police to mean 'a sum of money offered for the recovery of missing articles or for information'. As a verb *award* means to 'decide authoritatively on a point' (*award a decision*) as well as to 'allot' (*award a prize*).

awful *adj.*

Like *appalling* and *astonishing* this word has lost all the strength of its original meaning, and has become so colloquial that for serious description *awe-inspiring* should be used instead.

ay, aye *adv.*

As a poetic form of *ever*, the second spelling is more common, and the pronunciation is usually (ei). As an interjection meaning 'yes', the pronunciation is generally (ai), as in *aye, aye, Sir*.

B

back formation

In the history of language an *agent noun* is usually formed by the addition of a suffix to the stem of a verb, e.g. *teacher* from *teach*; *accompanist* from *accompany*. However, in some cases a verb has been invented from a noun or an adjective, e.g. *burgle* from *burglar*; *laze* from *lazy*; *diagnose* from *diagnosis*. This is

known as a *back formation*. Many formations
of this kind are colloquial, especially when
they are new, e.g. *enthuse* from *enthusiasm*;
process from *procession*.

background *n.*
This is a useful word when it is used for 'a
miscellaneous collection of facts which contri-
bute to a situation,' but it is often used inaccurately in bureaucratic jargon in the place
of such words as *cause, reason, qualifications* etc.,
e.g. *The background to his decision was his dislike
of living in a town,* where *The reason for* would
be better.

bad- see WELL-

bail, bale *v. n.*
The first of these spellings is always used for
bailing out a person, in the sense of 'releasing a
prisoner by acting as security for his return'.
For 'emptying water from a boat' or 'escaping
from an aeroplane by parachute' either can
be used, but *bale out* is more usual.

ballad ('bæləd), **ballade** (bæ'la:d) *n.*
A *ballad* is 'a narrative poem in simple form
(often with a refrain)', e.g. *Sir Patrick Spens,
Chevy Chase* etc. The form, which goes back at
least to the fifteenth century, has been
revived by many poets such as Scott, Tenny-
son and Coleridge, and is now often used for
popular songs of the more sentimental kind.

The term *ballade* is a much narrower one, and is used of a poem with three stanzas of eight lines each, concluding with a short final stanza of four lines, e.g. Chaucer's *Compleynt of Venus*. It is also used as a title for pieces of music by Chopin and later composers.

banal *adj.* **banality** *n.*

These words have been imported from France, and they are used mostly by critics. For *banal*, pronounced (bə'naːl) or ('beinəl), 'commonplace', 'trite', 'trivial, or 'vulgar' could be used. A *banality* is a 'truism' or 'platitude'.

bank see LEFT BANK

barbarian, barbaric, barbarous *adj.*

All these words are loosely used to indicate 'uncivilized behaviour' as well as 'roughness' and 'primitive strength'. There are some distinctions, however, in their more precise application. In ancient times the word *barbarian* meant 'foreign', and it is now used to describe 'the savage, uncivilized tribes from the north who attacked the Greeks and Romans and eventually overthrew them and their civilization'. *Barbaric* is sometimes used for an artistic quality associated with primitive life, e.g. *The curtain rose on a scene of barbaric splendour.* *Barbarous* suggests 'cruelty' and 'inhuman behaviour', e.g. *She received the most barbarous treatment from her captors.*

barbarian, barbarism, barbarousness, barbarity n.

The noun *barbarian* is used of 'an uncivilized person'. *Barbarism* and *barbarousness* mean 'the absence of civilization or polish in a person or group', e.g. *We were shocked by the barbarousness of his behaviour*; *The children were found to be living in a state of barbarism*. *Barbarity* is the quality of 'ruthless cruelty', e.g. *The attack was pressed home with the utmost barbarity*. The word *barbarism* has a special meaning in connection with language; it denotes 'a word or phrase ignorantly formed or used', e.g. [*beneficient*] for *beneficent*.

basis n.

The phrases *based on, on the basis of* are properly used where there is a sense of 'something fundamental on which something else is constructed', e.g. *His conclusions were based on the figures for the past year*. But in commercial and Civil Service jargon they are often used to take the place of shorter, simpler words, e.g. *The successful candidate was chosen on the basis of his knowledge of the subject* when *for his knowledge of* would be sufficient.

bathos n.

An 'anti-climax', 'a sudden descent from the sublime to the ridiculous'. It can be deliberate, as in Pope's lines

Here thou, great Anna! whom three realms obey,
Dost sometimes counsel take—and sometimes tea.

or unintentional:

The feathered race with pinions skim the air—
Not so the mackerel, and still less the bear.

(J. H. Frere: *Progress of Man*)

It can also arise out of an unsuccessful attempt to achieve PATHOS (q.v.).

bay see GULF

bay window, bow window

A *bay window* is one which projects from the wall of a house. If it is curved it can also be called a *bow window*.

because *conj.*

1. This word is often used redundantly instead of *that*, e.g. [*The reason I am coming is because I want to see you*] where *reason* has already expressed the idea of *because*.

2. It can lead to ambiguity when it follows a negative statement, e.g. *I am not coming to see you because I want to go to the concert.* This could mean either *I am not coming to see you, as I would rather go to the concert* or *I am not coming to see you just for the sake of going to the concert.* A comma between *you* and *because* would make the meaning clearer.

beg *v.*

The use of this word in business letters, e.g. *We beg you will accept our apologies for the delay,* is an outdated form of servile politeness which can be replaced by a more matter-of-fact and everyday form of writing, e.g. *We apologise for the delay*.

begging the question

This accusation is often loosely made in an argument when it is felt that an opponent is 'shifting the ground of discussion' or 'being unfair'. It does not imply that he is evading a straight answer to the question. Strictly it means that he is arguing from an assumption that is itself open to argument, or is drawing unjustified conclusions, e.g. *In an argument on the merits of a Prime Minister, it is begging the question to say, "Of course he's a good leader, he would not be in the job otherwise."*

begin, commence, start *v.*

Begin is the most useful of these words. It is followed by an infinitive or present participle, e.g. *I am beginning to feel old*. *Commence* is more formal, and is followed by a present participle, e.g. *The government has commenced negotiating an agreement*. *Start* is used for physical motion, and has an element of suddenness. It too is usually followed by a present participle or infinitive, e.g. *The car started moving* (or *to move*).

behalf, behoof *n.*

To act *on behalf of* someone means simply 'act as his agent or substitute', e.g. *The deputy chairman will act on behalf of Mr. Brown at this meeting. In behalf of implies 'an act or speech in defence or praise of someone', e.g. She spoke warmly in his behalf. Behoof is an archaic form.*

beholden *adj.*

A slightly archaic word meaning 'indebted' or 'obliged'. The erroneous form *beholding* is now obsolete.

beloved *adj. n. past part.*

This word has three syllables when used as an adjective or noun, e.g. *my beloved* (bi'lʌvid) *country*; *Beloved, thou hast brought me many flowers / Plucked in the garden* (Elizabeth Barrett Browning). When used as a past participle, it has two syllables, e.g. *beloved* (bi'lʌvd) *by his countrymen.*

below, under, beneath, underneath *adv. prep.*

Below describes the relative positions of two separate things, e.g. *He was fishing below the waterfall*; *His position in the firm was below his brother's*; *Below the first-floor window there was a small flower bed.* *Under* implies a closer relative position, e.g. *He bathed under the waterfall*; *He was under his brother's authority.* The use of these two prepositions overlaps in phrases like *below* or *under a certain age.*

Beneath is slightly archaic and pedantic when used in *the grass beneath your feet*, but is preserved as the only possible word in phrases with a moral note, e.g. *beneath contempt*.

Underneath is mostly used where there is a sense of close physical covering, e.g. *In the desert there is often water underneath the sand*. It is also used in connection with the hidden qualities of people, e.g. *He may seem ambitious but he is a modest man underneath*.

beside *prep.* **besides** *adv. prep.*

Beside is a preposition, meaning 'alongside of', e.g. *He sat down beside her*; *You look tall beside him*. *Besides* is an adverb or preposition meaning 'in addition to', e.g. *Have you no clothes besides those?*; *Besides knowing some Greek, she was fluent in Italian*.

better *adj.*

Colloquial when used for *well*, e.g. *He has been ill but is almost better now*.

between *prep.*

Between you and me not [*you and I*]. *Between* can be used with more than two objects but there is usually a sense of sharing or of separate relationships, e.g. *The children divided the apple between them*; *Agreements were made between the different countries*. (Where a more vague and general sense is required, *among* can be used, e.g. *They discussed it among themselves*). *Between* can be followed by a plural noun, e.g. *They saw a path between the trees*, or by a noun followed by *and* and another noun, e.g. *You must not come between a man and his wife.* *Between* is loosely used in the following ways:—

1. In place of *after*, e.g. [*Between each sentence he took a deep breath*].

2. Followed by *or* instead of *and*, e.g. [*I was offered a choice between whisky or brandy*].

beware *v.*

This word is now usually followed by *of* before a noun or present participle, e.g. *Beware of the bull*; *Beware of going too near the edge of the cliff.*

bi-annual, biennial *adj.*

Bi-annual means 'twice a year', *biennial* 'every two years'. Compounds made with *bi-* lead to great confusion, e.g. *bi-monthly*, which can mean either 'twice a month' or 'every two months'. *Twice-monthly* and *two-monthly* are much clearer terms.

Bible *n.* **biblical** ('biblikəl) *adj.*

The Bible has a capital letter but should not be put in inverted commas or italics. The adjective *biblical* is spelt without a capital.

bibliography (bibli'ɔgrəfi) *n.*

A *bibliography* is 'a list of works used in the preparation of a book'. It enables the reader to pursue the subject of the book further.

bicentenary, bicentennial see CENTENARY

big, great, large adj.

Generally speaking, *big* and *large* are inter-changeable and are used for size and quantity, while *great* has come to mean 'leading', 'supreme', 'important', 'in a high degree', e.g. *a great actor, great courage, great developments.* Where it is used for size, there is usually a suggestion of impressiveness as well, e.g. *The building was entered through a great courtyard.* Influenced by journalism, *big* has begun to take over the use of *great* meaning 'important', e.g. *This job requires a big man. Big* and *great* are often used colloquially as terms of abuse, e.g. *You're just a big fool; Take your great foot off my toe,* but *big*, like *large*, can also have the sense of 'generous', as in *that's big of you; large-* (or *big-*) *hearted.*

billion adj. n.

In Great Britain this is 'a million million', in France and the U.S. it means 'a thousand million'.

biography n.

'A life written by someone else'; an *autobiography* is 'the story of the writer's own life'.

blame v.

It is acceptable to say *I blame you for all the trouble* but not [*I blame all the trouble on you*]. Strictly this should be *I put the blame for all the trouble on you.*

54

blessed *adj.*

She was blessed (blest) *with a cheerful disposition* (sometimes written *blest*). It is more blessed ('blesid) *to give than to receive.*

blond, blonde *adj. n.*

The adjective is usually spelt without the *e*; the noun, when it means 'a fair-haired woman', can be spelt with or without the *e*; when it refers to the silk *blonde-lace* it always retains *e*.

bloom, blossom *n. v.*

In their literal senses, *bloom* is used for the flower of a plant which is grown for its flowers, *blossom* for flowers which will lead on to fruit, e.g. *The daffodils are in full bloom; There is no blossom this year on the cherry trees.* Similarly, in figurative use, *bloom* and *blooming* imply fulfilment; *blossom* and *blossoming* imply promise, e.g. *The arts of painting and sculpture were blooming in Italy during the fifteenth century. At the school concert his blossoming talent was noticed for the first time.*

blueprint *n.*

'A drawing or diagram in white on blue paper'; hence the popular use of the word for 'a detailed plan'. (see STYLE)

born, borne *past part.*

The past participle of the verb to bear is *borne* except when it refers in the passive voice

55

to birth, e.g. *I have borne your complaints too
long* but *He was born with a silver spoon in his
mouth.* The past participle in the active voice
is also *borne*, e.g. *She has borne too many children*,
and when *by* follows in the passive voice, e.g.
He was the first of the children borne by her.

both ... and, both of, both

Both is sometimes redundantly followed by
as well as, e.g. [*Both his father, as well as his
mother, treated him unkindly*] (*Both his father and
his mother*). *Both of* implies more of a separate
existence for the things described than *both*,
e.g. *Both of her brothers have given her the same
advice*; *She took it in both hands.*

bottleneck n.

A useful metaphor to describe 'the slowing
down of a flow when it has to pass through a
narrow channel', as when traffic from several
directions converges and enters a narrow
street, or supplies are held up through faulty
distribution. Like many verbal short cuts it is
too much used and produces absurdities like
[*We must do our best to iron out this bottleneck*];
[*There is a world-wide bottleneck in machine tools*].

bow window see BAY WINDOW

brackets see PUNCTUATION

brain, brains n.

There is no strict rule for the use of the singular
and plural forms of this word, but the plural is

more often used for the physical sense, e.g. *knock his brains out*, and in informal phrases such as the *brains of the family*, while the singular often appears in more figurative phrases such as *He has that tune on the brain* and in compounds such as *brain drain*.

breakdown n.

Where this word is used for the analysis of figures it is sometimes intended figuratively, where it might be taken literally, e.g. *The Opposition leader asked for a breakdown of all the houses built since the war.*

brethren, brothers n.

Brethren is an archaic plural of *brother* which is still preserved in special cases, particularly in the Church and for members of some organizations such as Trinity House, Freemasonry etc. *Brothers* can be placed either before or after a name, e.g. the *brothers Grimm* or the *Marx Brothers* but the latter is more common. *Sisters* always follows the name.

brim-ful adj.

Always hyphenated. (see PUNCTUATION, HYPHENS)

British adj. n. **Britain, Britisher, Briton** n.

British is the correct adjective for any person or thing belonging to or made in Great Britain or the British Isles. *Britisher* is an Americanism and *Briton* is not much used

57

except for *the Early Britons*. In England and on the Continent there is a tendency to use *English* for *British*.

broad, wide *adj.*

These words overlap in many of their uses and are both opposites of *narrow*. *Broad* can imply 'amplitude', 'strength' or 'generosity', and 'disregard for small issues', e.g. *broad-shouldered, broad farce, taking a broad view of someone's conduct* or *a broad interest in a subject*.

Wide refers to the distance between two points—*a wide doorway, a wide margin*—and can be used for 'extensive' rather than 'deep', e.g. *a wide knowledge of languages, a wide experience*. A *broad view* of a situation is a 'tolerant' one, a *wide view* is an 'extensive' one.

broadcast *v.*

The past tense and past participle *broadcasted* have given way to the universal use of *broadcast*.

brothers see BRETHREN

burlesque (bəːˈlesk) *adj. n.*

'A comic imitation of a literary or dramatic work; not a serious satire'.

burned, burnt *v.*

The second form is more often used with an object, e.g. *He hastily burnt the incriminating document* but *It burned quickly, giving off only a thin wisp of smoke.*

but *conj. prep. interj.*

1. [*We could not start the car but found the battery was flat.*] *But* used as a conjunction should imply a contrast or contradiction. It is often used where *and* would be better (as in the example above); there the second clause is an extension of the first rather than a contradiction. Cf. the following two examples of correct usage:—*My uncle was very old and had a weak heart. My uncle was very old, but he was still young at heart.*

2. When used as a preposition meaning 'except', *but* is followed by the pronoun forms *me, him, her, them, us* if there is no following clause, e.g. *Everybody has heard the story but me.* However, when *but* is followed by a clause (and usually preceded by a negative), *I, he, she, they, we* are used, e.g. *Nobody but I heard the story.* (A more natural way of saying the same thing would be *I am the only one to have heard the story.*)

3. *But* used as an interjection with an adjective, e.g. *But lovely! But definitely!*, is an old-fashioned colloquialism. However, it can be used at the beginning of a sentence to provide emphasis in both formal and informal writing, e.g. *You may think I am exaggerating. But I can assure you that these figures are correct.*

4. [*It was quite clear that nobody wanted to go on*, but *some decided to stay behind*, yet *the leaders thought they ought to continue*, however *finally it was agreed to go part of the way*.] The above is an example of how long sentences are badly stitched together by conjunctions, such as those unitalicised, to avoid repeating *and*, in a way which ignores the proper function of *but*, *yet*, *however*. The sentence could be rewritten as: *It was quite clear that nobody wanted to go on and some decided to stay behind. The leader, however, thought they ought to continue and finally it was agreed to go part of the way.*

by *prep. adv.* **bye** *n.*

By makes some compounds with a hyphen, some without, e.g. *by-election*, *by-law*, *by-pass*, *by-play*, *by-product*, *by-walk*, *by-way*; *bygone*, *bypath*, *bystander*, *byword*.

The spelling *bye* is used in sporting terms and is equally acceptable in *bye-election*, *bye-law* and the phrase *bye and bye*.

C

c.

An abbreviation of the Latin *circa*, meaning 'about', used with dates in parenthesis, e.g. *This is one of his early paintings (c. 1800)*. When the date is not in parenthesis, it is more usual to use *about*, e.g. *About the year 1800 the artist painted this picture, which was his first portrait.*

calculate *v.*

The use of this word particularly in the U.S. for *consider*, e.g. *I calculate he'll be a great man one day*, is typical of the way many precise or technical terms have been taken into ordinary speech and given a much wider and more general meaning. Examples come from many fields of knowledge and activity, but in particular from mathematics and psychology, e.g. *to the nth degree, percentage, ambivalent, inhibition.* (see STYLE)

can, may *v.*

Can (past tense *could*) expresses the power to do something; *may* (past tense *might*) has an element of doubt or involves permission, e.g. *He has so much talent that he can do what he likes; I have no authority over him; he may do as he likes.* The use of *can* instead of *may* for asking permission is colloquial, e.g. *Can I go home now?*

cannon, canon *n.*

The first is 'a large gun'. The second can be either 'a member of the chapter of a cathedral'; 'a rule or standard by which something is judged', as in *the canons of good taste*; 'the established law of the church'; 'the books of the Bible accepted by the Church'; 'a form of musical composition'.

cannot, can not, can't *v.*

　1. *Cannot* is written as one word except where *not* refers to something other than *can*, e.g. *The ability to drive a car can not only increase mobility but also give confidence.*

　2. *Can't* is sometimes loosely combined with *seem*, e.g. [*I can't seem to get up this morning*] for *I can't get up* or *I seem unable to get up.*

cant see LANGUAGE TERMS

canvas, canvass *n. v.*

　The material is spelt *canvas* and so is the verb meaning 'cover something with canvas'. To 'solicit votes or business' is *canvass*, and its noun is spelt the same way.

capable see LIABLE

capital letters see PUNCTUATION

carcase, carcass *n.*

　Both spellings are acceptable. The plural forms are *carcases* and *carcasses*.

case *n.*

　1. This word is often used superfluously, though it has many legitimate uses, e.g. 'a medical case'; 'a case at law'; 'an argument' (*He put up a very good case*); 'an example' (*It's a typical case of bad planning*); 'circumstances' (*I do not believe in making exceptions, but in this case it would be worth it*). However, it would be better omitted in sentences like these: *In the case of vegetables there has been a steep rise in*

prices. (*The price of vegetables has risen steeply*). *You should dial 999 in the case of an emergency.* (*You should dial 999 in an emergency*). In official jargon *case* is often used to blunt the force of a statement, e.g. *if this were the case* rather than *if this were true*.

2. *In any case* can be ambiguous because it has different meanings in formal and informal usage, e.g. *Despite the alternatives offered, we cannot accept your conditions in any case* (i.e. *under any circumstances*); *I'm afraid I'm just too busy to come and see you this Friday. In any case, my wife is borrowing the car that day* (i.e. *besides, furthermore*).

cast, caste (ka:st) *n.*
Cast is the spelling for most uses of this word including all those connected with the verb meaning 'throw'; 'the actors in a play'; 'anything formed in a mould' (*cast-iron*); 'the characteristics of a person' (*He was of an enquiring cast of mind*); 'a squint' (*He had a cast in one eye*). *Caste* is reserved for 'an exclusive and hereditary class of persons'. It appears in the phrase *to lose caste*.

category *n.*
Used in official jargon for 'class' or 'division'.

catholic *adj.* **Catholic, Roman Catholic** *adj. n.*
With a small initial letter, *catholic* is a slightly archaic word for 'liberal' or 'universal', e.g.

His tastes are catholic. Catholic, with a capital letter, was originally used for the whole Christian church but is now generally confined to meaning the *Roman Catholic* Church or religion, as opposed to the *Protestant*.

cause, reason *n.*

The *cause* is 'that which is responsible for an event', e.g. *The heavy rainfall was the cause of the floods.*

Reason implies human agency and 'the act of reasoning not necessarily corresponding to the facts of the case', e.g. *The cause of his departure was the threat of war; his reason for going was to visit his uncle in Switzerland.*

cease *v.*

This word is becoming archaic except in phrases like *cease fire* (noun or verb), *cease work* and in legal and official pronouncements.

cello see VIOLONCELLO

Celt (kelt) *n.* **Celtic** ('keltik) *adj.*

This is the usual spelling and pronunciation.

centenary *n.* **centennial** *adj.*

A *centenary* is 'a hundredth anniversary of an event'. *Bicentenary* (200 years) and *tercentenary* (300 years) are established terms, but for higher multiples it is easier to say *four-hundredth anniversary* etc.

Centennial is an adjective meaning 'occurring once every hundred years'.

centre, middle *adj. n.*

Centre is used in a more precise sense than *middle* especially in geometry where it is 'a single point rather than a central area'. It is also used figuratively with the meaning of 'a focal point', e.g. *She was the centre of attention*, and for 'a point where activities converge', e.g. *a community centre*. It is not used of 'time' or 'action' or 'quality' as *middle* is, e.g. *his middle years*; *He was in the middle of shaving*; *material from the middle range*. *Centre* is a more genteel word and, surprisingly, is found in politics, e.g. *He is a little to the right of centre*, where *middle* would seem more appropriate but is not used. *Center* is the American spelling.

century *n.*

The twentieth century began in 1901, the nineteenth in 1801, not in 1900 and 1800 as is sometimes thought. In a passage of continuous writing it is better to use *the eighteenth century* than to write the *18th century*.

ceremonial *adj. n.* **ceremonious** *adj.*

Ceremonial is a noun or adjective used of a formal occasion.

Ceremonious is an adjective only, and is more often applied to people or behaviour, e.g. *None of the ceremonial was omitted*; *He made a most ceremonious entrance.* (For CEREMONIOUS FORMS OF ADDRESS see LETTER-WRITING)

certainty, certitude *n.*

Certainty can mean either 'the state of being certain or inevitable' or 'a person's state of conviction'. *Certitude* is only used for the second, e.g. *It was a certainty that the government would fall*; *He expressed his certainty* (or *certitude*) *that the government would fall*.

chairman *n.*

This word can be used of either sex, but a woman can be addressed as *Madam Chairman*. (SEE FEMININE FORMS)

challenge *v.* **challenging** *adj.*

This word has been so much over-used by journalists that it has lost its original meta-phorical meaning and is now applied to any difficult situation which has to be met, e.g. *The government will have to meet the challenge of rising unemployment* (cf. *problem*).

chance *v.*

Chance is more formal and pedantic than *happen*, which it is better to use.

character *n.*

This word means 'the sum of the qualities of a person, place, situation, or thing'. It is loosely used instead of words like *kind*, *sort*, *nature*, e.g. *His efficiency was of a ruthless character* (*nature*); *I suspect that some of his transactions are of a shady character* (*kind*). (SEE KIND; NATURE)

charge *n.*

Ambiguity can arise in a sentence like *The prisoner was in charge of the guard*. *In charge of* means 'in authority over', whereas *in the charge of* means 'under the authority of'. There is no doubt which is meant in, e.g. *The girl was in charge of her younger sister* or *The bus was in the charge of the driver*.

check *n. v.* **cheque** *n.* **check up on** *v.*

For the noun meaning 'draft on a bank' the spelling in the U.S. is *check*, in Britain *cheque*. (In the U.S. the verb *check in* is used for depositing baggage and for reporting at an airport). *Check up on* is often used where *check* would be sufficient, e.g. [*Will you check up on the facts?*]

cheerful, cheery *adj.*

Cheerful can describe either a mood or a person's nature; *cheery* overlaps with both these meanings, but can also have a sense of vulgar, ostentatious cheerfulness.

childish, childlike *adj.*

Both these words have the neutral sense of 'belonging to childhood' when applied to a child; but when used of an adult, *childish* implies contempt for a disagreeable quality particularly associated with childhood, while *childlike* expresses admiration for a quality which most people have lost, e.g. *He showed a*

67

childish lack of control over his temper; *The child-like innocence of her ways.*

china see PORCELAIN

Chinee *n.* **Chinese** *adj. n.*

Chinese can be either singular or plural. Like *Jap* and *Nigger*, *Chinee* is a colloquial and derogatory term which gives offence.

chock-full *adj.*

This word always has a hyphen.

choice *adj. n.*

1. Used as an adjective in advertising, this word can mean 'chosen as the best of its kind' but it is often almost meaningless (cf. *prime*, *selected*, *quality*).

2. As a noun it is sometimes loosely used instead of 'chance' or 'opportunity', e.g. [*You are offered the choice of a free tablecloth with your soap*] where there is no question of selection. A choice can be made of one out of several things, e.g. *He offered her a choice of books to read*; and between two or more things, in which case *between* is followed by *and*, not by *or*, e.g. *a choice between black, white and red.*

Christian name *n.*

The terms *forename* and *first name* are equally acceptable and sometimes more appropriate.

chronic *adj.*

In medicine this word is used for 'a long-term condition', the opposite of *acute*; colloquially it often means *severe* or *tiresome*, as well as 'continuous'. The adverb is *chronically*.

circumlocution

'A roundabout manner of speech or writing', 'the use of many words where few would do'.

circumstances *n.*

This word can be preceded by either *in the* or *under the*, without any clear difference of meaning.

city *n.*

Strictly speaking, this word should only be used in Britain of 'a town which has been given the title by Royal Charter' (not necessarily a cathedral town), but it is now generally used for any large town. *The City* means the 'City of London', the small area of the capital which is the centre of banking and commerce for the whole country.

clad see CLOTHED

claim *n. v.*

[*He claimed that it will soon be impossible to drive a car into the centre of the town.*] This example illustrates the colloquial use of *claim* to mean 'assert', 'believe', 'hold', or 'maintain'. *Claim* is appropriately used in: *Charles Edward, the Young Pretender, claimed the English throne*; *Cases can be claimed from the left-luggage official by means of this ticket*, where it has the sense of 'stating a right of possession'.

69

classic *adj. n.* **classical** *adj.*

These very confusing words overlap in many of their uses. They can both refer to 'the ancient civilizations of Greece and Rome', a student of which is a *classic* or *classicist* and his studies *classical* or *the classics*. Anything which is 'typical' or 'recognized as excellent in its class' is more likely to be *classic* than *classical*, e.g. *Anthony Trollope was a classic Victorian novelist.* (without necessarily having any connection with classical authors). *The Derby is a classic of the flat-racing season.* But we can also have a *classic example of bureaucratic inefficiency. Classical architecture* has the style and proportions of Greek and Roman architecture, but *classical music* is a more complex and loosely used term. It is sometimes used of 'the main tradition of European composition since the sixteenth century' and at other times is opposed to *romantic, modern* or *popular.* In literature the old distinction between *classical,* meaning writing which is 'elegant, balanced, conforming to rules', and *romantic,* meaning writing 'in which the form is regarded as less important than the content', is no longer regarded as useful.

clause

'A group of words which forms part of a sentence'. A clause has a subject and a complete verb, and so could stand alone unlike a PHRASE (q.v.) A sentence can consist of one clause or several, joined by a conjunction or a relative pronoun. The simplest way of joining two (or more) clauses is to form a sentence with *and* or *but*. However, many sentences have a main clause and one (or more) subsidiary clauses, where the subsidiary clause takes the place of a noun, adjective or adverb and expands the sense beyond the powers of a single word, e.g. *I fear rain tomorrow* (noun object), *I fear that it may rain tomorrow* (noun clause); *He discovered some valuable gold coins* (adjective), *He discovered some gold coins which an expert valued at thousands of pounds* (adjective clause); *We had to leave early* (adverb), *We had to leave before dawn broke* (adverbial clause). (SEE SENTENCE; OF)

cleanliness ('klenlinis), **cleanness** ('kli:nnis) *n.* *Cleanness* is 'the state of being clean', e.g. *The cleanness of his collar left much to be desired.* *Cleanliness* is 'the habit of keeping clean'.

clench see CLINCH

clergyman, minister, priest *n.* In Britain *clergyman* usually means 'a minister of the Church of England', *minister* means 'a clergyman of a Nonconformist church', and *priest* is the term used by Roman Catholics

71

and Anglicans. These three informal usages are partially interchangeable.

clever *adj.*

Often this adjective is loosely used in the sense of 'knowledgeable' or 'difficult to understand', e.g. *Such clever people would never want to talk to me*; *It is no good trying to understand such a clever book.* Its more accurate use is illustrated in phrases like *He's a clever little monkey*; *It is a very clever way to get round the difficulty*, where it is used to mean 'ingenious', 'intelligent', 'adroit'.

cliché see STYLE

client, customer *n.*

A *customer* buys things, a *client* uses professional services. It is sometimes considered more polite to call a *customer* a *client*, but this is a euphemism.

clinch *n. v.* **clench** *v.*

These two forms are interchangeable in some of their uses, such as 'fix securely', or 'settle an argument or bargain'. For the physical actions connected with 'grasping firmly' or 'making tense' *clench* is used, e.g. *clench your fist (or your teeth)*. When two boxers or wrestlers are grappling at close quarters, the term used is *clinch*.

close, shut *v.*

Close is the more general term for 'the opposite

72

of open', *shut* describes the physical action, e.g. *See that the door is closed when you leave; There's too much air coming in, you'd better shut the window; The shops shut at six; They close all day on Thursdays.*

clothed, clad *past part.*

Both these words are current forms of the past tense and past participle of *to clothe. Clad* is sometimes archaic, e.g. *clad in rich brocade,* and is always related to some specific kind of clothing, e.g. *clad in oilskins; lightly clad.* It is colloquial when used by itself, e.g. *We'll have breakfast as soon as you're clad. Clothed* is more often used in the figurative sense, e.g. *The hill was clothed with pine trees.*

c/o

This abbreviation of *care of* is used in addressing letters. It should be used only before the name of a person, and not before the name or number of a house.

coherence, cohesion *n.*

Both these nouns mean 'sticking together'. *Coherence* when applied to speech or writing has come to mean 'intelligibility and consistency', e.g. *We thought he must have been drinking, there was so little coherence to his speech.* The figurative use of *cohesion* is for groups etc., e.g. *The war increased cohesion between social classes.*

collect ('kɔlekt) *n.* (kə'lekt) *v.*

The verb means 'bring together', e.g. *I am collecting money for charity*; *He collects stamps*; *Uncovered food collects flies*. It is colloquially used for 'fetching a single object or person' e.g. *I will collect you after school*. The noun means 'a prayer'.

collective nouns see NUMBER; OF

college *n.*

A few schools have always been known as colleges, e.g. *Eton* and *Winchester*, and others have imitated them. But in speech or writing the term is generally reserved for places of higher education.

collusion *n.*

This noun implies 'co-operation for an anti-social purpose', e.g. *It was unknown whether the rebels acted singly or in collusion*.

colonies *n.* **colonial** *adj.*

Originally these were the terms applied to British territories overseas, but since most of them have now become independent, the use of these words has been replaced by *Commonwealth*, both as noun and adjective.

colons and semicolons see PUNCTUATION

colossal *adj.*

This word meaning 'immense in size' has been debased through over-use and is used for 'excellent', 'outstanding', 'impressive'.

comic, comical *adj.*

The first of these is used for something deliberately funny, e.g. *a comic turn on the stage.* the second for something unintentionally amusing, e.g. *Her face was a comical sight when she heard that she had mistaken the vice-chancellor for the janitor.*

commas see PUNCTUATION

commence see BEGIN

commercial jargon see STYLE

common see MUTUAL

common sense see PUNCTUATION, HYPHENS

comparative

The form of an adjective or adverb indicating a higher degree, e.g. *newer*; *more alarming*; *better*; *more rapidly.* (see SPELLING, ADJECTIVES). These forms are sometimes loosely used where no comparison is intended, e.g. [*He is the kind of person who always takes the easier way*].

compare *v.*

This verb is followed by *to* when it is used in the sense of 'liken', 'point out a resemblance', e.g. *He compared the garden to a jungle,* and by *with* when a detailed comparison is made, e.g. *In my next lecture I shall compare seventeenth-century French drama with Classical Greek theatre.*

complement, compliment *n.*

The first of these is 'something which completes', the second 'an expression of admira-

75

tion or regard', e.g. *The ship had its full complement of officers and men; The leading lady received
many compliments on her performance.* (see
SUPPLEMENT)

compounds

A *compound word* is 'one made by joining two
or more words together', e.g. *blackboard, half-
wit, go-between, teaspoonful.*

comprehend see APPREHEND

compress ('kɔmpres) *n.* (kəm'pres) *v.*

comprise, include *v.*

The work comprises the following duties: (implies
that these are all the duties). *The work includes
the following duties*: (implies that there may be
others).

concave, convex *adj.*

Concave means 'curving inwards', 'hollowed';
convex means 'curving outwards'. A *convex
lens* is thicker at the centre than at its edges.

concern see WITH

concert *n. v.*

The noun is pronounced ('kɔnsət), the
verb is mainly used in the past participle
(kən'sə:tid), e.g. *concerted action.*

conduct ('kɔndʌkt) *n.* (kən'dʌkt) *v.*

confidant *n.* **confident** *adj.*

The noun is an anglicised French word meaning 'someone to whom one entrusts one's
intimate secrets' and, when applied to a
76

woman, it has a final *e*. The pronunciation is
(kɔnfidænt). *Confident*, meaning 'feeling or
showing assurance', and *confidant* are both
related to the verb CONFIDE (q.v.)

confide *v.*

To *confide in* someone is to 'open your heart to
them', 'tell them your secrets', e.g. *Her heart
was breaking, and she had no one to confide in*. To
confide something *to* someone is to 'entrust it
to them', 'hand it over', e.g. *She confided her
personal documents to her lawyer*.

conflict ('kɔnflikt) *n.* (kən'flikt) *v.*

conjunction

The grammatical term for 'a word used to
join the parts of a sentence'. *And, as, because, or,
that, unless* are conjunctions. *Both . . . and,
either . . . or, neither . . . nor*, and *not only . . . but
also* are known as *correlative conjunctions*. They
must be carefully placed before the words
they are joining, not [*She neither looked to right
nor left*] but *She looked neither to right nor left*.
(SEE EITHER . . . OR; NUMBER)

conjure *v.*

The pronunciation is (kən'dʒuə) when the
sense is 'appeal to solemnly', e.g. *I conjure you
to hear my case*, but ('kʌndʒə) when it means
'perform conjuring tricks' or 'call up in the
imagination', e.g. *He conjured up the idea of a
perfect building*.

connection, connexion n.

Both spellings are used. *In connection with* is often used where one word would suffice, e.g. *The agent called to see him in connection with (about) his insurance policy.*

conservative adj.

This word is often used to describe estimates, figures etc. where a simpler one such as *low* or *moderate* could replace it.

consider see REGARD

constructional, constructive adj.

Constructional means 'to do with construction', e.g. *constructional toys; the constructional details of a building.* *Constructive* means 'helpful', 'positive', the opposite of *destructive*, e.g. *Have you any constructive suggestions?*

contemptible, contemptuous adj.

Contemptible means 'worthy to be despised, scorned', e.g. *He tried hard, but the results were contemptible. Contemptuous* means 'scornful', e.g. *Seeing that I failed to understand, he gave me a contemptuous look.*

content adj. n.

Used as an adjective meaning 'happy', and as a noun meaning 'satisfaction', the pronounciation is (kən'tent). The more familiar noun is *contentment*, except in phrases like *to his heart's content.* As a noun meaning 'that which is contained', the plural form is commoner, though the singular is preserved for 'the essential matter of a book or speech'. *It was a well-delivered speech, but I could not agree with its content*; *Show me the contents of your suitcase.* Both these uses have the pronunciation ('kɔntent,-s).

contiguous see ADJACENT

continual, continuous *adj.*

Continual means 'always going on' or 'frequently repeated', e.g. *Their shortage of money was a continual worry. Continuous* means 'uninterrupted', but not necessarily spread over a long period, e.g. *There was a continuous noise of hammering next door.*

continuance, continuation, continuity *n.*

Continuance and *continuation* share the sense of 'the act or state of continuing', e.g. *The continuance* (or *continuation*) *of his grant depends on his good examination results. Continuation* has the added sense of 'an extension', 'a further instalment', e.g. *There will be a continuation of the debate next week for pupils who are interested. Continuity* is 'the state of being continuous', 'consistency', and is used in radio and the cinema in this way.

contraction

Contracted forms such as *isn't, we'll* are only used in conversation, in personal letters, and dialogue.

contrary, converse, opposite *adj. n.*

When pronounced (kən'treəri) this word is an adjective and means 'peevish', 'given to making difficulties'. ('kɔntrəri) can be an adjective or a noun. *On the contrary* implies difference, but not necessarily the opposite, e.g. *I did not go to London, on the contrary I went to Paris. Converse* implies a switching round of roles, e.g. *It isn't true that I went to see James; the converse is the truth; he came to see me. Opposite* could be substituted in the second example, but it has a more absolute meaning than the other two, as a statement can have only one opposite, e.g. *I did not go to London, I did the opposite and stayed at home.*

converse *adj. n. v.*

As adjective and noun meaning 'opposite' this word is stressed ('kɔnvəːs); the verb meaning to 'tell', 'hold a conversation' is pronounced (kən'vəːs). (see CONTRARY)

convex see CONCAVE

co-respondent ('kouris'pɔndənt) *n.* **correspondent** (,kɔris'pɔndənt) *n.*

A *co-respondent* is 'a person named in a divorce suit as having committed adultery with a wife or husband'. A *correspondent* is 'a person writing letters' or 'one sending regular articles to a newspaper or magazine, e.g. *foreign correspondent.*

corroborate, verify *v.*

These words are sometimes used as if they were interchangeable, but they have their own different meanings. To *corroborate* is to 'provide fresh evidence of the truth of something', 'confirm', e.g. *His story, unbelievable as it seemed at first, was corroborated when the second messenger arrived.* To *verify* is to 'check the truth of', e.g. *His whole theory turned out to be false, because he had not verified the facts on which it was based.*

council, counsel *n.*

A *council* is 'a meeting' and 'those who meet'; individually they are *councillors*. *Counsel* means 'advice', and those who give it are *counsellors*. *Counsel* is also the legal term for 'a barrister', always used in the singular form.

counterpart *n.*

A confusing word, as it can have two almost opposite meanings:—

1. 'equivalent' or 'similar', e.g. *In Britain the robin is a small bird, but its counterpart in America is much larger.*

2. 'complement', 'something opposite but corresponding', e.g. *The right-hand glove is the counterpart of the left.*

of course

This expression is often used, especially by journalists, in a spirit of condescension, to emphasize a fact unlikely to be known to the reader, e.g. *He was descended, of course, from the famous John Brown, the American hero.*

credence ('kri:dəns), **credit** ('kredit) *n.*

To *give credence* means to 'believe', e.g. *We gave no credence to his reports*, and has no other meaning though it is sometimes inaccurately used for 'credit', 'support', e.g. [*His smart appearance gave credence to the story that he was rich*].

credible, creditable, credulous *adj.*

Credible means 'believable', e.g. *It is hardly credible that time should have passed so quickly*; *Creditable* means 'worthy of praise', e.g. *His efforts this term have been most creditable*; *Credulous* means 'easily hoodwinked', 'too ready to believe', e.g. *Only the credulous will accept the official figures*.

creole (kri:'oul) *adj. n.*

This word is used to describe a native of the West Indies or Spanish America, whose parents were both Europeans. Such people, especially if there is an expatriate community in the country, tend to speak a language compounded of the European language and their native language. (see MULATTO; QUADROON)

criterion

Plural *criteria*.

cult *n.*

From meaning 'religious worship' this word has become popularly used for 'a temporary enthusiasm or craze', e.g. *The cult of the open-air life.*

curb *n. v.* **kerb** *n.*

The first form is used for the verb meaning 'check, hold in, restrain', for the noun where it refers to 'part of a horse's harness', and in the figurative sense of 'restraint', e.g. *Try to curb your impatience.* For the edge of a pavement the form *kerb* is more often used.

curtailed words see ABBREVIATION; APOCOPE

customer see CLIENT

cyclopedia (shortened form of **encyclopedia**) see DICTIONARY

cynic *n.* **cynical** *adj.*

The word *cynic* is now only used as a noun, meaning 'a person of a sceptical temperament', while the adjective is always *cynical.*

czar, tsar, tzar *n.*

The first is the usual spelling.

D

dare *v.*

This verb has two meanings. With the first, which is 'have the courage to do something', it can make two kinds of sentence:—*He dare not say anything* or *He does not dare to say anything.* (SEE NEED)

The second meaning is 'challenge or defy someone to do something', e.g. *He dares me to tell the police what I heard*; *My friends dared me to climb the tree.* *Durst* is an archaic form of *dared*. *Dare say* is written as two words, even when it means 'expect', 'imagine', e.g. *I dare say he will be late.*

dashes see PUNCTUATION

data *n.*

This Latin plural is still used with a plural form of the verb, e.g. *Make sure your data are correct.* (SEE SPELLING, NOUNS)

dates

1. The usual forms for the date at the head of a letter are *2 July 1946* or *July 2nd 1946.* The first is better as it builds up logically, day-month-year, and avoids the necessity for *-st*, *-nd* or *-th*. It is better to avoid putting the whole date in numbers, e.g. *2.7.46* because the order is different in the U.S., so to an American it would mean '*7 February 1946*'.

2. In writing pairs of dates there should be either *from . . . to . . .*, e.g. *He was abroad from 1910 to 1912*, or a hyphen, as in *He spent the years 1910-12 abroad.* There is no need to use both.

3. A.D. comes before the figures. B.C. after them.

4. Where there are pairs of years it is only necessary to give as much of the second one as will make it clear, e.g. *1760–1*, *1762–70*, *1762–1800*. (see CENTURY; TWENTIES)

in this day and age

This is an overworked cliché which adds nothing to *in these days*, *at this time*.

decided, decisive *adj.* **decidedly, decisively** *adv.*

Decided means 'firm', 'definite', or 'of a resolute nature'; *decisive* is not usually applied to people: it means 'important', 'final', e.g. *There is a decided touch of frost in the air*; *She is a woman of decided character, and will be sure to get her own way*; *The decisive battle of the war was fought on that day*; *At the decisive point in the match rain stopped play*. *Decidedly* means 'definitely', 'undoubtedly' and is often placed before the verb, e.g. *She decidedly preferred to live by herself* (cf. *She frequently came to see us on Sundays*). *Decisively* means 'firmly', 'conclusively'.

decimate *v.*

This verb means strictly to 'eliminate one out of ten', but it has become loosely used for any large-scale reduction in numbers, and absurdly in phrases like [*The enemy was decimated by* 50%].

85

décor, decoration n.

Decoration is the general term for 'ornament', 'the act of decorating'; *décor* is the word used for a stage setting.

defective, deficient adj.

Defective comes from the noun *defect*, and means 'imperfect in quality', while *deficient* refers to a deficit or deficiency, and means 'inadequate in quantity', 'insufficient', e.g. *When the water supply was deficient the sanitary measures were bound to be defective.*

defensible, defensive adj.

Defensible is used of 'something that can be defended', *defensive* for 'something used in the act of defending', e.g. *His line of conduct was defensible as it was the only practicable one; Britain sold the aeroplanes on the condition they were to be used only for defensive purposes.*

definite, definitive (di'finitiv) adj.

Definite means 'firm', clear'; *definitive*, which is sometimes loosely used in the same sense, strictly means 'final', 'absolute', e.g. *I made a definite offer for the house; This will surely be the definitive edition of his Works.*

definitely adv.

This word has ceased to be of value for adding emphasis and is often used without much meaning instead of *yes*, and in sentences like *It's definitely beginning to rain.*

delimit *v.*

Delimit can mean either 'define limits and fix boundaries', e.g. *The boundary wall delimited his land*, or 'end a restriction', the opposite of 'limit', e.g. *The Board of Trade has delimited the import of sugar*.

delusion, illusion *n.*

A *delusion* is 'a firm belief in something false or untrue, usually lasting', while an *illusion* can be temporary and voluntary, e.g. *Napoleon suffered from the delusion that his army was irresistible; While the manager was away she enjoyed the illusion of being in full charge*. These words can be interchangeable, e.g. *If we take it that our difficulties are over we are under a delusion or an illusion*.

dependent *n.* **dependant** *adj.*

(cf. *descendant*)

depends *v.*

It is becoming pedantic to follow this word invariably by *on*, e.g. *It depends on what he says*. But when there is a subject other than *it*, the custom is to follow with *on*, e.g. *The price depends on the state of the market. It all depends* is colloquial.

deprecate, depreciate (di'priːʃieit) *v.*

To *deprecate* means to 'express strong disapproval of something', e.g. *The Home Secretary deprecated the use of corporal punishment in schools. Depreciate* can be either intransitive or transitive, and means 'lose value' or 'belittle', e.g. *A machine will depreciate if allowed to get rusty; This author's works will one day be widely read, no matter how much the critics depreciate them now; All my shares have depreciated lately.*

descendant *n.* **descendent** *adj.*

The first means 'one who is descended from an ancestor', as in *I am a distant descendant of a thirteenth-century French Count. Descendent* is an adjective meaning 'descending' but now very rarely used, because of its similarity in spelling and pronunciation to *descendant.*

(cf. *dependent*)

devoted, devout *adj.*

Both these words have the sense of 'zealously dedicated', but whereas *devoted* can be used of a *husband, servant, admirer* etc., *devout* is mainly used in a religious context, meaning 'pious, passionately religious'. The word is occasionally used to mean 'eager', as in the phrase *I devoutly hope*. Both words come from a Latin word meaning to 'vow'.

dialect see LANGUAGE TERMS

dialogue *n.*

This is 'direct speech, the words written as they would have been spoken'. (see PUNCTUATION, INVERTED COMMAS)

88

dictionary, encyclopedia, lexicon n.

Dictionaries and *lexicons* both give a list of the words in a language arranged alphabetically with their meanings and often their pronunciation and derivation. If the language is a foreign one a translation is given, and it may be two-way, i.e. *English-French, French-English.* An *encyclopedia* is also arranged alphabetically; it contains classified information on all branches of knowledge or on some or one of them, e.g. *an encyclopedia of gardening.* The term *dictionary* is becoming more popular for the single subject encyclopedia. *Handbooks* and *Companions* are also frequently arranged in this way.

different *adj.*

This word can be followed by either *from* or *to;* the occasional awkward use of *than* is probably due to confusion with *other than,* e.g. [*His results were different than those he had received before*]. Sometimes the adjective is incorrectly used where the adverb is required, e.g. [*He speaks different from the way he used to speak*], presumably by analogy with *he looks different.* *Think* and *feel* can be used with either form according to the sense, e.g. *The new carpet feels different from the old one. When you have read his letter I am sure you will feel differently towards him.*

digraph ('daigrɑːf), **diphthong** ('difθɔŋ) *n.*

Digraph is a phonetic term for a vowel sound which is really two, although written with either one or two letters, e.g. *time, tame, tome, bough, boy, beer*. Diphthong is the term used for 'two letters forming one sound in a word', e.g. *æ* in *orthopædic* and *œ* in *amœba*.

dilemma *n.*

This word is loosely used for 'a problem or difficulty'. Strictly it should be kept for cases where there are only two possibilities of action, e.g. *Forced to leave either her husband or her children, she found herself in a dreadful dilemma.*

diminish, minimize *v.*

To *diminish* is 'make less or become less', e.g. *The dangers of driving diminish as roads are improved*. To *minimize* is to 'make as little as possible of something', 'underestimate', e.g. *It does not pay to minimize the dangers of the journey.*

diminutives

These are nouns which have been altered in form to express smallness, usually by the addition of a suffix, e.g. *flatlet, kitchenette, duckling.*

direct speech see PUNCTUATION, INVERTED COMMAS

disinterested, uninterested *adj. past part.*

These words are often confused: *disinterested* means 'having no personal advantage at

90

stake', 'having no axe to grind'; *uninterested* means 'having no interest in a subject', e.g. *He gave disinterested support to the cause, for he had nothing to gain by its success; I tried to infect him with some enthusiasm, but he remained uninterested.* The noun form from *disinterested* is *disinterestedness*; from *uninterested* it is *disinterest.*

dispersal, dispersion *n.*

Dispersal is 'the act of dispersing', e.g. *The police quietly effected the dispersal of the crowd*; *dispersion* is 'the resultant state of having been dispersed', e.g. *The wide dispersion of the family made it difficult to get in touch with all the members.*

dissociate *v.*

This, not [*disassociate*], is the opposite of *associate.*

distinct, distinctive, distinguished *adj.*

Distinct means 'clear', 'easily recognized', e.g. *I noticed a distinct coolness in his manner.* Followed by *from* it means 'separate', 'different', e.g. *Let us keep the legal view distinct from the moral one.* *Distinctive* is applied to a characteristic particularly associated with a certain object, e.g. *You cannot fail to recognize him by his distinctive style of dress.* It is often used by critics for a quality they find hard to define, e.g. *his distinctive style.* *Distinguished* means 'exceptional', 'eminent'.

distinction *n.*

There are three uses of this word:—

1. 'The process of distinguishing between things', e.g. *Distinction between innocence and guilt is sometimes difficult even for the wisest judge.*

2. 'The characteristics which make things different', e.g. *One of the chief distinctions between an apple and a pear is the difference in their shape.*

3. 'The quality of being distinguished', e.g. *a composer of great distinction.*

distrust, mistrust *v. n.*

Mistrust is a weaker word than *distrust*, it means to 'have doubts' rather than to 'have no trust in'. *The villagers seemed friendly enough but we mistrusted their politeness; He mistrusts his own abilities; I distrust his promise to repay me.*

do *v.*

1. This verb is used as an auxiliary in negative or interrogative sentences, e.g. *Did you have a good time?* where *Had you a good time?* would sound slightly pedantic. In the U.S. *Do you have a newspaper?* is a simple question relating to the present, whereas here it implies a continuing process, i.e. *Do you take a newspaper?* rather than *Do you have one now?*

2. *Do* is used for emphasis or persuasion, e.g. *I do mean it, Do come and see me.*

3. Difficulties of consistency arise when *do*

is used as a substitute verb to avoid repetition (a) of a passive, e.g. [*He told me to be photographed, but I did not do it*] (instead of *have it done*), (b) of a verb which has not actually been used, e.g. [*Instructions were not forthcoming though the authorities had promised to do so*] (instead of *promised to issue them*), (c) of *be* or *have*, e.g. [*He has not been to a university as I have done*] (instead of *have*).

4. It is used redundantly in *Will he come? I think he will* (*do*).

5. The negative interrogative forms are *Didn't you have a good time?* or the rarer form, found chiefly in Scotland, *Did you not have a good time?*

Doctor see PUNCTUATION, FULL STOPS; LETTER WRITING

donate *v.*

A formal word for 'give', a back formation from the noun *donation*. A person who gives is a *donor* or *donator*, one who receives is a *donee*.

double comparatives and superlatives

Phrases like [*more lovelier, most highest*] are no longer acceptable in speech or writing.

double negatives

Sometimes these are useful because they express a limited doubt or a subtle difference from the affirmative, e.g. *He was not unhappy at school.* Otherwise they are used to add a tone of formality and obscurity to official language, e.g. [*Nevertheless on no account do we not want to be considered unwilling to negotiate*].

double passives

Some of these have become acceptable, e.g. *All the prisoners were ordered to be shaved,* where *prisoners* is the subject of both *ordered* and *shaved,* but this does not apply to [*All the houses were ordered to be pulled down*], which is confusing. It could mean either *All the houses were earmarked for demolition* or *It was ordered that all the houses should be pulled down.*

double subject see NUMBER

doubt *n. v.* doubtful *adj.*

These words are followed by *whether* or *if* in a positive statement, e.g. *I doubt whether we shall have enough food,* and by *that* in a negative one, e.g. *I am not at all doubtful that we shall have enough.*

doubtless, no doubt

Both of these are used with the sense of 'probably', often with a tone of irony, e.g. *No doubt you know more about it than I do.* For emphasis, and to express certainty, the phrases used are *undoubtedly, without a doubt, beyond (a) doubt.*

draft *n. v.* draught *n.*

These words come from different senses of the

94

verb *draw*. *Draft* can mean 'a sum of money drawn from a bank', or again 'a rough plan', as in *This is only the first draft*. In the U.S. it is used for the conscription of men whose names are drawn by the selection board, and for those who have been conscripted in this way. *Draught* is used for 'a drink', for 'beer drawn from the barrel,' for 'a cold current of air', and 'a ship's displacement', and in the plural in the game of *draughts*.

drier *adj. n.* **dryer** *n.*

The first of these spellings is the only correct one for the comparative form of *dry*. For the noun meaning 'a machine for drying things' both spellings are acceptable, but *dryer* is more common.

drink, drank *v.* **drunk, drunken** *adj. past part.*
Despite the danger to his health, by midnight he had drunk more whisky than anyone else; He drank three glasses of water at half time. (cf. *sing* and *sink*). *Drunk* describes 'a temporary state of intoxication', *drunken* 'a habitual one'.

due to

This is not strictly acceptable in an adverbial phrase instead of *owing to* or *because of*, e.g. *Due to the illness of the chief actor, the play had to be withdrawn*, but its colloquial use in this way is increasing.

dues see TAX

duteous, dutiful *adj.*

   Duteous, like *beauteous*, *bounteous*, *piteous* and
   plenteous, is not part of current everyday usage.

dye

   Present participle *dyeing*.

E

-eable see SPELLING, ADJECTIVES

each *adj. pro.*

   Like *every*, this word gives rise to doubts about
   whether the verb used with it should be
   singular or plural. When *each* is used as an
   adjective with the subject of a sentence or as a
   pronoun, a singular verb is used, e.g. *Each
   car was noisier than the last*; *Each was given his
   own bed*. When it is a pronoun referring to an
   antecedent, it takes its number accordingly,
   e.g. *They arrived late at night, and were each
   given a bed*. Between each (see BETWEEN). *Each
   other* can be used for more than two people,
   e.g. *The children were taught that they must all
   return each other's books*.

economic, economical *adj.*

   Economic means 'governed by the laws of
   economics', 'practicable', 'giving a fair
   return', e.g. *Although she is my friend, I am going
   to charge her an economic rent for the room.*

Economical is 'concerned with economy', 'thrifty', e.g. *an economical person* or *way of living*.

effect *v.* see AFFECT

effective, effectual, efficacious, efficient *adj.*

All these words are connected with the verb *effect* and share the meaning 'capable of producing results', but they have different applications. *Effective* can also mean 'showy', 'successful', and is applied to colour schemes, dress, the arts. *Efficient* is used for people in the sense of 'being competent', and for methods and machines which achieve their purposes. *Effectual* lays more emphasis on results, e.g. *No propaganda has so far been effectual in reducing smoking*. *Efficacious* is only used of medical remedies and treatment, e.g. *efficacious in the treatment of coughs*.

egoist, egotist *n.*

Both these words refer to a person who is 'self-centred'; an *egoist* acts selfishly and always in his own interest; an *egotist* may merely talk too much about himself or try to attract attention to himself. The adjectives are *egoistic* or *egoistical*, *egotistic* or *egotistical*.

ei, ie see SPELLING

either ('aiðə*) or ('i:ðə*) *adj. pro.*

Either can only be used where there are two people or things being described; if there are more, *any* must be used. The verb following it is always singular, even if it refers to two groups, e.g. *The French are playing the Russians this afternoon, but I cannot tell if either has won.*

either .... or

If there are two singular subjects the verb is singular, e.g. *Either the bank or the post office is sure to be open.* If one or both subjects are plural, so is the verb, e.g. *Either the candidate or his parents are to sign this form.*

eke out *v.*

This means 'make something in short supply go further', e.g. *We eked out the meat with large helpings of potato; She eked out her small capital by taking in boarders.* The object of this verb is the substance in short supply; it is wrongly used in [*They eked out a miserable existence*].

elder *adj. n.* **eldest** *adj.*

This adjective is now chiefly used to denote seniority among the members of a family, e.g. *my eldest* (rather than *oldest*) *sister*. However, it is still retained in *elder statesman* and *elders of the Presbyterian Church.*

eligible ('elidʒəbl), **illegible** (i'ledʒəbl) *adj.*

Eligible means 'suitable', 'qualified for election', 'fit and worthy to be chosen'. *Illegible* describes writing which is 'unreadable'.

else *adv.*

1. [*You must buy a ticket, else you can't come with us.*] Being an adverb, *else* cannot join two

clauses as a conjunction does, so the above sentence should be: *You must buy a ticket or (else) you can't come with us.*

2. [*The explosion in the High Street turned out to be nothing else but a car backfiring.*] *Else* is followed by *than* not *but*, so either *nothing else than* or *nothing but* should be written. (cf. *other*; *more*)

3. The genitive forms *anyone else's*, *someone else's* are used, but with *who* there is a choice between *whose else* and *who else's*, the former being more common.

emend see AMEND

emigrant, immigrant *n.* **migrant** *adj. n.*

An *emigrant* is a person leaving a country to settle in another; when he arrives there he is known as an *immigrant*. *Migrant* can be used of humans in demographical surveys as a noun, but is generally used as an adjective for birds which move to warmer or cooler areas in different seasons.

eminent *adj.*

This means 'outstanding', 'distinguished', e.g. *an eminent surgeon*. It is sometimes confused with *imminent*. (see IMMANENT)

encyclopedia see DICTIONARY

enough see SUFFICIENT

enquire, inquire *v.* **enquiry, inquiry** *n.*

To some extent these verbs are interchangeable, but *to enquire* has the simple meaning 'to ask', whereas *to inquire into* is 'investigate'. So an *enquiry* is usually 'a request for information', an *inquiry* 'a formal investigation'.

ensure, insure *v.*

To *ensure* is 'make certain', e.g. *I will start early to ensure that I arrive in time.* To *insure* is 'protect by insurance', e.g. *She insured her jewels against theft.*

enthuse see BACK FORMATION

envelop (in'veləp) *v.* **envelope** ('envəloup) *n.*

equable, equitable *adj.*

Equable means 'uniform in intensity', 'not variable', e.g. *He always went to the Channel Islands for his holiday because of the equable climate.* It can also be used to describe a person's nature, meaning 'unruffled', the opposite of *precipitate*. *Equitable* can also be used of people in the sense of 'fair-minded', as well as of a *decision, reward, appointment* etc. where it has the sense of 'just'.

equally *adv.*

As is unnecessary after this word, e.g. *Her skill at cooking was remarkable, and her sewing equally good* (or *and her sewing as good*), not [*equally as good*]. In formal speech or writing *equally with* is used, e.g. *I value his opinion equally with my own.*

-er, -or see SPELLING, NOUNS

-er, -est, more, most see SPELLING, ADJECTIVES

ere *prep.*

   Archaic form of *before.*

escalate *v.*

   A back formation from *escalator* (see STYLE). The original meaning of 'increase by stages' has developed recently into the sense of 'increase in an uncontrolled or disproportionate way', e.g. *Some people believe that the escalation of the war is inevitable.*

especially, specially *adv.*

   Especially means 'to a great degree', e.g. *I was especially happy that day. Specially* means 'for a particular purpose', e.g. *I was specially asked to meet him.* These words are loosely used as if they were interchangeable, e.g. [*It was specially kind of you to ask me*]; [*The trees were planted especially for the occasion*]. *More especially* is sometimes used, but *more* is quite superfluous: [*We can expect colder weather, more especially in the north*].

Esperanto see LANGUAGE TERMS

essay see ASSAY

etc. (ˌetˈsetərə)

   This abbreviated form of the Latin *et cetera* is widely used. It can refer to either people or things, meaning 'and the others' or 'and the rest', but it is not used in formal writing.

&c. is sometimes found, particularly in commercial documents.

euphemism ('ju:fəmizm), **euphony** ('ju:fəni), **euphuism** ('ju:fju:izm) *n.*

In the first of these a less disagreeable word or phrase is substituted for a more accurate but more offensive one, e.g. *underprivileged* for *poor*, and many ways of referring to *death* and *dying* such as *passing on* or *at rest*. *Euphony* means 'pleasantness of sound'; *euphuism* is a literary term for 'an affected, elaborate and bombastic style of writing current in the late sixteenth and early seventeenth centuries.'

even see ONLY

-ever *suffix adv.*

As a suffix *-ever* may be added to the words *who, which, what, when, where, how* written as one word, e.g. *whoever, however,* etc. When used colloquially for emphasis, it is not joined to a preceding adverb, e.g. *Where ever did you get that hat? How ever shall we get there?*

every *adj.* **everyone, everybody** *pro.*

Every is followed by a singular verb and pronoun, e.g. *Every book is in its place. Everyone* and *everybody* vary according to whether the emphasis is on the group or the individuals, e.g. *Everybody wants to do his best; Everyone was cheering their loudest.* When the emphasis is on separateness, it is written as two words, e.g. *He wrote to every one of his friends to tell them the news.* (see EACH)

every day, everyday

The first of these is an adverbial phrase, e.g. *I see him every day*, the second an adjective, meaning 'ordinary', 'usual', e.g. *To him it was an everyday sight.*

except, excepting *prep.*

Used as a preposition, *except* is followed by *me*, *him*, etc., not *I*, *he* etc., e.g. *They were all ready except me* (see BUT). As a conjunction for *unless*, it is archaic, e.g. *Except you obey me, you will be punished. Excepting* is used instead of *except* where it follows *always*, *not*, *without*.

exceptional, exceptionable *adj.*

The first means 'unusual', 'outstanding', e.g. *He shows exceptional talent.* The second means 'objectionable'. 'something to take exception to', e.g. *His behaviour was exceptionable.*

excess *n.*

This word, which has the meaning of 'too much of something', 'more than usual', is sometimes confused with ACCESS (q.v.)

exclamation marks see PUNCTUATION

explicit see IMPLICIT

extempore (eks'tempəri), **impromptu** (im-'prɔmtju:) *adj. adv.*

As *extempore* can be either an adjective or an adverb, there is no need for [*extemporary*] or

103

[*extemporarily*]. It refers to 'a speech or performance given without notes or previous preparation', while an *impromptu* speech is one the speaker was not expecting to have to give.

exterior, external; interior, internal *adj.*

As adjectives, either *exterior* and *external* or *interior* and *internal* are interchangeable, but the use of *exterior* always implies an *interior* and vice versa. *External* has the additional meaning of 'superficial', 'inessential'. Cf. the following examples: *There is a strong lock on the exterior door* (implying that there is also an interior door); *I am judging from external evidence* ('outside the subject itself'); *He told the interior story of prison life* ('from the inside'); *This arrangement is purely an internal one* ('not concerning those outside').

F

factitious, fictitious, fictional *adj.*

Factitious means 'engineered', 'artificially accentuated'; its antonym is *spontaneous*. *Fictitious* means 'counterfeit', 'unreal', 'untrue'. A *factitious event* is 'one which is contrived so as to achieve more excitement and interest than it is worth', e.g. television games or some kinds of advertising. A *fictitious event* is one that is incorrectly reported to have taken place. *Fictional* means 'occurring in fiction'; its antonym is *non-fictional*.

farther *adj. adv.* **further** *adj. adv. v.*

Further is the commoner of these two words—which are for the most part interchangeable—and is also used as a verb. *Farther* is slightly more often used where physical distance is concerned.

feasible *adj.*

This word has one of the meanings of *possible*, 'practicable', 'able to be done', but it is often incorrectly used for *probable*, e.g. [*It is feasible that he won't paint the house if it rains*].

female *n. adj.* **feminine** *adj.*

Female is used as a noun as well as an adjective, and states the sex of human beings or animals, e.g. *The female lion is called a lioness*. *Feminine* is only an adjective and is used for the characteristics of the sex, e.g. *feminine grace, feminine intuition*. (cf. *male* and *masculine*)

feminine forms

These are occasionally used in professions and occupations, and some are well established, e.g. *actress, heroine, postmistress*. It is more general now to use the masculine form and add *woman* when necessary to differentiate, e.g. *woman doctor*. Words like *mayoress* are useful because they describe a separate function. The suffix *-ette* is usually avoided though now accepted in *usherette*.

ferment (fə'ment) *v.* ('fə:ment) *n.* **foment** (fou'ment) *v.*

The literal meaning of *ferment* is 'undergo or cause fermentation'. Yeast is used to ferment sugar, causing it to effervesce and make bread rise. Figuratively it is used for 'stir up trouble'.

Foment is also used in this sense, but it is better to confine its use to the literal one of 'applying a hot dressing to an infected part of the body', e.g. a boil.

few *adj. n.*

This word is a noun in *a few*, meaning 'a small number', 'some', 'not none', e.g. *The strawberries were nearly over but we found a few. Few*, as an adjective, is the opposite of *many*, e.g. *There were so few strawberries that it was hardly worthwhile picking them.* (Cf. *little* and *a little*: *Little remains to be said on this subject. I hope you will tell us a little of what you know.*) *A good few, quite a few* are colloquial expressions. *Comparatively few* is often used where there is no comparison.

(see COMPARATIVES)

fewer see LESS

fictitious, fictional see FACTITIOUS

finalize *v.*

Official and commercial jargon, used instead of the obvious and satisfactory words *complete* and *finish*.

flaunt, flout *v.*

These words are often confused though their meanings are almost opposite. To *flaunt* is 'wave or display something in an ostentatious way', e.g. *flaunt one's riches*. To *flout* is 'mock at', 'defy openly', 'insult', e.g. *flout the law*.

floor, storey *n.*

In Britain the *first storey* of a building is the one above the *ground floor*, in the U.S. it is the one at ground level. Note the plural *storeys*.

focus *n.*

This word can only be used in connection with eyes and vision, not with ears and sound. The plural is *focuses* or *foci*. Past tense is *focused*.

folk *n.*

This is a collective noun so there is no need for a plural, though *folks* is sometimes used colloquially. Used for 'people' especially for 'one's relatives' it has a homely sound, e.g. *Let's go and visit the old folks*.

Folklore is written as one word, but most other compounds are written as two, e.g. *folk dance*, *folk song*, if there is no chance of

107

ambiguity.   (see Punctuation, hyphen)

as follows

This is an impersonal phrase, so it is always used in the singular form, regardless of number.

foment see FERMENT

for-, fore *prefix*

Where the prefix means 'away', 'out', 'not', it is spelt *for-* as in *forgo, forswear, forget, forlorn forbid.* Fore- has the sense 'before', 'former', 'in front of', e.g. *foresee, foretell, foreground, foreboding. Forbear* is a verb meaning 'desist', 'not do something': *forebear* is a noun meaning 'ancestor'. *Forego* is to 'go before', archaic except in *a foregone conclusion*; *forgo* means 'deny oneself something'.

forbid, forbad(e) *v.*

Forbid is correctly used in *I forbid you to see my daughter again; It is forbidden to walk on the grass.* It is used loosely for 'prevent', e.g. *Decency forbids my telling you more. Forbad* is a commoner form of the past tense than *forbade*. (see PROHIBIT)

forbidding *adj.* **foreboding** *n.*

Forbidding means 'stern', 'menacing'. Foreboding is 'a presentiment', 'grim threatening.'

forceful, forcible *adj.*

Both these words are adjectives from *force*, but *forcible* has the more literal meaning of 'by force', e.g. *We had to use forcible means to keep her from going back to the burning house* or *We had to use force ... Forcible* can also have the more metaphorical sense of 'cogent' and it overlaps with *forceful* to mean 'vigorous', 'energetic', 'impressive', e.g. *a forceful personality, a forceful argument.*

FOREIGN WORDS AND PHRASES

Borrowing from other languages is a continuous process, and no firm line can be drawn between words which are recognized as foreign and those which have been absorbed into the English language. Some distinction in their use can be made according to which of the following categories they fall into.

The first consists of expressions which have retained their native form, sometimes abbreviated, and which have usually no familiar equivalent. It includes Latin phrases like *anno Domini, ad hoc, etcetera, de facto;* French social and cooking terms like *au pair, paté, soufflé;* and Italian musical terms like *concerto, allegro.* These require no indication of their foreign origin in writing, and have a recognized English pronunciation.

The other class of words and phrases is most frequently found in literary and learned

works, and in the conversation of people who
have read or travelled widely, or wish to
give the impression of having done so. It is
no longer safe to assume that all educated
people have a knowledge of Latin, so the use
of tags and quotations from that language is
becoming rare, but French, German, and
Italian words are constantly used and offer
many pitfalls. If they are likely to be unfamiliar to the reader they should appear in
italics in print, and in single inverted commas
in writing. When the writer is not very familiar with the language from which he is
borrowing he can easily make mistakes in
either the form or the meaning of what he
borrows, as when [*cri de coeur*] is written for
cri du coeur, or *arrière pensée* used in the sense of
'afterthought'. Pronunciation raises another
difficulty as it is impossible to give a fully
correct sound to a foreign word in the middle
of an English sentence, while to anglicize it
completely may give an appearance of
ignorance. Generally a compromise pronunciation is used.

Clearly the best course to follow when considering the use of foreign phrases is to look
for an English equivalent. If there is none
care should be taken that both form and meaning are correct, and that their use makes for

clarity and precision rather than obscurity and affectation.

Some of the most commonly used foreign words and phrases are given in the Appendix. These are not necessarily recommended for use in writing, but are listed to help those who meet them in reading.

forename see CHRISTIAN NAME

for ever *adv.*

Usually written as two words.

foreword, preface, introduction *n.*

All these words can be used for the introduction to a book. A *preface* is often written by someone other than the author.

former, latter *adj.*

These words are only used in formal writing and do not help to produce clarity; *first* and *second* are more familiar, and have the additional advantage of not limiting the writer to two nouns or names.

forms of address see LETTER WRITING

forward, forwards *adv.*

Sometimes these forms are interchangeable, but *forward* is becoming commoner. It is the one most often used in questions of time; *forwards* is used to denote a direction.

fragile, frail *adj.*

Both these adjectives mean 'easily broken or destroyed', but *fragile* has the narrower sense

111

of 'liable to snap or break', 'delicate', e.g.
This china is fragile, do not touch it. *Frail* is also
used metaphorically, e.g. *a frail old man* or
human frailty which describes 'moral weakness'.

framework *n.*

A word often appearing in official jargon
(see STYLE) instead of simpler phrases, e.g.
*He could only consider the problem within the
framework of the housing situation* (*in connection
with housing*). (cf. *context, landscape*)

free *adj.*

This has the compounds *freeborn, freehold,
freelance, freemason, freethinker* written without a
hyphen, and the following written with one:
free-hand, free-spoken, free-wheel.

free-will *adj.* **free will** *n.*

The hyphen is used strictly in accordance
with the part of speech. It appears in the
adjective, e.g. *A free-will offering,* but not in
the noun, e.g. *The doctrine of free will.*

French words see FOREIGN WORDS AND
PHRASES

-ful *suffix*

Nouns ending with this suffix make their
plural by adding a final *s* not one in the
middle, e.g. *teaspoonfuls, platefuls, handfuls.*

full stops (periods) see PUNCTUATION

funeral *n.* **adj.** **funereal** (.fju'ni:əriəl) *adj.*

Funeral is a noun in use as an adjective, so it

112

can only describe something connected with a funeral, e.g. *a funeral procession*, whereas *funereal* means 'gloomy', 'dismal', 'like a funeral', e.g. *The dark wallpaper made the room funereal*, or *His clothes were funereal*, i.e. gloomy enough to be worn at a funeral.

further see FARTHER

G

gala ('gɑːlə) or ('geilə) *n.*

Gallic, Gaelic *adj.*
Gallic refers to the Gauls or the French, and is used for some French attributes, e.g. *Gallic wit*. *Gaelic*, pronounced ('geilik) or ('gælik), means pertaining to the Gaels, i.e. the Highland Scottish Celts, and is the word for their language.

gallop, galop *n. v.*
The second spelling is the dance. Both verbs have past tense *-oped*, present participle *-oping*.

gaol, jail *n.*
Both spellings are acceptable in ordinary writing, and are both pronounced (dʒeil), but legal and official English writing uses the first.

gambit *n.*
A fashionable word loosely used for 'any opening move or statement'. In chess it means 'the

sacrifice of a pawn or piece', implying willingness to lose it for the sake of later gain.

gap *n.*

In journalism this metaphor for the 'difference between two sets of things' is often loosely used and its literal meaning forgotten, e.g. *The trade gap widens* makes sense, but *The credibility gap builds up suspicion* does not, because a gap cannot build.

garbled *adj.*

Though it is often used to mean simply 'confused' the full meaning of this word is 'distorted, often by a deliberate selection of facts, to support one's evidence', e.g. *a garbled version* of an eye-witness's story.

gender *n.*

This word is only used in grammar, and not otherwise as a synonym for *sex*.

generic, genetic *adj.* **genetics** *n.*

Generic is the adjective from the Latin word *genus*, which is used, especially in botany and zoology, to signify 'a class or an order'. It is in this way contrasted with a *species*, which is 'a smaller, more closely-knit group within a genus', and the adjectives *generic* and *specific* are used as antonyms. *Genetic* refers to creation and reproduction; the noun *genetics* means 'the study of heredity in individuals or of the physiology of reproduction'. (see -IC, -ICS)

genie, genius, genus n.

Genii is the usual plural form of *genie*. *Genius* (see TALENT) adds the suffix *es*, while *genus*, meaning 'a class' or 'an order', has the Latin plural *genera*.

gentility, gentleness n.

Gentility is the noun corresponding to the adjective *genteel*, and is mostly used of manners and a way of life, e.g. *Though shabbily dressed, she was obviously a person of some gentility.* Gentleness is 'the quality of being gentle' and is used of people and actions, e.g. *He picked up the injured child with great gentleness.*

gentle adj.

This word is archaic in phrases such as *gentle reader, the gentle art*.

gentleman n.

This word is disappearing from general use because of its class connotation. It is rare now to hear an honourable and considerate person described as *a perfect gentleman*. It is retained in the opening of speeches, e.g. *Ladies and Gentlemen*, and in titles such as *Gentlemen of the Jury*. The abbreviation *gent* is unacceptable.

gibe, gybe, jibe n. v.

Gibe and *jibe* are both used for the verb meaning 'taunt'; for the nautical term meaning to 'swing the sail from one side of the boat to the other' the spelling is *gybe*.

gimmick *n.*

A colloquial word which has rapidly become accepted in formal writing. It means 'a trick or device to secure publicity', and is generally used with grudging admiration.

gipsy, gypsy *n.*

Both spellings are used, the second is commoner in the plural *gypsies*.

glance, glimpse *n.*

A *glance* is primarily 'the act of looking', and 'the brief view obtained while taking it' is a *glimpse*; but the two overlap in sentences like *A brief glance* (or *glimpse*) *was enough to show him all he wanted to see*, though the meaning would not be exactly the same. You *take* or *have a glance* at something but you *catch a glimpse* of it.

God, god *n.*

A capital letter is used for reference to a single supreme deity and in direct address; a small letter for the idea of one deity among several, e.g. *a pagan god.*

good- see WELL-

goodbye, good-bye, good bye

All these forms are used.

goodwill *n.* **good-will** *adj.* **good will**

Goodwill is the form used where it refers to 'one of the assets of a business', e.g. *The ironmonger is selling the premises and the goodwill of his business.* The hyphenated form is the adjective, e.g. *He was making a good-will visit. Good will* is used for active or passive support, e.g. *Can I be sure of your good will towards the project?*

got, gotten *v.*

I have got to, meaning 'I must', is acceptable in all but the most formal speech and writing. *I have got,* expressing possession, is unnecessarily though very widely used. The past participle *gotten* is used in the U.S., but in British English it appears only in the phrase *ill-gotten gains.*

gourmand ('guəmənd), **gourmet** ('guəmei) *n.*

Both these words describe 'lovers of food', but the first implies gluttony, the second connoisseurship, the well-informed appreciation of good food and wine.

grand, great- *prefix.*

Grand is always used, without a hyphen, for the generations twice removed from one's own in the direct line, e.g. *grandfather, grandson.* For the generations beyond this *great* is added, with a hyphen, e.g. *great-granddaughter.* For niece, nephew, aunt and uncle *great* is usually preferred, although *grand* is still used.

gray, grey *adj.*

Both these spellings are used, *grey* more often.

Greek, Grecian *adj.*

The first of these is the one more often used to describe anything to do with Greece and its language; *Grecian* is kept for occasions where there is a question of style, e.g. art, architecture, facial outline (as in *Grecian nose*).

gulf, bay *n.*

Both are 'inlets of the sea'. A gulf is larger and deeper, and usually has a narrow entrance, e.g. *the Persian gulf*. A bay is wider at the mouth than a gulf, e.g. *the Bay of Biscay*.

gybe see GIBE

H

had see WERE

half, halves *adj. adv. n. prefix*

When *half* refers to a singular noun or pronoun it is followed by a singular verb; when it refers to a number it is plural, e.g. *half a pound is enough, half a dozen are needed*. In compound nouns and adjectives a hyphen is used, e.g. *a half-bottle of wine*, but not when it is used as an adverb, e.g. *the bottle was half empty*. Some words like *halfpenny* and *halfway* are written as one. Very occasionally the word *half* is loosely used for *part*, e.g. [*Divide it into three halves*].

halfpenny *n.*

This word has two plurals, *halfpence* and *half-pennies*. (see PENNY)

handful

Plural *handfuls*

hanged, hung *past part.*

Hanged is only used in connection with capital punishment, e.g. *The prisoner was sentenced to be hanged.*

hard, hardly *adv.*

Hard is the usual form of the adverb in the sense of 'in a hard way', 'energetically', though *hardly* is sometimes used. One reason for preferring *hard* is to avoid confusion with *hardly* in the sense of 'scarcely', which could occur in, e.g. *He was hardly hit by the Depression.* (see SCARCE; WITHOUT)

harmony, melody *n.*

Both these words are used in the general sense of 'musical sound', but the special meaning of *harmony* is 'the combination of notes played simultaneously to form chords', while *melody* is 'a succession of notes forming a tune'.

have *v.*

To have something done, e.g. *to have your house painted*, is British usage, but *to have some-one paint your house* is general in the U.S. On the other hand *We had our car stolen* is used in the U.S. for a simple passive.

haven n. **harbour** n. v. **port** n.

A *haven* provides 'a natural shelter for a ship';
a *harbour* can be natural or constructed and
provides 'anchorage for shipping'; a *port* is 'a
town with a harbour used by trading ships'.
They are used indiscriminately in metaphor,
e.g. *a haven of refuge, to harbour a grudge, any
port in a storm.*

haver ('heivə) v.

This is a Scottish and Northern English word
meaning to 'talk nonsense'. It is loosely used
for *dither* or *hesitate*.

head- *prefix*

Most compounds of this word are made
without hyphens, e.g. *headland, headmaster,
headstrong.* Exceptions are *head-dress, head-
hunting, head-on.*

hectic *adj.*

A fashionable word for 'excited' or 'exciting',
'very, very busy'. Medically it is used for
'feverish flushing'.

help v.

If there is direct participation it is not strictly
necessary to follow this word by *to*, e.g. *May I
help you (to) cross the road?* But where the verb
following help is a separate action *to* does
appear, e.g. *You have helped me to understand the
truth.*

[*I cannot help but be surprised*] uses a mixture

of *I cannot help being* and *I cannot but be*, either of which is preferable.

heredity (hi'rediti), **heritage** ('heritidʒ), **inheritance** *n.*

Heredity is often loosely used to mean 'ancestry', e.g. [*His manner was overbearing because he was conscious of his heredity*]. The true sense is 'the biological process of transmitting characteristics from parents to offspring', as in *Heredity accounts for the heavy jawbones that are characteristic of Early Man*. *Heritage* is something to which one is born or to which one succeeds as an heir, e.g. *The castle proved to be a costly heritage*. In the last example, *inheritance* could also have been used, but only *heritage* is used in a metaphorical sense, e.g. *The Dales are the heritage of every Yorkshireman*.

hesitance, hesitancy, hesitation *n.*

The first of these forms is obsolete, the other two are both used for 'reluctance to act', and for 'speech impediments'. *Hesitancy* is more often used to describe the personal characteristics which cause the *hesitation*, e.g. *His natural hesitancy made him slow to decide*.

high, highly *adv.*

Both these forms are used. *High* is more common for descriptions of distance from the ground, *highly* when the meaning is in a high degree, e.g.; *He was highly successful.*

high, tall *adj.*

There is a good deal of overlapping between these two, but some distinction. Strictly, *high* refers to distance from the ground, *tall* to the proportions of the object being described, e.g. *a high hill, a tall man. High* is most often used in the figurative sense, e.g. *high ideals*, and *tall* in the colloquial expression *a tall story*, meaning 'an exaggerated account'.

historic, historical *adj.*

Historic is now only used (and tends to be overused) for 'deserving a place in history'; it can describe either a building of some antiquity or an occasion deserving to be remembered. *Historical* means 'concerned with history', e.g. *a historical novel*, or 'known to have existed', e.g. *a historical character* as opposed to a mythical one.

hoard, horde *n.*

A *hoard* is 'a secret stock of something', e.g. money or arms. A *horde* is 'an unruly or unwanted crowd of people', originally savage tribes, in these days trippers, shoppers, Press photographers etc.

homonym,   homophone,   synonym, antonym

Homonym is the term used for words which are spelt alike but which have different meanings, e.g. *bark* for 'the outer covering of the trunk and branches of a tree' or 'the noise made by a dog'; *spoke* for 'the past tense of *speak*' or 'part of a wheel'; *see* for 'look' or 'a diocese'. *Homophones* are 'pairs of words which sound the same but have different spellings and meanings', e.g. *so, sew; ale, ail. Synonyms* are 'words which have approximately the same meaning, though they may have other meanings which are not the same', e.g. *leave, quit; shut, close; guest, visitor; fatherly, paternal. Antonyms* are 'words with opposite meanings'.

Hon.

1. The abbreviation for *honourable*. It is used for members of Parliament, who refer to each other as *the honourable member for X*, and not by name. It is also used for members of titled families who have no titles themselves, e.g. *the Hon. Mrs. X*, and for the holders of certain offices, e.g. judges, members of the Privy Council.

2. As an abbreviation for *honorary* it is applied to the officials of societies when they are unpaid, e.g. *Hon. Sec.*

hospitable ('hɔspitəbl) or (hə'spitəbl) *adj.*
The accent on the first syllable is more general. Both pronunciations are acceptable.

how *adv.*
How can seem ambiguous after verbs like *tell, describe* and *show*. In [*He told me how he came to*
123

London and found work there], it could be replaced by *that* or omitted; in [*She told me how
she brought up her children*], *how* probably means
'in what manner' and it would therefore be
clearer to write *She told me her way of bringing
up her children.*

however *adv. conj.* **how ever**

When this is used as a conjunction, or as an
adverb to mean 'in whatever way', it is
written as one word, e.g. *It may be hoped,
however, that truth will prevail. However we look
at it, the plan is impossible.* When used to point
a contrast it is always followed by a comma,
and preceded by one if it comes in the middle
of a sentence. When *ever* is used after *how*
solely for emphasis, it is written separately,
e.g. *How ever did you manage it?* Sometimes
it is used unnecessarily after *but*, e.g. [*. . . but
without your help, however, we should not have
succeeded*]. (see BUT)

human, humane *adj.*

These words were once interchangeable, but
humane is now reserved for the narrower
meaning of 'merciful', 'considerate', 'kind',
e.g. *The prisoners all received humane treatment.*

humans *n.*

A word which is only acceptable when used in
contrast with animals; in other cases *human
beings* is more appropriate.

hung see HANGED

hypercritical ('haipə'kritikəl), **hypocritical** (,hipə'kritikəl) *adj.*

Sometimes confused. The first means 'excessively critical', the second 'insincere', 'pretending to be virtuous when one is not', e.g. *His great-aunt was hypercritical about washing hands before taking food or even a cup of tea; He was a great hypocrite about the amount he gave to charity.* The noun forms are: from *hypercritical*, hypercritic and hypercriticism; from *hypocritical*, hypocrite ('hipəkrit) and hypocrisy (hi'pɔkrisi).

I

I *pro.*

It is I is preferable to *It is me* in written English but the second, through use and habit, is now acceptable. [*Between you and I* (*he, she etc.*)] is ungrammatical. (see ONE)

-ible see SPELLING, ADJECTIVES

-ic, -ics *suffix*

Many words ending in *-ics* are singular and take a singular verb when regarded as a subject for study, e.g. *mathematics, physics, ethics, dynamics, statistics, politics,* but are treated as plural when related to an individual, e.g. *Physics is taught at my school, but my* *mathematics are too weak for me to join the class.*

idiom

The customary expressions of a country or a group of people are known as its *idiom*. Whereas grammar is subject to rules, idiom is not, so it is the harder part of a foreign language to grasp and use confidently. The idiom of one's own country is mostly picked up by ear, and this book is only concerned with idiomatic customs which are not familiar to everybody, such as those concerned with the use of PREPOSITIONS (q.v.) Many figurative expressions have become idiomatic; one is more likely to say *He was as deaf as a post* or *He was stone deaf* than *He was completely deaf.* (see also LANGUAGE TERMS)

ie, ei see SPELLING, NOUNS

i.e., e.g.

i.e. is short for the Latin *id est*, meaning 'that is (to say)', and leads on to another way of saying the same thing, e.g. *He spoke for the reformers, i.e. those who were eager for change*: *e.g.* is short for the Latin *exempli gratia*, meaning 'for the sake of example', and is used instead of *for example*, *for instance*, as in *We must increase our foreign exports, e.g. to Portugal.* Neither is used in speech or in formal writing.

if, whether, though *conj.*

If is often used ambiguously, e.g. [*Let me know*

if you are coming], where it could mean either *whether you are coming* or *if you decide to come.* Though is clearer than *if* in such sentences as *He was an impressive, if alarming figure.* (see PROVIDED THAT)

ignoramus

Plural *ignoramuses*

ilk *adj.*

Of that ilk is used in Scotland when a person's name is the same as that of his ancestral estate, e.g. *Mackintosh of that ilk.* It does not mean 'clan', 'family' or 'name'. It is loosely used as an archaic way of saying *of that kind.*

ill see SICK

ill- see WELL-

illegal, illegitimate, illicit, unlawful *adj.*

Illegal has the simple meaning 'contrary to the law of the land', e.g. *It is illegal to drive an unlicensed vehicle. Illegitimate* is the term used for a child 'born of unmarried parents' and for an 'unwarranted' conclusion in an argument, e.g. *I told him I was leaving, and he drew the illegitimate conclusion that I had been dismissed.* It can also mean 'unseemly' or 'unreasonable'. *Illicit* overlaps with *illegal*, but is particularly used for activities which are legal in some circumstances, e.g. *illicit diamond-buying. Unlawful* can mean 'contrary to moral and religious laws' rather than to the law of that

land, e.g. *Their marriage was unlawful in the eyes of God. It is unlawful* (though not *illegal*) *for a Moslem to drink wine; his religion forbids it.*

illegible, unreadable *adj.*

Illegible means 'badly written', 'difficult to read'; *unreadable* means 'too dull and uninteresting to read'.

illusion see DELUSION

image *n.*

An overused fashionable word for 'the public's view of a person or organization'. *The spitting image of* is a colloquial usage meaning 'exactly like'.

imaginary, imaginative *adj.*

Imaginary is used for 'something which is unreal', e.g. *He found all kinds of imaginary difficulties. Imaginative* is usually a word of praise, used of a person or of the treatment of a subject in art, music, literature etc.

immanent, imminent *adj.*

Immanent is a word used in philosophy and religion when speaking of the Deity as pervading the universe; *imminent* is used of something likely to happen soon, usually a danger, e.g. *He saw that a storm was imminent; The soldier feared imminent death.*

immigrant see EMIGRANT

immunity, impunity *n.*

Immunity means 'freedom', 'exemption from

some obligation or from attacks, especially of infections', e.g. *The Prime Minister cannot claim immunity from criticism*; *Immunity from smallpox can be obtained by vaccination*. Impunity means 'freedom from punishment or ill consequences', e.g. *He cannot take risks with impunity*.

imperial, imperious *adj.*

Imperial is the adjective from *empire* and *emperor*; *imperious* means 'domineering', 'arrogant'. Although one can say *an imperious tone of voice* or *an imperious greeting*, *imperial* should only be used to refer to an emperor or the qualities of 'majesty,' 'opulence' etc. which may be thought typical of imperial rule.

impersonate SEE PERSONATE

implicit, explicit *adj.*

Implicit means 'implied' 'not put into words', e.g. *There was an implicit understanding between them that the subject should not be mentioned*. *Explicit* means the opposite, e.g. *I cannot understand what you want unless you are more explicit*, i.e. 'explain more fully'.

imply, infer *v.* **implication** *n.*

The two verbs are often confused, though their meanings are almost opposite. To *imply* is to 'suggest or hint', to *infer* is to 'deduce', e.g. *He implied in his speech that his country was determined to resist force, from which we inferred that war was a possibility*. An *implication* can

129

mean 'something implied' or 'the act of
implying', but belongs also to the verb
implicate, 'to involve', e.g. *The official said he
would investigate the matter, but the implication
was that he thought it unimportant*; *The driver's
implication in the crime was never proved.*

impracticable, impractical, unpractical
adj.

Impracticable is used for things which are
'impossible to carry out', e.g. *His schemes were
so impracticable that they were never put into action.*
Impractical is much less used than *unpractical*
to describe people who 'lack a practical
or realistic nature', and for activities which
are 'possible but not convenient'.

impromptu see EXTEMPORE

in-, un-, non- see SPELLING, ADJECTIVES

in, at *(with names of places) prep.*

In is always used for residence or time spent
in countries, e.g. *She lives in Germany. I spent my
early days in Italy.* This also applies to cities,
e.g. *I shall see you in London*, but for small
places like villages, *at* is used, e.g. *The film
was shot at Dunbar.* For places of work, *in* is
used for shop, office, bank, etc., *at* for a
specific building, e.g. *at the Central Library,
the Polaris Base, the Royal Hotel* etc.

incidentally *adv.*

Like *actually*, this is often used superfluously,

but it can be useful to introduce an after-thought or a cross reference.

inclined to

I am inclined to think reduces the force of the statement it precedes, and is used by those who wish to avoid committing themselves.

include see COMPRISE

incognito (in'kɔgnitou) or (inkɔg'ni:tou)

This means 'a false name' such as is used by famous people not wishing to be recognized. It can be used as an adjective but is commonest as an adverb, e.g. *To travel incognito.*

inconsolable, unconsolable *adj.*

The first of these forms is generally used.

inculcate, inoculate, indoctrinate *v.*

Confusion between the first two of these leads to *inculcate* being followed by *with* instead of *on* or *into*; its meaning is 'impress upon the mind', e.g. *Week after week he inculcated his ideas on (into) his students.* The figurative use of *inoculate* is 'fill' 'imbue', e.g. *He inoculated the rest of the party with his courage. Indoctrinate* means 'fill the mind with a particular doctrine or set of principles'.

indifferent *adj.*

The old meaning of 'impartial' is archaic now, but there are two distinct modern meanings:

1. 'unresponsive', 'not affected by', e.g. *She was indifferent to his pleading.*

131

2. 'of poor quality', 'mediocre', e.g. *She made an indifferent teacher.*

individual *n.*

Use of this word instead of 'person' is either facetious or contemptuous, e.g. *We were confronted by a shabby individual with a two-day's growth of beard.* It is properly used when contrasting a person with a society or group, e.g. *Exceptions cannot be made for individuals.*

indoctrinate see INCULCATE

indoor *adj.* **indoors** *adv.*

The use of these two words is shown in: *Badminton is an indoor game; Stay indoors, it is raining.* (cf. backwards, outdoors, upstairs)

infer see IMPLY

infinitely *adv.*

This word is loosely used for *considerably* or *greatly*.

infinitive see VERB

inflammable, inflammatory *adj.*

Inflammable means 'easily set on fire' or figuratively 'highly excitable'. *Inflammatory* is only used figuratively and means 'producing excitement', e.g. *He made an inflammatory speech, urging the miners to strike.*

inflict *v.*

To 'impose suffering or a penalty', followed by *on*, e.g. *He inflicted severe penalties on all the prisoners.* (see also AFFLICT)

inform *v.*

Much used in commercial and bureaucratic jargon, e.g. *I beg to inform you that your order is being attended to*; *We are informed that the delay in answering your communication has been unavoidable.* *Tell* could be used instead, or the whole phrase omitted.

ingenious, ingenuous *adj.*

The first means 'clever in an original way', e.g. *an ingenious plan*, whereas the second means 'simple and childlike' or 'frank', 'sincere', e.g. *the blushes of ingenuous shame* (Gray's *Elegy*).

inheritance see HEREDITY

-in-law *suffix*

Formerly used for 'parent by a second marriage of one of the partners', where we now say *step-*; now used only for 'the relationship of one marriage partner, to the other partner's family', e.g. *Mother-in-law*, the mother of one's spouse, *daughter-in-law*, a son's wife.

inoculate see INCULCATE

in order that

This is followed by *may* or *might*, e.g. *In order that nothing may be forgotten*, but can often be replaced by *that* or *so that*.

inquire see ENQUIRE

inside *adv. n. prep.*

This word is only followed by *of* when it is

133

used as a noun, e.g. *the inside of his mouth* but *inside the time allowed*.

insofar, in so far *adv.*

This is generally written as three separate words. It is formal and often used where *so far*, *although* or *except that* would be clearer and simpler.

inst., prox., ult.

Commercial jargon meaning 'the present month', 'next month' and 'last month' respectively.

instinct, intuition *n.*

Both these words describe a way of achieving knowledge, or reaching a decision, without using reason or exterior observation. To some extent they are interchangeable, but for 'a quality of mind' *instinct* is used, e.g. *He had an instinct for picking the best.* For 'immediate perception' *intuition* is used, e.g. *Intuition told us what to do when the moment for action arrived.*

insure see ASSURE; ENSURE

intelligent, intellectual *adj.*

Intelligent means 'having natural cleverness and being quick to understand'; an *intellectual* person is one who is 'mainly devoted to mental activity'.

intense, intensive *adj.*

These words are not interchangeable in all contexts. We speak of *intense excitement, intense*

134

suffering, intense concentration, but of *intensive* (i.e. 'thorough') *study of a book, intensive cultivation of the soil, intensive preparations for a bombardment.*

into, in to

These are written as one word when used as one preposition, e.g. *into the future*, and separately when used as an adverb and a preposition together, e.g. *He went in to fetch his hat*; *Entries should be sent in to the secretary.*

intransitive verbs see VERB

intuition see INSTINCT

invalid *n. adj.*

Meaning 'a sick person' this is pronounced ('invəli:d); as an adjective meaning 'having no legal force', i.e. the opposite of *valid*, it is pronounced (in'vælid) e.g. *The deceased's will was invalid, as there was only one witness to it.*

inverted commas see PUNCTUATION

irony

This term is used for various situations, all of which have the common feature of a double meaning and a more enlightened viewpoint. *Irony* can be used for verbal mockery, where the indirectness of the speaker is not fully understood by the victim but appreciated by other listeners who are 'in the know'. Some novelists (Henry Fielding is an example) adopt an ironical standpoint when introducing a character. There is also *Dramatic Irony*, where a character in a play or novel says something which has no particular significance to him, but means far more to the audience or reader. The *Irony of Fate* is a literary convention used to great effect in Greek tragedy; it describes an unexpected turn of events which makes a mockery of hopes and expectations almost at the moment of their realization. (see SARCASM; SARDONIC)

-ise, -ize see SPELLING, VERBS

italics

The term given in printing to sloping type, as opposed to the usual upright or Roman. It can be the equivalent of inverted commas, underlining, or spoken emphasis, and is used as follows:—

1. For the names or titles of books, plays, newspapers, films, ships etc. Where a title begins with *The* this is usually included in the italics, e.g. I have been reading *The Canterbury Tales*, but newspapers are more often referred to thus: He was a regular reader of the *Guardian*. *The* is not included in the names of ships: They sailed in the *Queen Elizabeth*. (see PUNCTUATION, INVERTED COMMAS and CAPITAL LETTERS)

2. Foreign words and short phrases are printed in italics (longer passages in inverted

136

commas), unless they have become fully anglicised, e.g. He was glad to be back on terra firma, but: He spoke as if his victory was a *fait accompli*. This is a matter for the individual writer to decide, but if authority is required, lists are given in *Rules for Compositors and Readers at the University Press, Oxford.*

3. For emphasis. Italic type can be used to indicate words which would be marked by the tone of voice in speaking, or by underlining in writing, e.g. "I wish you *were* coming." This is useful in writing dialogue, especially in plays, but should be used sparingly elsewhere.

its *poss. adj.* **it's**

Its, as a possessive adjective, has no apostrophe, e.g. *The cat was cleaning its paws. It's,* with an apostrophe, is an abbreviation for 'it is' or 'it has', e.g. *It's difficult to say how long it will take; It's started to rain.*

J

Jacobean, Jacobin, Jacobite *adj. n.*

Jacobean refers to 'the reign of James I and to anything characteristic of it', especially architecture or furniture. *Jacobin* describes 'the extreme democratic group in the French

Revolution'. The *Jacobites* were 'the supporters of the exiled James II and his descendants', especially the Old and the Young Pretender (Bonnie Prince Charlie) as the lawful claimants to the British throne. They were most active in Scotland during the eighteenth century.

jail see GAOL

jargon see LANGUAGE TERMS

journal, magazine *n.*

A *journal* was formerly a daily paper, but the term is now used for weekly and monthly periodicals. It is for a limited class of readers, e.g. *British Medical Journal* (for medical practitioners). A *magazine* is usually for general readers, and contains entertaining or informative articles.

journalese

A form of jargon (see STYLE). A term used to describe the second-rate style of some journalists.

judgement, judgment *n.*

Both forms are accepted, the second is more generally used.

judicial, judicious *adj.*

Judicial is used for anything 'concerned with the processes of the law', especially for anyone 'acting in the rôle or manner of a judge', e.g. *speaking in a judicial capacity*. *Judicious* is used for the 'qualities supposed to be found in judges, such as wisdom and prudence', e.g. *He spoke in a judicious way of the rights and wrongs of the case.* It can also mean *discreet*, e.g. *My remarks were very judicious; Make a judicious selection of books for holiday reading.*

just *adv.*

This word is often used superfluously, e.g. [*It is just exactly a year since he died*]. Used for 'absolutely' it is colloquial, e.g. *I am just certain I am right.*

K

kale, kail *n.*

Both spellings are used, the first is more general especially with compounds such as *kale-field*, *sea-kale*. The spelling *kail* is used in Scotland, e.g. *kail-runt*, 'a cabbage stem', and *kail-yard*, 'a cabbage patch'. Also in *the Kailyard School*, a group of Scottish sentimental writers.

Kent *n. adj.* **Kentish** *adj.*

Both these forms are used adjectivally, the second being commoner. There is a traditional distinction between a *Kentishman* and a *Man of*

Kent, according to his birthplace, east or west of the River Medway.

kind *n.*

Kind of and *sort of* are often loosely and superfluously used, e.g. [*I feel kind of lonely*]. [*Those kind of*] is often written ungrammatically instead of *that kind of* or *those kinds of*, e.g. [*I did not know that you made friends with those kind of people*].

kindly requested

A redundant phrase used in business jargon instead of *asked*.

kith and kin

This is often used as if it were an expression like *wear and tear*, in which the repetition of sounds reinforces the meaning. *Kith* means 'people known to us, rather than related', so the phrase means 'friends and relations.'

kneel

Past participle and past tense *knelt* or *kneeled*.

knit, knitted *past part. past t.*

When used literally, the past participle and past tense of *knit* are *knitted*, e.g. *It was a beautifully knitted garment.* In figurative use it is *knit*, e.g. *All his stories had well-knit plots.* An exception is its use with *brows*, where it is usual to say *with knitted brows*.

know-how *n.*

An American expression for 'technical or

expert knowledge', which has become an accepted term.

L

-l, -ll
(For single or double *l* in words such as *fulfil* see SPELLING, VERBS)

laboratory *n.*
Usually pronounced (ləˈbɔrətəri) in British English, (ˈlæbərətəri) in U.S.

lack *n.*
Though this word means 'the absence of something necessary or expected', e.g. *lack of common sense, of hygiene* etc., it is loosely used for 'absence' in a purely negative sense, e.g. *He showed a lack of nervousness.*

laden see LOADED

lady *n.*
As an indication of sex this word has been replaced by *woman*, e.g. *woman doctor*, except in cases where class or gentility is emphasized, e.g. *lady help*. As a term of respectful address *Madam* is used. (see LETTER-WRITING)

laid see LAY

lama, llama *n.*
The first is 'a Tibetan priest', the second 'a South American animal like a camel'.

LANGUAGE TERMS

kinds of English

Old English or *Anglo-Saxon* is the term for the English Language as it was spoken up till 1100-50, after which *Middle English*, in which Chaucer wrote, continued till about 1500. The language spoken since that time is known as *Modern English.*

Basic English is a simplified form of the language which has a vocabulary of about 850 words and is intended for international use.

King's (or Queen's) English means grammatically correct speech or writing.

Pidgin (or Pigeon) English is a jargon formed by a blend of English with Chinese or another oriental or an African language for communicating with the natives, originally for trade. *Melican takee plenty chow-chow* is an example of Chinese Pidgin.

Standard English is the accepted form of the language.

general language terms

cant is used for a jargon or private language, as in *thieves' cant.* It can also have the sense of hypocritical moral or religious talk or writing.

dialect is a local or regional form of a language, sometimes differing so much from the standard speech of the country as to be unintelligible to the outsider, sometimes varying only in accent and to a small extent in vocabulary. The French word *patois* is sometimes used.

Esperanto is an artificial language intended for universal use.

gibberish is speech which is incomprehensible to the hearer because it is nonsensical, too rapid, or too learned.

idiom can mean the forms of expression peculiar to a country (see separate entry) or simply a *language* or *dialect*. It is also used for one person's characteristic way of speaking or writing.

jargon is the special vocabulary of an art or science, trade, sport, occupation or group of people. Its use can be irritating to others, especially when it occurs in journalism (*journalese*) which sometimes offends the reader by its lack of taste, grammar or logic. *Officialese* is the jargon of those in power, and here the pitfalls are obscurity, pomposity, and the concealment of vague and illogical thinking. (SEE STYLE)

lingo is used colloquially for a language or vocabulary one does not understand.

lingua franca is a language used over a wide area by people of different races, especially that used in the Eastern Mediterranean by traders and sailors from many countries.

linguistics is the study of language and speech.

slang. This term for very informal and colloquial speech can cover many variations from standard usage, not merely the invention of new words. It can cover a change in pronunciation (*Oh Yeah?*) or stress, *I shall be delighted* (meaning the opposite); or an abbreviation like *telly*. Slang words and phrases are also added to the language by imitating sounds (*swoosh*), running words together (*cuppa*), borrowing from other countries (*O.K., pronto*), using a proper name (*gamp*). Slang sometimes becomes current through the widespread imitation of a witticism or a clever piece of advertising. It is also the expression of the desire of a group of people to resemble each other and to be unintelligible to others; school slang is an example of this. Wars also create a large number of slang expressions, partly owing to close association and partly to a desire for humorous relief. Although the term is often used reproachfully it is one of the ways the language is enriched, and many of our accepted words were considered slang when they were first used, for example *mob*, an abbreviation of the Latin *mobile vulgus* 'the fickle crowd', which was severely frowned on in the seventeenth century. But slang words are not usually considered suitable in formal writing.

rhyming slang is a cockney device in which a phrase is substituted for a single word e.g. *trouble and strife* for *wife*, *plates of meat* for *feet*.

vernacular. Used as a noun this means 'the native language of a country', homely everyday speech as opposed to a literary language. As an adjective it means 'native' or 'in dialect'.

languor *n.*

The letter *u* is silent in this word ('læŋgə) and in *languorous* ('læŋgərəs) but it is pronounced in *languish* ('læŋgwiʃ) and *languid* ('læŋgwid).

large see BIG

last, latest *adj.*

Latest means 'last up till the present', *last* means 'last of all', 'final', but there are exceptions such as *last year*, *last week*, *last night*. *Last century* is incorrect. Accepted usage is *in (during) the last century*.

late *adj.*

Confusion arises over the use of this word instead of *former* or *ex-*, when it might also mean 'dead', e.g. *the late rector of this parish*.

Latin words see FOREIGN WORDS AND PHRASES

latter see FORMER

laudable (ˈlɔːdəbl), **laudatory** (lauˈdeitəri) *adj.*

Laudable means 'praiseworthy' and is used of people and their actions; *laudatory* is used to describe written or spoken praise of someone's work, e.g. *I could see that she was making a laudable effort*; *His new book has received laudatory reviews.*

lawful, legal *adj.*

These words overlap in many of their uses, but *lawful* has a wider application, and is used for moral law as well as that of the country. *Legal* refers only to the law of the land, and is always used when the sense is concerned with the law, e.g. *the legal profession, legal proceedings.* (see ILLEGAL)

lay, lie *v.*

Lay is a transitive verb with the past participle *laid*, past tense *laid*. It cannot be used without an object, unlike *lie*, which has past participle *lain*, past tense *lay*, and can only be intransitive. There is commonly confusion both in speech and writing. *The hen laid an egg in the henhouse which lay on the hill* is correct.

leading question

A *leading question*, a term used in law and often misused to mean ['a question which makes evasion impossible'], is 'one which suggests the answer wanted by the questioner'. In a court of law, counsel often asks *leading questions* in order to elicit the desired answers, e.g. *You didn't know the lift was out of order, did you?* which leads to the answer *No.* Such questions are used in cross-examination to obtain contradictions.

left bank

This is the side of a river which is on your left-hand side when facing downstream.

left hand, left-handed *adj.*

Left hand means 'on the left side'; *left-handed* describes 'a person who habitually uses the left hand instead of the right'.

leg *n.*

A term used in journalism to describe one stage of a journey or of a sporting event, e.g. *the first leg of the tournament.*

legal see LAWFUL

legible see ILLEGIBLE

legislation, legislature *n.*

Legislation is 'the act of making laws', the *legislature* 'the body which makes the laws', e.g. *What government was responsible for this piece of legislation? He was an outstanding member of the legislature.*

lend see LOAN

less, lesser *comp. adj.*

Fewer is used instead of less when it is a question of number, *less* is reserved for describing quantity except where it is associated with a numeral, e.g. *less water, fewer bottles of beer, two bottles less*. Another word is usually substituted for less when it follows *a*, e.g. *I would like less* but *I would like a smaller helping. Lesser* is a double comparative of *little*, used only as an adjective meaning 'smaller', 'less important', e.g. *The lesser celandine*; *Don't waste time on these lesser matters*.

-less *suffix*

This suffix is used to make adjectives from nouns, and (only rarely) from verbs. A hyphen is needed where there would be three *l*s in succession, e.g. *smell-less*, but not where there are two, e.g. *soulless*.

lest *conj*.

A slightly archaic form of *unless*, which is followed by *should*, not by *would* or *will*, e.g. *They spoke in whispers lest they should be heard*.

let *v*.

In the sense of 'allow' this verb is transitive, and takes an accusative pronoun even where it is the subject of the next clause, e.g. *She will let him and me go if I ask her. Let the dog alone* has become an acceptable form of *Leave the dog alone. Let go* and *leave go* are sometimes followed by *of* before the object, but *of* is necessary if a pronoun is the object, e.g. *Let go the anchor*; *Let go (of) the rope*; but *Let go of it at once*.

LETTER-WRITING AND FORMS OF ADDRESS

Correspondence can be broadly divided into two kinds, *personal* and *business or official*, but these categories often overlap. Where important business is being transacted between friends, as might be the case with a lawyer and his client, it is as well to keep personal messages separated in some way, as the business part of a letter may need to be consulted, later and by different people.

Apart from invitations there is no need for advice on the forms to be used in *personal* letters, though some of the points given below for guidance in writing business and official letters may be useful.

forms used for addressing people

Letters to men can be addressed as follows:—
Mr. Bates, Mr. T. Bates, or *Mr. Thomas Bates*. If the courtesy title *Esq.* is used the surname must be preceded by a first name or initials, and letters be put after the Esq. e.g. *Thomas Bates Esq. M.A.* Young boys can be addressed as *Master*. The plural form *Messrs.* is only used with the names of business firms which contain a personal name *Messrs. Jackson & Sons*.

Married women are identified by their husband's first name or initial, e.g. *Mrs.*

R(obert) Henderson, but widows usually appear as *Mrs. M(ary) Henderson.* It is useful for women signing letters to unknown correspondents to add *Mrs.* or *Miss* in brackets to their signatures.

Professional titles are used instead of Mr. etc. as in *Dr. H. Stevens, The Rev. Simon Clifford,* or occasionally combined as in *Professor Sir Henry Armitage.* Members of the Privy Council have the title *Rt. Hon.* which is followed directly by the name, except where there is a title, e.g. *The Rt. Hon. Clement Attlee,* the *Rt. Hon. Viscount Hall.* First names are always used with the titles *Sir* and *Dame* as in *Sir Laurence Olivier, Dame Margot Fonteyn.*

Orders, decorations, degrees, qualifications and *letters denoting professions* appear in that order, Degrees start with the lowest, but orders start with the highest, *Joseph Halliday Esq. O.B.E., D.S.O., M.A., F.S.A., M.P.* Orders and decorations are usually included in addresses, but qualifications etc. are only used where appropriate, as when writing to a person in his official capacity.

A table of ceremonious forms of address appears overleaf. The forms given for beginning and ending letters are those used only in the most formal correspondence. The modern trend is towards greater informality, so that a very ceremonious preliminary letter beginning *My Lord* and referring to him as *Your Lordship* (rather than *you*) may be followed in later letters by the less formal opening *Dear Lord* (*name*) and end *Yours faithfully* or *Yours sincerely*. Peers of all ranks below that of Duke may be addressed informally in this way.

Similarly a less formal approach can be used in correspondence with the other dignitaries listed.

Whitaker's Almanac and *Who's Who* are useful books to consult when corresponding with people in important positions.

Rank or title	Form of Address
THE QUEEN	The Queen's Most Excellent Majesty OR Her Majesty Queen Elizabeth II
ROYAL PRINCE	His Royal Highness Prince (*Christian name*) OR [*if a duke*] His Royal Highness the Duke of
ROYAL PRINCESS	Her Royal Highness the Princess (*Christian name*) OR [*if a Duchess*] Her Royal Highness the Duchess of
AMBASSADOR (British)	His Excellency (*followed by rank*) H.B.M's Ambassador and Plenipotentiary,

OF ADDRESS

Begin	*End*
Madam, OR May it please your Majesty, (Your Majesty)	I have the honour to remain, Your Majesty's faithful subject,
Sir, (Your Royal Highness)	I have the honour to remain, Your Royal Highness's most dutiful subject
Madam, (Your Royal Highness)	I have the honour to remain, Your Royal Highness's dutiful and obedient servant,
Sir, My Lord, etc. (*according to rank*) (Your Excellency)	I am, etc. (*according to rank*), Your obedient servant,

153

ARCHBISHOP	His Grace the Lord Arch-bishop of
ARCHDEACON	The Venerable the Arch-deacon of
BARON	The Rt. Hon. the Lord
	OR
	The Lord
BARONESS	The Rt. Hon. Lady *(Surname or title)*
BARONET	Sir *(Christian name and surname)*, Bt.
BARONET'S WIFE	Lady *(surname)*
BISHOP	The Right Rev. the Lord Bishop of
	OR
	The Lord Bishop of
BISHOP (Suffragan)	The Right Rev. the Bishop Suffragan of
BISHOP (Roman Catholic)	The Right Rev. the Bishop of
CARDINAL	His Eminence Cardinal *(Surname)*

154

My Lord Arch-
bishop,
(Your Grace)
Venerable Sir,
	I have the honour to be,
	   Your Grace's obedient
	   servant,
	I have the honour to be,
	   Your obedient servant,

My Lord,
(Your Lordship)
	I have the honour to be,
	   Your Lordship's
	   obedient servant,

Madam,
(Your Ladyship)
	I have the honour to be,
	   Your Ladyship's
	   obedient servant,

Sir,	I am, Sir, Your obedient servant,
Madam,	I am, Madam, Your obedient servant,

My Lord Bishop,
OR
My Lord,
(Your Lordship)
	I have the honour to be,
	   Your Lordship's
	   obedient servant,

Sir, OR Right Reverend Sir	I am, Sir, Your obedient servant,
As above	As above

My Lord Cardinal,
OR
My Lord,
(Your Eminence)
	I have the honour to be,
	   Your Eminence's obedi-
	   ent servant,

CLERGY	The Rev. (*Christian name and surname*)
CONSUL (British)	Esq., H.B.M's Consul-General, Consul, Vice-Consul, *as may be*
COUNTESS (Wife of Earl)	The Rt. Hon. the Countess of
DAME (Order of the British Empire)	Dame (*Christian name and surname*)
DOCTOR	[*if an M.D.*] (*Christian name and surname*) Esq., M.D. [*if an M.B., Ch.B. etc.*] Dr. (*Christian name and surname*) [*if an F.R.C.S.*] Mr. (*Christian name and surname*)
DOWAGER (and Widows of Baronets)	The Rt. Hon. the Dowager Duchess (Countess, etc.) of OR The Rt. Hon. (*Christian name*) Countess of
DUCHESS (not Royal)	Her Grace the Duchess of
DUKE (not Royal)	His Grace the Duke of

Dear Sir, (formerly Reverend Sir)	I am, dear Sir, Your obedient servant,
Sir,	I am, Sir, Your obedient servant,
Madam, (Your Ladyship)	I have the honour to be, Your Ladyship's obedient servant,
Dear Madam,	No set form
No set form	No set form
As for Duchess, Countess, etc.	As for Duchess, Countess etc.
Madam, (Your Grace)	I have the honour to be, Your Grace's most obedient servant,
My Lord Duke, (Your Grace)	I have the honour to be, Your Grace's most obedient servant,

EARL	The Rt. Hon. the Earl of OR The Earl of
JUDGE (High Court)	The Hon. Sir OR *[if not a Knight]* The Hon. Mr. Justice *(surname)*
JUDGE (County Court)	His Honour Judge *(surname)*
KNIGHT	Sir *(Christian name and surname)* K.C.B. etc.
KNIGHT'S WIFE	Lady *(Surname)*
LORD MAYOR	*(For London, York, Belfast, Dublin)* The Rt. Hon. the Lord Mayor of OR The Rt. Hon *(Christian name and surname)* Lord Mayor of *(For others)* The Right Worshipful the Lord Mayor of

My Lord, (Your Lordship)	I have the honour to be, Your Lordship's most obedient servant,
Sir,	I have the honour to be, Sir, Your obedient servant,
Sir,	I have the honour to be, Sir, Your obedient servant,
Sir,	I am, Sir, Your obedient servant,
Madam, (Your Ladyship)	I am, Madam, Your obedient servant,
My Lord, (Your Lordship)	I am, my Lord Mayor, Your obedient servant

LORD MAYOR'S WIFE	The Rt. Hon. (*or* Hon. *according to husband's title*) the Lady Mayoress of
MARCHIONESS	The Most Hon. the Marchioness of
MARQUESS (or Marquis)	The Most Hon. the Marquess of
MAYOR	(*For certain cities*) The Right Worshipful the Mayor of (*for others, and towns*) The Worshipful the Mayor of
MAYOR'S WIFE	The Mayoress of
MEMBER OF PARLIAMENT	According to title, with the addition of *M.P.*
PRIVY COUNCILLOR	The Rt. Hon. (*Christian name and surname*)
SECRETARY OF STATE	H.M. Principal Secretary of State for (*department*)
VISCOUNT	The Rt. Hon. the Viscount
VISCOUNTESS	The Rt. Hon. the Viscountess

My Lady Mayoress, OR Madam, (Your Ladyship)	I am, my Lady Mayoress, Your obedient servant,
Madam, (Your Ladyship)	I have the honour to be, Your Ladyship's obedient servant,
My Lord Marquess,	I have the honour to be, My Lord Marquess, Your obedient servant
(Your Lordship) Sir (or Madam),	I am, Sir, (or Madam), Your obedient servant,
Madam,	I am, Madam, Your obedient servant,
Sir,	I am, Sir, Your obedient servant,
According to rank	According to rank
Sir,	I am, Sir, Your obedient servant,
My Lord, (Your Lordship)	I have the honour to be, Your Lordship's obedient servant,
Madam, (Your Ladyship)	I have the honour to be, Your Ladyship's obedient servant,

postal addresses *The Post Office Guide* gives full information on addressing letters both to this country and abroad. The form recommended for Great Britain has the Post Town in capital letters, followed by the county in small letters, followed by the post-code for those towns which have them, e.g.

Miss Joan Bannerman,
6, Overton Drive,
HORSHAM,
Sussex
postcode.

style and form The meaningless formalities which used to be general in business and official letters, e.g. [*We are in receipt of your favour of the 29th inst*]; [*I am directed by the Regional Commissioner to inform you that etc.*] have given way to a more simple, direct and friendly way of writing in which the main consideration is to give the information in a form which can be readily understood, arranged in a logical manner, and conveying a helpful frame of mind. A writer who can imagine himself in the position of the person receiving the letter is most likely to achieve this.

Offices and firms are likely to have their own conventions in the matter of layout etc., but there are some accepted customs:—

address If the address of the writer is not printed it should be written or typed in the top right-hand corner. The date should come under it, and below this on the opposite side should be the name and address of the person or firm to whom the letter is written. Occasionally this is put at the bottom left-hand corner of the sheet. (see DATES)

beginning and ending of letters The form used depends on the relationship between the correspondents, but the main point to be remembered is that each kind of opening has its equivalent closing phrase. A table of those most commonly used is given below:—

Very formal

Sir, Gentlemen, Madam, Mesdames,	I am, Sir, *or* I remain, Sir, Your obedient servant, Stanley Edwards.

Formal

Dear Sir(s), Dear Madam, Mesdames	Yours faithfully, Yours truly,

When correspondent is known

Dear Mr. Macdonald, Dear Mrs. Price,	Yours sincerely, Yours truly,

Between friends

Dear Price,

Dear Arthur,

My dear Price,

My dear Arthur,

} Yours ever,
Yours
affectionately,

A common grammatical mistake is to start or finish a letter with a clause which is not attached to any subject e.g. [*In reply to your letter of the 16th June the book you mention is no longer in stock*]; [*Hoping to hear that the goods have arrived safely, Yours faithfully, A. G. Simpson*]. These could be written *In reply to your letter of the 16th June, I am sorry to have to tell you that the book you mention is no longer in stock*; *Hoping to hear that the goods have arrived safely, I am, Yours faithfully*.

postscript 'An afterthought added to a letter'. It is abbreviated to PS. not [P.S.]. An additional postscript is abbreviated to PPS.

invitations These should be answered in the form in which they are sent. An informal letter beginning *Dear Mary, We are giving a party at 8.30 on January the first and hope you will be able to come*, should be answered by a similar letter. A formal invitation beginning *Mrs. Dalrymple at home*, or *Mr. and Mrs. Dalrymple request the pleasure of your company* should be answered in the third person *Mr. and Mrs. Richardson have much pleasure in accepting*

*Mrs. Dalrymple's kind invitation for . . . or Mr.
and Mrs. Richardson thank Mrs. Dalrymple for her
kind invitation for . . . but owing to a previous
engagement regret they are unable to accept.* Replies
in the third person should not be signed.

Further information can be found in
Modern Business Correspondence by L. Gartside.

liability *n.*

This word has the legal sense of 'the condition
of being answerable', 'bound to pay'. It is
often loosely used for 'responsibility', e.g.
He admitted his liability for the accident. It is
colloquial to use it for 'handicap', 'disadvantage', e.g. *It was a liability for him to have
to look after his younger brother.*

liable *adj.*

This word is often loosely used instead of
more appropriate adjectives such as *likely,
capable, apt*, e.g. *People are liable to misunderstand
if you behave like that.* In law it means 'responsible', e.g. *We must find out if the tenant is
liable for the repairs to the roof.* (see APT)

libel, slander *n. v.*

These words are used indiscriminately to
describe 'false or defamatory statements
about behaviour or character', but there is a
legal difference between them: a *libel* must
appear in writing or in print; a *slander* is only
spoken.

liberalism, liberality n.

Liberalism spelt with a capital means 'the views and practice of the Liberal Party', with a small initial *l* it is used for 'the quality of tolerance and breadth of outlook', e.g. *His father was shocked to hear of the liberalism of his opinions. Liberality* means 'generosity', e.g. *She distributed gifts at Christmas with her usual liberality.*

licence n. license v.

The difference in spelling between the noun and verb forms of this word also occurs in *advise* and *practise.*

lie see LAY

lifelong, livelong ('livlɔn) or ('laivlɔn) adj.

The first of these means 'throughout life' and is used in ordinary prose, the second means 'lasting', 'enduring', and is poetical.

lighted, lit past part.

Either form is acceptable for *light* in its usual sense, and for when it means 'come on unexpectedly', e.g. *He lighted (or lit) on the exact spot where the treasure was hidden.* When used as an adjective meaning 'illuminated,' 'ignited' or in compounds, *lighted* is commoner, e.g. *a newly-lighted fire.*

lightening pres. part. lightning n. adj.

Lightening is the spelling used for the present participle of the verb *lighten*, e.g. *lightening his load. Lightning* is the noun for 'the flash in a thunderstorm', and for the adjective used figuratively, e.g. *lightning speed*.

like see PREPOSITION

like *v.*

I would, in the sense of *I should like to,* is complete but pedantic. *I would like to point out* is more general than *I would point out.* (see SHOULD and WOULD)

-like *suffix*

The hyphen is only needed when words are made up specially for the occasion, e.g. *He wriggled, eel-like, into bed.* Established words like *godlike* are written as one.

likely *adj. adv.*

Likely is only used with *very, most* or *more.* In other cases it is replaced by *probably.* To use it as in [*He will likely come tomorrow.*] is archaic or dialect, and unacceptable. (see LIABLE)

limit see DELIMIT

limited *adj.*

This word is often used as a euphemism, e.g. *He is a man of limited ability,* where the writer does not want to commit himself to making too insulting a remark.

linage ('lainidʒ), **lineage** ('liniidʒ) *n.*

Linage is 'the number of lines on a page'; *lineage* means 'ancestry, descent'.

lingo see LANGUAGE TERMS

lingua franca see LANGUAGE TERMS

linguistics see LANGUAGE TERMS

lit see LIGHTED

literally *adv.*

A word too often used without thought to its meaning, e.g. *I had no lunch, so I was literally starving*; *The record-holder literally flew round the track*. In these cases *practically* or *virtually* can sometimes replace it.

little see FEW

loaded, laden *adj. past part. past t.*

Loaded is the past participle and past tense of *load*; *laden* is the adjective in general use, though *loaded* is used, e.g. to describe 'weighted dice', and colloquially for 'very rich' or 'drunk'.

loan *n.*

This word is no longer used as a verb except in the U.S. The verb is *lend*, e.g. *Will you lend (not [loan]) me your dictionary?*

loathe (louð) *v.* **loth, loath** (louθ) *adj.*

The verb is *loathe* meaning 'dislike intensely', e.g. *Some vegetarians loathe eating meat*. The adjective *loath* or *loth* means 'reluctant', e.g. *He was lo(a)th to go further*.

locale (lou'ka:l), **locality, scene** *n.*

Locality means 'neighbourhood', 'a more or less definite area surrounding a known

168

point', e.g. *Someone new has just moved into our locality*; *Wordsworth saw the daffodils in the locality of Ullswater*. It can also have the sense of 'an ability to find one's bearings in unfamiliar territory'. *Locale* has a particular modern meaning of 'the scene where a film is being shot', but it has the wider sense of 'forming a background to some event', e.g. *This lake is the locale of the flamingoes in the breeding season*. In many cases *scene* is the more natural word, but *locale* contains more of a sense of continuity, e.g. *the scene of the murder* but *the locale of the witches' sabbath*. (see VENUE)

locate *v.*

This word is often used for 'find', but it has a more precise meaning, to 'find out the exact position of', e.g. *He located the town on the map*. It is absurdly used in *He was late because he could not locate his shoes*.

look see WATCH

loose, loosen *v.*

To *loose* (the opposite of to *bind*) is 'set free', 'undo', 'free from fastenings', e.g. *loose the prisoner*, *loose the dog*. To *loosen* (the opposite of to *tighten*) means 'slacken', e.g. *loosen the rope*. (see UNLOOSE)

Lord, Lady see LETTER-WRITING

lot of, lots of

This phrase is treated as an adjective, so the

169

verb used with it agrees with the noun or pronoun which follows it, e.g. *A lot of people were frightened; Lots of us are thinking of going; A lot of snow has fallen.* (cf. half)

loud, loudly *adv.*

Loud and *loudly* are used to describe an action 'producing a great volume of sound', e.g. *He called loud* (or *loudly*) *enough to awake the dead. Loudly* can also imply 'vehemence or strength of feeling' e.g. *I told them the plan, but they disagreed loudly with it.*

lure see ALLURE

luxuriant, luxurious, luxury *adj.*

Luxuriant is used to describe anything 'growing abundantly or in profusion', e.g. *a luxuriant bank of ferns. Luxurious* is associated with richness and extravagance, e.g. *a luxurious fur coat. Luxury* is now often used as an adjective in advertising and usually means 'expensive', e.g. *a luxury cruise.*

M

madam ('mædəm), **madame** (mæ'dɑːm)

Madam is the form used for addressing a woman politely or respectfully in speech or writing, the equivalent of *sir*, e.g. *Madam Chairman, Dear Madam.* It is abbreviated to

Ma'am (ma:m) in speech. *Madame* is the French form, equivalent to *Mrs.*, plural *Mesdames* (mei'da:m), abbreviated to *Mme.*, *Mmes.*

magazine see JOURNAL

Mahomet(an), Mohammed(an) n. adj.

The first of these is the more popular form, the second is that used by scholars.

major, minor adj.

Originally these words were comparatives meaning 'greater', 'less', but they are now commonly used, especially in politics and journalism, instead of *important, chief* and *unimportant, secondary*, e.g. *a major disagreement, a minor issue.*

majority n.

This word can be followed by a singular or plural verb according to the sense in which it is used. It is singular when it means 'a large, or the greater, number', especially of votes, e.g. *His majority was overwhelming,* or when the sense is collective and implies a minority, e.g. *The future of the scheme was in doubt, but a majority was clearly in favour of continuing it.* Where it is used for a collection of individuals it is followed by a plural verb, e.g. *A great many people were injured in the train accident, but the majority were allowed home after treatment.* It is loosely used for 'most', especially when applied to quantity rather than number, e.g. *The majority of my work is done in the office.* *Great* can be used with *majority* to describe 'a large numerical superiority', but the use of *greater* or *greatest* with it is clearly redundant.

make shift *v. phr.* **makeshift** *n. adj.*

malapropism

This is the confusion of words which have an accidental likeness and approximately similar sounds but different meanings, usually with comic effect. The word comes from Mrs Malaprop who was noted for such blunders in Sheridan's play *The Rivals*.

Two examples are: *He was a very placid man, not easily decomposed* (discomposed) and *As headstrong as an allegory* (alligator) *on the banks of the Nile.*

male, masculine see FEMALE

mandatary *n.* **mandatory** *n. adj.*

Both words, as nouns, mean 'a person to whom a mandate is given'. The second (but not the first) as an adjective means 'obligatory', e.g. *Buying a licence for your television set is mandatory.*

mankind *n.*

Always treated as a singular noun, e.g. *Mankind has its own remedy.*

manner *n.*

When used in the sense of 'way', 'method',

this word does not need to be followed by *how*, but has *of* or *in which* after it, e.g. *His intentions were good, but not his manner of carrying them out.* Educated speakers generally prefer *well-* or *ill-mannered* to *good-* or *bad-mannered.*

manuscript *n.*

The singular is abbreviated to MS., the plural to MSS., in writing but not in speech, so when written, the article preceding the abbreviation is *a* not *an*.

many *adj.*

Used with a singular verb only after the phrase *many a-*, e.g. *Many a fool has been taken in by it* or *There's many a slip 'twixt cup and lip.*

marathon *n.*

This word means 'a long distance race', but it is popularly used for any prolonged contest, e.g. *a pie-eating marathon*, or *a marathon bridge match.*

margarine (ˌmɑ:dʒəˈri:n) or (ˌmɑ:ɡəˈri:n) *n.*

Pronounced either way; variations are local. The south-eastern pronunciation is the first.

marginal, minimal *adj.*

These words are often used in politics and journalism where 'very slight' or 'slightest possible' would be more direct, e.g. *His height gave him a marginal advantage over his opponent.*

marquis, marquess (ˈmɑ:kwis) *n.*

The first spelling is now generally used, though

some English nobles prefer the second. The feminine form of both is *marchioness* (.mɑ:ʃə-'nes).

masculine see FEMALE

massif (mæ'si:f) *n.*

'A large mountainous mass'.

massive *adj.*

This word is useful in its literal sense of 'large and solid', e.g. *a massive piece of sculpture*, but is often loosely used in the figurative sense instead of words like 'powerful', 'concentrated', 'widespread', e.g. *a massive attack on poverty and disease* or *There is need for a massive building programme*.

masterful, masterly *adj.*

Masterful means 'commanding', 'strong-willed', and is generally used to describe behaviour, whereas *masterly* means 'highly skilled' and is applied to performances in sport and the arts, e.g. *The local professional gave a masterly performance in the final round*.

may, might *v.*

May (past tense *might*) is used as an auxiliary verb in two main ways:—

1. permissive, e.g. *He says I may go*.

2. expressing doubt, e.g. *He may come tomorrow*.

When *may* is used with a past tense it implies a possibility still open, e.g. *He may*

174

have got lost; when *might* is used there is no longer a possibility e.g. *He might have got lost* (but hasn't).

maybe, may be

Maybe is increasingly being used instead of *perhaps* and *possibly*, especially in speech. As a verb it is written as two words, e.g. *It may be that I shall turn out to be right.*

mean *adj.*

Three common meanings are: (a) 'low', 'base', 'insignificant', e.g. *His success was no mean achievement.* (b) 'niggardly', 'miserly' (c) 'unfair', unsportsmanlike', e.g. *to take a mean advantage of someone.*

means *n.*

This word is treated as plural when it means 'income', e.g. *My means are not enough to keep me in comfort*, but can be either singular or plural when the meaning is 'method', e.g. *This means of transport is cheaper than sending goods by road; Several means of transport are now available to the manufacturer.*

meantime, Mean Time, meanwhile

Meantime is more commonly used than *meanwhile* for the noun, e.g. *in the meantime*, but *meanwhile* is more often used for the adverb, e.g. *Meanwhile the doctor was bringing out his hypodermic.* The words are written separately in *Greenwich Mean Time.*

175

medieval, mediæval *adj.*

The first spelling is more general now.

medium *n.*

Spiritualists talk of *mediums*, but the plural form *media* is commoner in other senses of the word, such as 'means', 'agency' etc.

meet, meet with *v.*

To *meet* is simply to 'encounter'; to *meet with* has the sense of to 'suffer', to 'be subject to', e.g. *He met with much hostility, many disasters.* [*To meet up with*] is colloquial.

melody see HARMONY

melted, molten *adj. past part.*

Melted is the usual form; *molten* is used for materials which are normally very hard, such as metals, e.g. *molten lead* but *melted butter*.

mental *adj.* **mentality** *n.*

It is colloquial to use *mental*, (which means simply 'pertaining to the mind') as a synonym for *crazy*. *Mentality*, which used to mean 'intellectual power', has come to be used in a contemptuous way for a certain type of mind, or habit of thinking, e.g. *The mentality of a Civil Servant is of no use in a business enterprise.*

Messrs.

The plural of *Mr.* mostly used before the names of business firms. It can be used before one or more names, e.g. *Messrs. Archibald Cooper & Sons Ltd., Messrs. I. Robertson and*

C. Agnew, The Messrs. Barker. There is no equivalent for *Mrs.*

metaphor see STYLE; ANALOGY

meter, metre ('miːtə) *n.* **metric, metrical** ('metrik, -l) *adj.*

The first spelling is used for instruments of measurement and for compounds like speedometer (spiˈdɔmitə). It is also used in the U.S. and sometimes in Britain for the unit of length, and for the pattern of a line of verse, but *metre* is more usual. *Metric* is the adjective for the system of measurement, *metrical* for the form of verse.

meticulous (məˈtikjuləs) *adj.*

This word means 'over-exact about minute details', but it is often loosely used as a synonym for *careful.*

mews *n.*

Originally plural, when it meant 'the place or stables where the King's falcons were kept'. In the singular it now means 'stables or coach-houses converted into dwelling-houses', e.g. *He lives in a mews.*

mickle, muckle *adj. n.*

Now archaic except in dialect, these words are different forms having the meaning 'great' or 'a great quantity'. In the Scots saying, "*Mony a mickle maks a muckle*", the first word was originally *pickle* not *mickle.*

middle *adj.*

Some of the compounds made from this word are written as one word, e.g. *middleman, middlemost*; some have a hyphen, e.g. *middle-aged, middle-weight*; some are separate words, e.g. *The Middle Ages, the Middle East.* (see CENTRE)

middle class, middle-class

The hyphenated form is the adjective. (see PUNCTUATION, HYPHENS)

Midsummer, mid-summer('s)

June 24 is known as *Midsummer Day.* For describing a day in the middle of summer *mid-summer('s)* or *midsummer('s)* is used.

might see MAY

migrant see IMMIGRANT

mileage *n.*

This spelling is more common than *milage.*

million(s) *n.*

When used for a precise number there is no *s* at the end of this word, e.g. *The land is worth two million (pounds),* but the *s* is added when the word is used more vaguely, e.g. *It will cost millions of pounds.*

mimic

Past tense and present participle *mimicked, mimicking.*

mimsy see PORTMANTEAU WORD

minimal see MARGINAL

minimize *v.*

This means 'reduce to the minimum, the least possible amount', e.g. *We are taking every possible precaution, in order to minimize any danger to the members of the expedition.* It is loosely used to mean 'diminish', 'lessen' or 'underestimate', e.g. *It does not pay to minimize the difference between the two nationalities.*

minimum *n.*

This word is often used inaccurately in the sense of 'a little' rather than 'the least', e.g. [*He would have been thankful for the minimum of kindness from his neighbours*].

minister see CLERGYMAN

minor(ity) see MAJOR(ITY)

minus ('mainəs) *adj.*

Colloquial and jocular when used other than in a mathematical sense, e.g. *He was never seen minus his bicycle.*

mis- *prefix*

Compounds made with this prefix are written without a hyphen even when the result is a double *s*, e.g. *misspent*. *Mis-shapen* is sometimes an exception.

misrelated participle see PARTICIPLES

Miss, Misses

The Misses Franklin is old-fashioned but is used in formal invitations and in written addresses; in speech and informal writing it is *The Miss Franklins*. (see LETTER-WRITING)

mistrust see DISTRUST

Mohammed(an) see MAHOMET(AN)

molten see MELTED

momentary ('moumәntәri), **momentous** (mә'mentәs) *adj.*

Momentary means 'for a very brief time', e.g. *After a momentary hesitation he ran on.* Momentous means 'of lasting importance', e.g. *a momentous speech, decision, occasion.*

monogram, monograph *n.*

A *monogram* consists of 'two or more letters written together or intertwined to make a single design', and used for ornament or identification. A *monograph* is 'a treatise on one aspect of a subject'.

monologue, soliloquy *n.*

Both these words describe 'a long speech made by one person'; a *monologue* is usually addressed to other people, whereas a *soliloquy* is a theatrical device by which an actor expresses his private thoughts heard by the audience but not by the other characters, who are often onstage at the time.

moral(s) *adj. n.* **morale, morality** *n.*

The noun *moral* means 'the generalization that can be drawn from a story or set of events', e.g. *The moral of this is that it pays to insure your house against fire.* The plural *morals* and the adjective retain the idea of ethical standards, e.g. *I would vouch for his competence but not for his morals*; *We cannot call this a moral issue, for there is no question of right or wrong*. Morale (mɔˈrɑːl) means 'state of mind', 'the presence or absence of courage' and 'the will to resist', and is most often used of troops and nations in time of war, e.g. *The shortage of food is having a bad effect on the morale of the people*. Morality can mean either 'a system of morals' or 'moral rightness', 'virtue', e.g. *His behaviour was of doubtful morality*.

morbid, mordant *adj.*

Morbid is derived from the Latin word for 'disease' and is used in this sense in *morbid curiosity*, which means 'an unnatural curiosity about the niceties of death and disease'. The more general use of *morbid* is to mean 'unhealthy', 'excessively introspective'; it is most commonly confused with *mordant*, meaning 'biting', 'corrosive', in the phrases *morbid wit* ('an inclination to finding humour in topics which are normally treated with solemnity') and *mordant wit* ('an acid, usually sarcastic, way of expressing things').

more *adj. adv.*

Sometimes inaccurately used with comparatives. e.g. [*more easier, more inferior*] and absolutes, e.g. [*more perfect, more omnipotent*].

181

Verbs following *more than* are singular or plural according to the following noun, e.g. *More than one person has been drowned in this pool*; *More than ten people have been drowned in this river*.

Confusion can arise over use with *fewer than* and *less*, e.g. [*There were more than a quarter fewer than last year*]; [*My trunk is more than three pounds less heavy than yours*]. These would be better in the form *There were less than three quarters as many as last year*, or *The number was reduced by over a quarter compared with last year*; *My trunk is over three pounds lighter than yours*.

most *adj. adv.* **mostly** *adv.*

Most is often loosely used in speech for 'much', 'very', losing its sense of being a superlative, e.g. *I found it most beautiful*. In the U.S. it is colloquially used as a short form of *almost*, e.g. *I 'most died of laughing*.

Mostly has the meaning of *for the most part*, e.g. *People mostly prefer to go by car*, but it is sometimes clumsily used instead of the adverb *most*, e.g. [*His death was a great blow to those who mostly cared for him*.]

motion see RESOLUTION

motivate *v.* **motivation** *n.*

These words, more popular in the U.S. than in Britain, are often used unnecessarily instead of simpler words such as *impel* or *move*, e.g. *He was clearly motivated by anger against his victim.*

mow, mowed, mown *v.*

The past tense is *mowed*, past participle *mowed* or *mown. Mown* is generally found in compounds, e.g. *new-mown hay.*

much, very much, very *adj. adv.*

Much and *very much* are used with participles, e.g. *I was (very) much amused*, but adjectives are preceded by *very*, e.g. *I was very sad when she left.* Some participles however have become adjectival, so *very* is used with them rather than *much*, e.g. *excited, satisfied, celebrated, tired.* It is grammatically inaccurate, though fairly common, to say *that much* instead of *so much*, e.g. *I can't afford to pay that much for a new dress.*

much more, much less

These two phrases, particularly the second, are often used so that they offer a contradiction to the preceding part of the sentence, e.g. [*It is difficult to understand her attitude, much less to sympathize with it*]. This could be written . . . *and impossible to sympathize with it.*

muckle see MICKLE

mulatto (*fem.* **mulattress**) *n. adj.*

'The offspring of a white person and a Negro'. The derivation of the word is from Portuguese, meaning 'of mixed breed'. (see CREOLE; QUADROON)

must *n.*

Use of this word as a noun is colloquial, e.g. *Evening dress is a must for this function.*

mutual *adj.*

This word is often loosely used instead of *common* without the meaning of 'two-way' which belongs to it, e.g. [*They all shared a mutual liking for music.*] It is properly used in *He and his sister had a great mutual respect.* It was originally used when two, and *only* two, persons were concerned. In Dickens's *Our Mutual Friend*, however, the friend was common to two other persons. This deviation has helped to expand the use of the word in *mutual acquaintance, mutual friend* etc. It is redundant to speak of a *mutual agreement* because to have an agreement two parties must accept it.

N

naïve, naive *adj.* **naïveté, naivety** *n.*

As these French words have been only partially anglicised, their pronunciation and spelling vary; the commonest pronunciation is (nɑːˈiːv, nɑːˈiːvtei) and the usual spelling is the anglicised version.

naphtha (ˈnæfθə)

napkin, serviette (səˈviːˈet) n.

Both these words are used; preferences for one or the other are a matter of fashion.

nature n.

Like *character* this is a word often used to form a phrase where a simple adjective would suffice, e.g. *His thoughts were of a gloomy nature* (i.e. *gloomy*); *The accident was caused by the dangerous nature of the corner. The accident happened at a dangerous corner* would be better. (see STYLE)

naught, nought n.

Nought is the numerical term for 'nothing'. *Naught* appears in archaic phrases such as *set at naught.*

near by, nearby

Near by is an adverb, e.g. *He found he could get petrol near by; nearby* is an adjective, e.g. *He buys his petrol at a nearby garage. Neighbouring* is often a better word.

near, nearly adj. adv.

Near as an adverb, e.g. *He was near frozen to death,* is now only used in dialect.

necessarily (ˈnesiserili) adv.

Traditionally the accent is on the first syllable, but the difficulty of this pronunciation has led to a widespread use of the pronunciation (ˌnesiˈserili).

necessary, necessaries; necessity, necessities *n.*

These words overlap in the usual meaning of 'things which are necessary', but *necessity* has the additional meaning of 'compelling circumstances', 'poverty', e.g. *He lacked the necessaries for a comfortable life; Necessity compelled him to find work. Necessary* is usually plural except in the colloquial phrase *the necessary* (i.e. money).

need, want *v.*

The distinction between these two is often blurred, e.g. [*He wants to mind his own business*]. *Need* is impersonal and objective, *want* is subjective.

Need can be followed by three different constructions in statements and questions: (a) He need not *go*; Needn't he *go*? (b) He does not need *to go*; Doesn't he need *to go*? or He needs *to go*; He does need *to go*. Does he need *to go*? (c) He needs *a new coat*. (see REQUIRE)

negatives

1. [*I shouldn't wonder if he doesn't forget to come.*] It is sometimes forgotten that two negatives in the same sentence usually cancel each other out. The example could be taken

186

to mean *I shall be surprised if he forgets to come.*

2. [*All of us have not decided to stay longer.*] In this sentence it is doubtful whether the subject or the verb is intended to be negative. The two meanings could be expressed with greater clarity in separate sentences: *A few of us have decided to stay longer* and *We have all decided not to stay any longer.*

3. [*Nobody found the new shoe polish effective and demanded their money back.*] Did anybody ask for their money back? The second clause must either contain another negative (*... and nobody was happy until the money had been refunded*) or have a fresh subject (*... and everybody demanded their money back*).

(see SPELLING, NEGATIVE FORMS)

neither . . . nor see EITHER . . . OR

neologism

A newly invented word or phrase, or one used in a new way.

Newcastle upon Tyne but **Newcastle-under-Lyme**

nomenclature (nou'menklətʃə) *n.*

A system of names, terminology etc., for example the Linnaean system for classifying plants. It is sometimes loosely used for *name*, as in *He is setting up a new firm, but cannot decide on its nomenclature.*

none see NUMBER

norm, normalcy, normality *n.*

Norm means 'a recognized standard', e.g. *The daily output of the workers in this factory is below the norm.* *Normalcy* and *normality* both mean 'the state of being normal', e.g. *After the excitement of the fire it was difficult to return to normality.*

no sooner

Followed by *than*, not *but.*

not only

Sometimes misplaced, causing an unbalanced sentence, e.g. *The plan was not only impossible but misled the workers*, which could be written either as *Not only was the plan impossible, but it misled the workers* or *The plan was not only impossible but also misleading to the workers.*

notable, noticeable, notorious *adj.*

Notable means 'remarkable', 'worthy of notice', e.g. *a notable violinist; notable progress.* *Noticeable* means 'easily seen', e.g. *It is noticeable how much she has grown.* *Notorious* means 'widely known', generally in a bad sense, e.g. *His meanness is notorious*; *He was a notorious criminal.*

nothing see ELSE

nothing but

Used as the subject of a sentence this is treated as singular, e.g. *Nothing but a few crusts of bread was found in the kitchen.*

notice *v.*

This verb should not be used intransitively as in [*I have a mark on my coat but it doesn't notice*]. This should be either *nobody will notice it* or *it is not noticeable*.

nought see NAUGHT

noun

1. Nouns are increasingly used instead of adjectives in phrases such as *the enemy forces*, *the* Times *correspondent*, *the unemployment position*. This is a more compact way of saying *the forces of the enemy* etc. but it can lead to ambiguity especially in newspaper headlines such as: UNIVERSITIES PROBE FINANCE SCARE. FISH TALKS AT GRIMSBY. BULL GRANTS INCREASE.

2. *Proper nouns* give the name of a particular person, place, or thing, and are written with a capital letter: *John Smith*, *Paris*, *Daily Express*, *Salvation Army*. (see PUNCTUATION, CAPITAL LETTERS)

3. *Collective nouns* name a class or group of things or people: a *team* of players, *fleet* of ships, *suit* of clothes. (For the use of singular or plural verbs after these nouns see NUMBER)

noxious, obnoxious (əb'nɒkʃəs) *adj.*

Noxious is a far stronger word than *obnoxious*, which is a word much used in value judgments on other people, e.g. *What an ob-*

189

noxious person! The meaning of *noxious* is 'harmful', as in *a noxious gas*, whereas *obnoxious* means 'offensive', 'objectionable', either of which is to be preferred.

number

Only nouns, pronouns and verbs have any change of form to indicate whether they are singular or plural, e.g. *Mouse, mice; his, theirs; has, have.*

Collective nouns raise doubts about whether they should be used with a singular or plural verb. The solution depends on whether the emphasis is on the group as a unit or as a collection of individuals, as in *The team has been successful in every match,* but *The team have promised to be punctual. The committee has decided to reject the application,* but *The committee have disagreed.* It is important that any pronoun referring back to the collective noun should have the same number, e.g. *The class was told to bring money for its teacher's present,* or *The class were told to bring money for their teacher's present.*

The following examples of the correct form illustrate some of the cases where difficulties arise over number:—

A man and a woman were coming towards us.

A man, accompanied by a woman, was coming towards us.

There were a shilling and a sixpence in the purse.
There was a pair of shoes in the suitcase.
A pair of shoes was left in the cupboard.
None of us was able to remember his correct place
at the table.
Everybody who comes is to be welcomed at the door.
Among those present was the doctor.
Among those present were the doctor and his wife.
What results has all his work achieved?
What results have all his labours achieved?
One of Shakespeare's plays has to be read by all
students.
Both of the children were dressed in green.
Each of the children was carrying a coat.
Either the doctor or his partner is always available.
Neither the doctor nor his partner was available.
It is one of the best books on the subject that has
ever been written.

Mistakes usually arise where there is un-
certainty about which noun or pronoun in
the sentence is the true subject of the verb,
or about which noun a pronoun is replacing.
Once these points have been decided, there is
usually no difficulty about achieving consistency within the sentence. (see THERE;
EVERY; WHAT; EACH; EITHER; -IC; PRONOUN;
SUMMONS; AMID; VERMIN; WHEREABOUTS;
YOUTH)

number of

A *number of* can mean either 'some' or 'a large (or small) number', and is treated as plural accordingly, e.g. *A number of* (or *some*) *cases have occurred*; *A number of people were persuaded, though a few disagreed*. The number of is singular, e.g. *The number of workers who change their jobs is increasing.*

numerals

There is often some doubt as to whether one should use Arabic numerals, e.g. *462*, in descriptive writing or whether the figure should be written out, e.g. *four hundred and sixty-two*. The following are brief guidelines:

1. When the number is over a hundred and is not a round number, there is no need to write it out, e.g. *We now have 319 members in our Music Society*. When the figure is a round number, it is more usual to write it, e.g. *The present population of England is around forty-five million.*

2. When the number is a sum of money which can be written out easily, it should be, e.g. *This book costs thirty shillings* (or *one pound ten shillings*).

3. Fractions should always be written out, e.g. *The hall was only half filled.*

4. For decimals, figures should always be used. (see DATES)

O

o, oh *interj.*

O is an invocation or the expression of a wish, and is never followed by a comma or exclamation mark, e.g. *O how I wish you had told me.* Oh is generally used where the exclamation stands by itself, and followed by a comma or exclamation mark, e.g. *Oh! I forgot to tell you.*

object

In grammar, the *object* is the word or group of words which is controlled by the verb. The personal pronouns take the form *me, him, us* etc. when they become objects. An *indirect* object can usually be distinguished from a *direct* object, because a preposition (usually *to* or *for*) placed before the indirect object will make the meaning of the sentence clearer, as in:

I gave him his present. (*to* him)

I kept her a chair. (*for* her)

Why don't you get yourself a new car? (*for* yourself)

We all wished him the best. (*to* him)

object (əb'dʒekt), **subject** (səb'dʒekt) *v.*

To *object* is followed by *to* and a present participle, not an infinitive, e.g. *Surely you do not object to paying your share?* not [*you do not object to pay your share*]. Similarly *subject*, which appears more often in the form *be subjected to*, is followed by a noun or present participle. *He was constantly subjected to insults* or *to being insulted.*

object, subject *n.*

The wrong one of this pair of words is sometimes used with terms like *study, research, inquiry* etc. *Object* must always have a sense of purpose, either immediate or long-term. *The object of his research was to find out about Glasgow in the nineteenth century; The object of his research was to get a higher degree; The subject of his research was Glasgow in the nineteenth century.*

objective, subjective *adj.*

An *objective* statement is one which simply gives a fact, e.g. *I am forty years old; The film lasts four hours.* A *subjective* one has a personal colouring, e.g. *I am as youthful as ever although I am forty years old; The film is too long.*

oblivious *adj.*

This means 'unaware', 'forgetful', and is followed by *of*, not *to*, e.g. *She was oblivious of his presence.*

obnoxious see NOXIOUS

observance, observation *n.*

Observance means the act of 'complying with a law', 'following a custom', or 'celebrating a rite', e.g. *The police try to ensure the observance of the law*; *There is no longer so much observance of Sunday as a holy day*. Observation can mean 'the act and results of watching', 'the collection of information', or 'a remark or comment', e.g. *After close observation the nature of the illness was diagnosed*; *An observation which you made in the course of your talk started me thinking.*

occupation *n.*

In the sense of 'trade' or 'profession', this word is sometimes misused to describe the worker rather than the work, e.g. [*My occupation is a teacher*] rather than *My job is teaching.*

octopus

Plural *octopuses.*

oculist, optician *n.*

An *oculist* is 'a medical specialist in treating the eye'; an *optician* makes or sells spectacles or optical instruments.

odour *n.*

The adjective is spelt *odorous*. (cf. *humorous, valorous* etc.)

oe, ae, e see DIGRAPH

of *prep.*

This gives rise to various mistakes and inconsistencies:—

1. With collective nouns, where the number of the verb should generally follow the collective noun rather than the following

195

one, e.g. *A pile of sacks was* (rather than *were*) *left on the floor.* It is possible to be too correct over this, when the sense of the verb is closer to the second noun, e.g. *The crowd of spectators were* (rather than *was*) *all shouting different slogans.*

2. Where a sentence has several clauses, it is a common act of carelessness to switch from one preposition to another in introducing them, e.g. [*Without a thought of whether he was acting wisely, or about what the consequences would be, or how he could escape them, he went straight ahead*].

O.K.
Used as an adjective, noun and verb commercially, e.g. *I have O.K.d his figures*; otherwise its use is colloquial.

olden *adj.*
Used only in the phrases *in the olden days, olden times.*

older see ELDER

ominous *adj.*
Pronounced ('ɔminəs) rather than ('ouminəs).

on the contrary see CONTRARY

one *pro. suffix, prefix*
Makes the compounds *anyone, everyone, someone, oneself, no one.* It is used in three ways as a pronoun:—

1. In a simple numerical way, e.g. *She*

gave me three apples, and I ate one; *One of us has to go.*

2. In an impersonal way, as a substitute for *we, you, people in general*, e.g. *One is not allowed to talk in the library*; *One might think it a better plan*; *One must be able to protect oneself.*

3. To avoid the use of *I*, usually from false modesty or affectation, e.g. *One hopes one won't disgrace the others.*

one's *pro.*

The only possessive pronoun written with an apostrophe. *Yours, hers, theirs, its, ours* are written without, as is *oneself.*

only *adv.*

There can be ambiguity if this word is carelessly placed in the sentence, e.g. [*I can see you only after lunch*]; [*The directors only went to the meeting*]. It should be placed as near as possible to the word it qualifies, e.g. *I can see only you after lunch* or *I can see you after lunch only*; *Only the directors went to the meeting* or *The directors went to the meeting only. Only too pleased, delighted* etc. is colloquial, and in formal writing *only too* is often a weak way of saying *very, extremely*, e.g. *The tribes were only too anxious to make peace.* (SEE NOT ONLY)

on to, onto

On to is often used where one word would be sufficient, e.g. *If Smith retires, the work will fall on (to)* Brown's shoulders. *Onto* is a preposition, e.g. *They poured the sauce onto the pudding.* The words must be separated when *on* is itself an adverb, e.g. *We ran right on to the end of our road.*

onward *adj. adv.* **onwards** *adv.*

Onward is used for both adjective and adverb and is commoner than *onwards* which is used only as an adverb.

opera see OPUS

operative *n. adj.*

This word is used in bureaucratic and commercial jargon for *worker*, e.g. *cotton operative.* A fashionable use of it as an adjective is found in e.g. *The operative word* where it means 'important', 'significant' etc.

opposite see CONTRARY

optician see OCULIST

optimistic, pessimistic *adj.*

Strictly these words are only properly used to describe a person's belief that good or evil will prevail, but they are often loosely used for *hopeful* and *hopeless*, e.g. *He took a pessimistic view of his chances of passing the examination. The outlook for the country is not optimistic.*

opus ('ɔpəs) or ('oupəs) *n.*

Latin word meaning 'work', used for numbering musical compositions in the order in which they were written, e.g. *Beethoven's Symphony No. 4 in B Flat Major, Opus 60.* Also

used of literary works especially in the phrase
magnum opus, 'a masterpiece'. It can be used
for the whole of an artist's work, but *oeuvre*
is more common. The grammatical plural
opera is rarely used because of its confusion
with the meaning 'a musical drama'.

-or, -our *suffix*

In the U.S. there is a standard spelling *or*,
where we have two forms, e.g. *horror, tenor,
mirror*, but *honour, fervour, favour*. Where
adjectives made from these nouns end in *ous*
the *u* is dropped, e.g. *odorous, humorous*, but it
is kept before *-able*, e.g. *favourable, honourable*.

oral see AURAL

ordinance, ordnance *n.*

An *ordinance* is 'something ordered by
authority', 'a decree or regulation'. *Ordnance*
means 'artillery', but the word is also used
in *Ordnance Survey*, the detailed geographical
survey made for the government.

other *adj. adv. pro.*

Other is followed by *than*, not by *but*, when it
means 'different', 'separate', e.g. *I have heard
no opinions other than yours. But* or *except* are
sometimes used to emphasise an exception,
e.g. *There is no other possible course except
(but) devaluation.* (*each other* see EACH)

other than

Is often used pedantically, e.g. *I could not be*

other than amused by what he said instead of
I could not help being amused.

ought to, should *v.*

Ought to implies a stronger moral duty to do
something than *should*, e.g. *You ought to tell
her the truth*; *You should tell her if you feel cold.*
Ought is always followed by *to*, unlike *can*,
may etc. This is sometimes forgotten when they
are used together, e.g. [*You ought and can
manage it*] for *You ought to and can.*

ours *personal pro.*

Spelt without an apostrophe.

out- *prefix*

Compounds made from this prefix do not
usually have a hyphen even when there is a *tt*,
e.g. *outtalk.* The exceptions are phrases like
out-of-date, out-of-doors.

outright *adj. adv.*

This is the form of both adjective and adverb;
there is no need to add *ly* to make the adverb.

over- *prefix*

This prefix makes compounds without a
hyphen, e.g. *overloaded.*

overall *adj.*

The precise use of this word is for describing
the measurement between two extremities,
usually of a ship, e.g. *the overall length of the new
Cunarder.* It is used in modern jargon especially by journalists, in contexts where it has

little meaning and could be replaced by *complete*, *general*, *inclusive* or *total*, e.g. *The overall picture shows some improvements.*

overflow

Past tense and past participle *overflowed*.

overlook, oversee *v.*

Confusion arises when *overlook* is used in its former sense of 'oversee', 'supervise'. The modern meanings of this word are 'look over at', e.g. *My house overlooks the sea*, and 'fail to see' either through neglect, e.g. *He overlooked the instruction in the last paragraph,* or deliberately in order to condone, e.g. *She decided to overlook her husband's misconduct. I asked him to overlook my work* is therefore ambiguous, and would be more clearly expressed as *I asked him to look over my work.*

owing to see DUE TO

Oxbridge see PORTMANTEAU WORD

P

paid see SPELLING, VERBS

pan- *prefix*

Meaning 'all', 'the whole of', this prefix is most frequently used with national names, e.g. *Pan-African*, and joined to them with a hyphen.

pandit, pundit *n.*

The second is the commoner form for 'a learned Hindu'. It is popularly used for 'an expert or authority on a subject', often in a tone of mockery.

parable see ALLEGORY

paradox

'An apparently contradictory statement which contains an important truth', e.g. *The golden rule is that there are no golden rules* (Shaw); *The cruellest lies are often told in silence* (Stevenson)

paragraph

Passages of writing are divided into paragraphs to help the reader by separating different topics, different aspects of a topic, or the stages of an argument. Occasionally they consist of only one sentence, particularly where great emphasis is required, but usually they contain several sentences all related to the same idea. The end of a paragraph provides a natural pause, where the reader can make sure that he has grasped the last stage of the matter before passing on to the next. It often happens that one sentence in a paragraph states its subject, which is expanded by the others; in business correspondence and other forms of writing where the main object is to impart or discuss facts, it is most convenient to put this sentence first, but where there is a theoretical argument the most important sentence is often reserved to the end of the paragraph, where it provides a climax or a summary. Novelists can convey variations of pace in their books by their use of these visible breaks; they tend to use long paragraphs for passages of description and reflection, shorter ones for conveying action.

A new paragraph is indicated by starting a sentence on a new line, leaving a space on the left-hand margin of the page. When a letter or memorandum contains a number of points which may be discussed later, it is helpful to number the paragraphs, or to give them headings.

parallel see SPELLING, VERBS

paraphrase, digest ('daidʒest), **précis** ('preisi:), **summary** n.

A *paraphrase* is 'an alternative version of a passage of writing sometimes simpler than the original, sometimes fuller'. Verse can be paraphrased in prose, and prose in verse, e.g. metrical versions of scriptural texts. It can also be a free translation. *Digest, precis* and *summary*, all mean 'a shorter, concise version, picking out the main points'; *digest* is used for 'a classified summary of a quantity of ma-

terial', *precis* for a single passage, *summary* for
either.

parenthesis (pəˈrenθəsis)

'A word, phrase or sentence within a passage,
which can stand grammatically complete
without it', usually marked off by commas,
dashes or brackets, sometimes called *paren-
theses*, e.g. *The officer, who was a tall man,
stopped and spoke to me.* It is correctly used for
expanding or amplifying a sentence, not for
inserting a piece of unconnected information
as in [*I told him (I was thirty at the time) that
he should wait a little longer before publishing his
book*].

partially, partly *adv.*

These words are often used as if they were
interchangeable, but *partly* means 'concerning only a part', and is the opposite of
wholly; partially means 'not fully', and is the
opposite of *completely*, e.g. *His book, which was
written partly in English and partly in French,
was only partially completed when he died.*

participles

Present and *past participles* are parts of a verb
which can be used as adjectives, e.g. *your*
broken *promise*, or to help form a tense, e.g.
I have broken *my glasses. Present participles*
always end in *ing. Past participles* have a
variety of forms, sometimes the same as the

past tense: *hoped, burnt, begun, sold, blown, taken*. Both types can be used with a noun or pronoun as a simple adjective, e.g. *a forced confession, a* helping *hand*, or to form an adjectival phrase, e.g. Seeing *my distress he came to my help*; Left *on my own, I wondered what to do next*.

The use of participles gives rise to two common mistakes. The first is to write the sentence so that the participle is related to the wrong noun or pronoun, e.g. [*Crossing the street, a car stopped in front of him*] (*As he was crossing the street*). The other is to fail to supply any noun or pronoun to which it can be related, e.g. [*Disappointed in the hope of a quick settlement, there seems to be no chance of an early end to the strike.*]

A few participles may be used without being related to a noun in the main sentence, e.g. Considering *the circumstances*; Speaking of *holidays*.

(see SPELLING, verbs)

particular *adj.*

This word is often used loosely to add emphasis to *this*, e.g. Why did you choose this [*particular*] moment to come? In *I could not find the particular colour I wanted* it is properly used to mean 'special', 'exact'.

partly see PARTIALLY

party n.

Used in the sense of 'person' this is a legal term for someone signing a contract or taking part in a lawsuit, e.g. *neither party to the agreement may withdraw*. However its use is colloquial in place of *person*, e.g. *a certain party is considerably older than she pretends to be*.

pass v.

The past participle of this verb is *passed*, the adjective formed from it is *past*, e.g. *Time has passed slowly since you went away*; *The days are past when I could walk ten miles*; *The past six years*.

passive voice

The impersonal passive is often used in commercial and bureaucratic writing to avoid directness and responsibility, e.g. *It is not considered advisable to pursue the matter further*, rather than *We advise you not to pursue the matter further*.

past tense and past participles see SPELLING, verbs

patent n. v.

Usually pronounced ('peitənt) in G.B., ('pætənt) in the U.S.

pathos ('peiθɔs)

'A situation which evokes pity, either in life or art'. The original Greek word means 'suffering' and *pathos* seems to return to this

206

meaning in the phrase *the pathos of* (or *in*) *the situation*.

patois see LANGUAGE TERMS

pence, pennies *n.*

The plural form *pennies* is used where the emphasis is on the coins as separate objects, e.g. *There is a pile of pennies on the table*; *I have run out of pennies so I cannot use the stamp machine*; but *pence* is used where the purchasing value of the coins is concerned, e.g. *It will cost only a few pence. Halfpence* and *halfpennies* are used the same way.

Twopence is sometimes written *tuppence* in accordance with the pronunciation, but only in commercial or humorous writing.

pendant, pendent *adj. n.*

Either spelling can be used for this word, both as an adjective meaning 'hanging', and as a noun meaning 'an ornament which hangs round the neck'.

peninsula *n.* **peninsular** *adj.*

pennant, pennon *n.*

These forms are interchangeable; both mean 'a long narrow flag, generally nautical or military'.

people *n.*

Generally followed by a verb in the plural even when it means a nation, e.g. *The British people are determined not to give in.* (see NUMBER)

per *prep.*

A Latin preposition often pointlessly used in place of *by*, especially in commercial jargon, e.g. *I am sending your goods per rail.* It is more useful in phrases like *per month, per head*, but even here *a* could often be used. In *per capita*, the word *capita* is the plural of *caput* ('head') and is a legal term referring to a method of sharing property among several persons. It is sometimes mistakenly used for 'each person', e.g. [*They were paid five shillings per capita*].

per cent, percentage, proportion *n.*

Per cent is a recognized abbreviation and requires no full stop. It is often superfluously used in observations where no accuracy is intended, e.g. *Fifty per cent of my time is spent in teaching.* *Percentage* is loosely used for 'a small number' or 'a few', e.g. *A percentage of the soldiers refused to take part in the raid.* *Proportion*, which should imply a comparative relationship, is often used to mean simply 'a part', e.g. *A proportion of his time was spent in planning for the future.* Both words should be qualified by *large, small* etc.

perceptible, perceptive, percipient *adj.*

Perceptible means 'capable of being perceived' and is always followed by *to*, e.g. *The insect was so small that it was barely perceptible to the human eye; perceptive* means 'discriminating', 'having perception', e.g. *The conductor was very perceptive in spotting passengers who had not paid their fare*. It also has the more restricted meaning 'of sight', as in *the perceptive organs*. *Percipient* is a less common form of *perceptive*.

perfect *adj. v.*

The adjective *perfect* is an absolute term so *most* and *more* are not strictly needed with it, but it can mean 'approaching perfection' and be used comparatively in that sense, e.g. *His taste is more perfect than mine*. *Perfect fool, perfect nuisance, perfectly ridiculous* etc. are colloquial usage and rather old-fashioned. The verb is pronounced (pə'fekt).

periphrasis (pə'rifrəsis)

'The use of roundabout language', e.g. *The retiring Secretary was made the recipient of a cheque* where ... *presented with a cheque* would be more direct.

permissible, permissive *adj.*

Permissible describes an action which is allowed, 'not prohibited', e.g. *It is permissible to leave your car here*. *Permissive* describes an attitude of 'allowing something to be done without enforcing it', e.g. *In the Act there is a permissive clause which allows local authorities to provide free libraries*. In a wider sense it means 'liberal-minded', 'anti-disciplinarian', e.g. *The Permissive Society*.

permit *v. n.*

The verb *permit* is only followed by *of* when it means 'make possible', e.g. *The situation does not permit of any other course of action.* Otherwise it is followed by an infinitive, e.g. *My father will not permit me to marry before I am twenty-one* not [*My father will not permit of my marrying*]. The noun is pronounced ('pə:mit).

per proc., per pro., p.p.

These abbreviations are used by secretaries when signing letters in the absence of the principal, e.g. *p.p. Professor Giles Smethwick, Mary Evans.* The alternative is to use *for.* (see LETTER-WRITING)

persona, personage, personality *n.*

Persona in Latin is 'a person' or 'a mask worn by actors'. In psychology it means 'the aspect of the personality presented to the outside world'. *Dramatis personae* means 'the characters in a play, opera etc.' A *personage* is 'someone of importance', usually owing to birth or office, e.g. *I had no idea she was such a personage in the district.* A *personality* is a journalistic term for 'a celebrity', e.g. *racing personality of the year.*

persona grata

'An acceptable person' or 'someone temporarily in favour with someone else', e.g. *He was persona grata with all* not [*a persona grata*]. *Persona non grata* or *ingrata* is the opposite. (SEE FOREIGN WORDS AND PHRASES)

personable *adj.*

This means 'of pleasing appearance'.

personal(ly) *adj. adv.*

This is often used needlessly to reinforce *I*, e.g. *Personally I think it will rain today*, but it is useful for distinguishing between official and private opinions and actions, e.g. *The Minister gave me his personal views which were not those of the Cabinet.*

personality see PERSONA

personate, impersonate, personify (pəˈsɔnifai) *v.*

The first two of these words mean 'play the part of another person, either on the stage or for fraudulent purposes'. *To personify* is 'to embody' or 'be an outstanding example of a quality or characteristic', e.g. *She personified beauty for me when I was young*; *Our Olympic team personified all that was best in British sport.*

persons *n. pl.*

Used only in official language, e.g. *Persons requiring assistance*; *Persons found in possession of*; *Undesirable persons.*

perspicuous (pəˈspikjuəs), **perspicacious** (ˌpəːspiˈkeiʃəs) *adj.*

Perspicuous (noun *perspicuity*) means 'clear', 'easily understood' and is usually applied to an

211

explanation or a piece of writing, e.g. *I could not have understood it without the perspicuity of his description*. *Perspicacious* (noun *perspicacity*) means 'clear-sighted', and is used of people, e.g. *The observation showed the unusual perspicacity of the speaker*.

pertinent (to) *adj.*

'Relevant', e.g. *Your remarks are not pertinent to the discussion*. *Irrelevant* and *inappropriate* are antonyms, but not *impertinent*.

pessimistic see OPTIMISTIC

phenomenon (fi'nɔmənən), *n.* **phenomenal** *adj.* **phenomenally** *adv.*

Phenomenom means 'anything perceived by the senses', particularly in science. It is loosely used for anything remarkable, particularly the adjective and adverb *phenomenal(ly)* instead of *extraordinary, outstanding, unusual*, e.g. *He tore down the road at a phenomenal speed*; *The sale of long-playing records has been phenomenal*. Plural *phenomena* (fi'nɔminə).

phrase

The grammatical term for a group of words in a sentence which cannot stand alone, as it has no complete verb. It can take the place of a noun (*He has given up hoping for a letter*), an adjective (*I want a jar with a lid*), or an adverb (*She came slowly down the steps*). (see CLAUSE; SENTENCE)

physician (fi'ziʃən), **physicist** ('fizisist) *n.*

A *physician* is 'a doctor qualified to treat disease by medicine', but not a surgeon. A *physicist* is 'someone skilled in the practice of physics or a student of physics'.

pick, choose *v.*

These words overlap a good deal, but *pick* is generally used where there is an element of chance, *choose* where there is careful thought and the weighing of alternatives. One *picks* a winner in a race, but *chooses* a husband or wife.

picnic *n. v.*

Present and past participles *picnicking* and *picnicked*.

pidgin, pigeon English see LANGUAGE TERMS

pigmy, pygmy *n. adj.*

The preferred spelling is *pygmy*.

piteous, pitiable, pitiful *adj.*

All these words can mean 'pathetic', 'wretched' or 'worthy of contempt'. *Pitiful* has two additional meanings, 'deserving of pity' and more rarely 'merciful'. (see DUTEOUS)

plaid, tartan *n.*

A *plaid* is the garment worn over the shoulder by a Highlander. It is loosely used, outside Scotland, to mean *tartan*, which is the cloth of which *plaids* and *kilts* are made. It is generally pronounced (plæd) in England, but (pleid) in Scotland.

plateful *n.*
Plural *platefuls.*

plenteous, plentiful *adj.*
The first form is archaic. (see DUTEOUS)

plenty *n.*
Plenty used as an adjective without *of* is colloquial and unacceptable, e.g. [*There is plenty time*].

pleonasm ('pliːənæzəm)
'The use of more words than are necessary for the sense'.

plethora ('pleθərə) *n.*
'A superabundance.' In medicine 'an excess of red corpuscles in the blood'.

plurals
(For the plural forms of words ending in *eau, ics, c, ou, s, x, y,* and of numbers and proper names and titles, compounds and abbreviations see SPELLING, NOUNS. See NUMBER for the treatment of nouns and pronouns as singular or plural.)

pn-, ps-, pt-
Words beginning with these letters are always pronounced without the *p*, e.g. *pneumatic* (njuːˈmætik). The same is true of *ps* as in *psychology*, *pt* as in *ptarmigan*.

poetess *n.*
A woman who writes poetry is a *poet*, or if it is necessary to distinguish sex, a *woman poet*.

Poetess is out of date. (see FEMININE FORMS)

poetic, poetical *adj.*

There is no clear distinction between these words.

point of view see VIEW

politic, political *adj.*

Politic means 'cunning' or 'expedient', e.g. *His speech against nationalization was a politic move*; *It is not a politic moment to ask him to resign. Political* means 'associated with politics or government'.

politics *n.*

This word can be treated as singular or plural according to whether it is thought of as an activity or a system of beliefs, e.g. *Politics is a rewarding career*; *His politics* (i.e. 'his political views') *are right-wing.* (for other words operating in the singular and plural see -IC, -ICS).

porcelain, china *n.*

China is the general term; *porcelain* is usually reserved for the finest kind of semi-transparent earthenware.

portmanteau word

'An invented word made up of the sounds or parts of two words', e.g. *chortle* from *chuckle* and *snort*; *mimsy* from *miserable* and *flimsy*; *Oxbridge* from *Oxford* and *Cambridge.* Lewis Carroll invented many in his book *Through the Looking Glass.*

possessive forms

In the singular *'s* is used, as in *the dog's dinner*; in the plural the apostrophe is put at the end of the word, as in *in his parents' eyes*. (see SAKE) Proper names ending in *s* used to have the apostrophe only, and this is retained in certain traditional forms such as *Jesus' life*, *Moses' law*, *Keats' poetry*, and in poetry, but not with modern names, e.g. *the Williams's house*, *Thomas's party*. (see also Appendix of Proper Adjectives)

possible see FEASIBLE

post- *prefix*

Most compounds made with this prefix have a hyphen, whether it is used to mean 'after', or refers to the postal services, e.g. *post-dated*, *post-free*. The exceptions are mostly well established nouns like *postscript*, *postman*, *postgraduate*.

potent ('poutənt) *n.* **potential** (pə'ten ʃəl) *adj.* *Potent* means 'powerful', e.g. *a potent drink*, *a potent influence*. *Potential* means 'latent', 'existing in possibility but not in actuality', e.g. *a potential source of danger*; *potential ability to rise to the top*.

-p, -pp

(For monosyllables ending in *p* and the forms made from them, see SPELLING, VERBS).

p.p. see PER PROC.

practicable, practical adj.

Practicable describes 'something that can be done or carried out', e.g. The plan is not practicable because we have neither the men nor the tools required. Practical means 'efficient' and can describe the nature of a person or of an action or method, e.g. I have found a practical tool for the purpose.

practice n. **practise** v.

The noun is spelt with a c, the verb with an s. cf. advice, advise; licence, license.

pre- prefix

Usually makes compounds without a hyphen, except where there would be a double e, e.g. pre-existence.

precede, proceed v.

Precede, which means 'be in front of' or 'occur before (in time)', is sometimes confused with proceed, meaning 'go forward', 'go on with'. Their proper use is illustrated in: When it had finally been decided that the bishop should precede the vice-chancellor, the procession was allowed to proceed.

precipitate, precipitous adj.

Precipitate means 'hasty', e.g. precipitate flight of the enemy; precipitous means 'steep', e.g. precipitous descent down the cliffs.

précis see PARAPHRASE

preface n. see FOREWORD

prefer v. **preferable** ('prefərəbl) *adj.*

Makes participles *preferring, preferred* but the adjective is a comparative, so there is no need to precede it by *more*. e.g. *The second plan is [the more] preferable.*

prefix n. v. **preface**

The noun *prefix* ('pri:fiks) is used for 'the group of letters added at the beginning of a word to make a compound', e.g. *up-, inter-, re-, over-*. (For use of hyphens in these compounds, see PUNCTUATION)

The verb *prefix* (pri:'fiks) is often confused with *preface* especially in the placing of objects. The object of *prefix* is the thing prefixed, e.g. *He prefixed a bibliography to his book*. The object of *preface* is the thing to which something is added, e.g. *He prefaced his remarks with a few jokes.*

prejudice n. v.

Usually followed by *in favour of* or *against*; *to* only follows in the phrase *without prejudice to.*

preposition

A word which relates a noun or pronoun to the rest of the clause to form a noun phrase, e.g. *He looked at the clock*; *Do not go without me*. Pronouns used after a preposition are in the form *me, him, her, us, them, whom*. Sometimes two prepositions are used together, e.g. *up to, out of.*

It is pedantic to make a sentence sound unnatural to avoid ending it with a preposition, as in *I have nothing left for which to hope* rather than to write *I have nothing left to hope for*; but it is usual to avoid ending a sentence with more than one preposition, e.g. *I cannot remember which page we finished up at*, especially in formal writing. Some words are always followed by certain prepositions, and these are idiomatic.

The list below includes the most common linking of prepositions with verbs and adjectives. A verb following the preposition normally takes the *-ing* form, but where the infinitive is used, it is so marked.

Verb and preposition:

abide *by* or *in* (see ABIDE)
abstain *from*
account *for* ('explain')
accredit *to*
accuse . . . *of*
acquaint . . . *with*
acquit . . . *of*
agree *to* (e.g. *agree to a proposal*)
agree *with* (e.g. *agree with somebody about something*)
aim *at* (for *to* see AIM)

answer *for* ('take the responsibility for')

apologise *for*

appeal *to*

apply *to* (e.g. *apply to someone for something* or *apply oneself to something*)

approve *of* ('favour')

ask *about* or *after* ('enquire')

ask *for* ('request')

aspire *to*

atone *for*

attend *on* ('wait upon')

attend *to* ('deal with' or 'take notice of')

begin *to* or *by* (see BEGIN)

believe *in*

belong *to* or *with*

beware *of*

blame . . . *for* (for *on* see BLAME)

boast *about* or *of* ('brag')

border *on*

borrow . . . *from*

care *about* ('feel concern for' or 'be worried about')

care *for* ('like' or 'look after')

charge . . . *for* ('ask a price for')

charge . . . *with* ('accuse of')

compare *to* or *with* (see COMPARE)

complain *of* or *about*

conceal . . . *from*

confide *in* or *to* (see CONFIDE)

conform *to*

congratulate ... *on*

connive *at*

consent *to*

consist *of* ('be composed of')

consist *in* ('spring from', 'comprise')

correspond *to* ('be similar to', 'agree with')

correspond *with* ('write and receive letters')

count *for* ('be worth')

count *on* ('rely upon')

cure ... *of*

deal *in* ('trade in')

deal *with* ('take action regarding' or 'trade with')

defend ... *from*

delight *in* ('be delighted with')

depend *on* or *upon*

deprive ... *of*

despair *of*

deter ... *from*

die *of*

differ *from*

disapprove *of*

dispose *of*

dissent *from*

dissuade ... *from*

embark *for* ('set out on a journey to')

embark *on* ('engage in')

excuse ... *for* ('forgive')

221

excuse . . . *from* ('grant exemption from')

fail *at* or *in*

forgive . . . *for*

free *from*

gloat *over* or *upon*

hesitate *to* ('be reluctant')

hinder . . . *from*

hold *over* ('defer')

hold *to* ('abide by')

hope *for*

indulge *in*

inflict . . . *on*

inquire *about* ('seek information', see ENQUIRE)

inquire *into* ('investigate')

insist *on*

instruct . . . *in*

interfere *with*

join *in* ('participate')

join *to* or *with* ('unite')

jump *at* ('accept eagerly')

jump *to* ('move (over-hastily', e.g. to a con-
    clusion)

lean *on* (e.g. *He leant on a stick for support*)

lean *upon* (e.g. *He leant upon his father for financial
    support*)

live *for* ('be utterly engrossed in')

live *on* ('be reliant for life upon')

long *for* or *to* (e.g. *He longs for his twenty-first
    birthday*; *He longs to leave school*)

marvel *at*

meddle *in* or *with*

meet *with* ('encounter')

mistake . . . *for*

mourn *for* or *over*

part *from* ('leave')

part *with* ('renounce ownership of')

partake *of*

permit *of* or *to* (see PERMIT)

persevere *in* or *with*

persist *in*

pore *over*

prefer . . . *to*

present . . . *with*

preside *over*

profit *by*

quote . . . *on* ('use someone's actual words on some topic', e.g. *I quoted my professor on Renaissance painting*)

reckon *on* ('depend upon')

recover *from*

refer *to*

refrain *from*

rejoice *at*

rely *on* or *upon*

remind . . . *of* (e.g. *She reminded me of a girl I knew at school*)

remind . . . *to* (e.g. *She reminded me to buy something for dinner*) remonstrate *against* (e.g. *I remonstrated against the idea of moving into a tenth-floor flat*)

remonstrate *with* (e.g. *Although I remonstrated with the traffic warden, his decision did not change*)

repent *of*

reproach . . . *with*

reprove . . . *for*

restrain . . . *from*

send *for* ('summon')

struggle *for* (e.g. *The country was struggling for independence*)

struggle *to* (e.g. *He struggled to undo the knots*)

struggle *with* or *against* (e.g. *He struggled with the terrified horse*)

subject . . . *to*

succeed *in* ('be successful')

succeed *to* ('follow')

suffer *from* (see SUFFER)

suspect . . . *of*

sympathize *with*

think *about* ('consider', 'be interested in')

think *of* ('call to mind', 'have an opinion of' or 'consider'; see THINK)

threaten *with*

tire *of*

tyrannize *over*

warn . . . *of* (e.g. *I warned him of the train's approach*)

224

warn . . . *against* (e.g. *I warned them all against smoking*)
wonder *at*
yearn *for*
yield *to*

Adjective and preposition:

absorbed *in*
accustomed *to*
afflicted *with* (see AFFLICT)
afraid *of*
akin *to*
anxious *about* ('troubled')
anxious *for* ('greatly hoping')
apt *to* (+infinitive)
ashamed *of*
assailed *by*
assured *of*
astonished *at* or *by*
averse *to* or *from* (see AVERSE)
blessed *with*
blind *to*
bound *for*
capable *of*
characteristic *of*
clad, clothed *in* (see CLOTHED)
concerned *about* or *for* (e.g. *I was concerned about my aunt's behaviour*)

concerned *in* or *with* (e.g. *He was so deeply concerned in the affair that he offered his resignation*)

confronted *with* or *by*

conspicuous *for*

content *with*

convicted *of*

convinced *of*

credited *with*

decked *with* ('decorated')

deficient *in*

delighted *with*

dependent *on* or *upon*

deprived *of*

desirous *of*

determined *on*

devoid *of*

disappointed *at* or *by* (e.g. *I was disappointed at (by) my examination results*)

disappointed *in* or *with* (e.g. *He was disappointed in his team when they lost the Cup Final*)

eager *for*

endowed *with*

engaged *in* ('occupied in')

envious *of*

exempt *from*

faithful *to*

familiar *with* (e.g. *familiar with Greek*; *familiar with the gardener*)

favourable *to*
fond *of*
fraught *with*
free *from* or *of*
frightened *of*
full *of*
furnished *with* ('provided with')
galled *by*
geared *to*
good *at*
grateful *for*
grounded *in*
guilty *of*
hampered *by*
haunted *by*
hostile *to*
identical *to*
impervious *to*
implicit *in*
independent *of*
indifferent *to*
infested *with*
inherent *in*
innocent *of*
insensible *to*
inspired *by* or *with*
intent *on*
interested *in*
introductory *to*

jealous *of*
juxtaposed *with*
knowledgeable *on*
lacking *in*
laden, loaded (see LOADED)
liable *to* (+infinitive)
likely *to* (+infinitive)
loyal *to*
luxuriant *with*
marred *by*
merciful *to*
native *to* ('born in')
natural *to*
necessary *for* or *to*
noted *for*
noxious *to*
obedient *to*
offended *at* or *with* (e.g. *I was offended at the powerful smell*)
offended *by* or *with* (e.g. *I was offended by his mocking tone*)
overcome *with* or *by*
overpowered *by*
overwhelmed *by*
pampered *by* or *with*
parallel *to*
partial *to*
particular *about*
patient *with*

peculiar *to* ('belonging exclusively to')

perceptible *to*

perplexed *at*

pertinent *to*

perturbed *by* or *at*

pleased *with* or *at*

pliable *to*

polite *to*

popular *with*

pregnant *with* (e.g. *The clouds were pregnant with the coming storm*)

prejudiced *against*

preliminary *to*

proportionate *to*

proud *of*

qualified *for* or *to* (+infinitive)

receptive *to*

regardless *of*

related *to*

replete *with*

responsible *for* (e.g. *The night watchman was responsible for the security of the building after 5 p.m.*)

responsible *to* (e.g. *The plumber's mate was responsible to the plumber for ensuring that the joints were tight*).

sacred *to*

safe *from*

satisfied *with*

sceptical *of* or *about*
sensible *of* ('aware')
sensitive *to* (see SENSIBLE)
similar *to*
simultaneous *with*
sorry *for* or *to* (+infinitive)
stagnant *with*
subordinate *to*
suitable *for*
superior *to*
surprised *at*
suspicious *of*
synonymous *with*
terrified *of* or *by* or *at*
tired *of*
traditional *to*
typified *by* or *in*
uniform *with*
upset *by* or *at*
used *to* ('accustomed')
venerated *by*
vigorous *in* (e.g. *He was vigorous in the defence of party policy*)
young *in* or *at*

(see also GLANCE; IN, AT; MANNER; PREJUDICE; PROHIBIT; REPLACE; RESENTMENT; RESIGN; SUBSTITUTE; THINK; VARIANCE)

Many prepositions are also used as conjunctions, cf. *I have told no one but him*, where *but* is a preposition, and *I have told no one, but he may have*, where it is used as a conjunction. It is only in colloquial English that *like* is used in this way, to mean *as* or *as if* [*Can you dance like I can? It looked like it would rain.*] (see ADVERB; CONJUNCTION)

prescribe, proscribe *v.*

To *prescribe* is 'order or advise the use of', e.g. *treatment prescribed by a doctor.* To *proscribe* is to 'banish' or 'outlaw'.

present participles see SPELLING, VERBS

presume see ASSUME

pretence, pretension(s), pretentiousness *n.*

Pretence is 'the act of pretending', in both its senses of claiming and of feigning, e.g. *He makes no pretence to be richer than he is; You must not believe what he says, it's all a pretence.* *Pretension(s)* has only the sense of 'advancing a claim', e.g. *He has no pretension(s) to be a candidate for the presidency.* *Pretentiousness* means 'claiming or aspiring to more than one has', usually with presumption and arrogance, e.g. *His pretentiousness showed in the over-elegance of his house, the long words he used in conversation, and his constant references to aristocratic acquaintances.*

prevent *v.*

Prevent in the sense of 'stop' used without

from is colloquial, e.g. *prevent him going*. The more formal use is *prevent him from going* or *prevent his going*.

priest see CLERGYMAN

primate ('praimət) *n.*

This word has two distinct meanings:—

1. 'The head of a church', e.g. *The Archbishop of Canterbury*.

2. 'A member of the highest order of mammals, which includes man and monkeys'.

prime, primary, primitive *adj.*

Prime means 'most important', 'essential', 'of first quality', e.g. *Prime Minister*, *prime beef*. *Primary* means 'earliest', 'original', 'elementary', e.g. *primary colours*, *Primary school*. *Primitive* means 'uncivilized', 'rough', 'prehistoric', e.g. *Their civilization was still in a primitive state*.

principal *adj. n.* **principle** *n.*

Principal means 'chief', e.g. *my principal aim*; *the Principal of the college*. A *principle* is 'a moral or physical law', e.g. *He is acting against his principles*; *the principles of astronomy*.

probable *adj.*

Not to be used with an infinitive on the analogy of *likely*, e.g. [*I think it is probable to rain today*.] This should be either *I think rain is probable today* or *I think it is probable that it will rain today*. (see FEASIBLE; LIKELY)

proceed see PRECEDE

process *v.*

Process ('prouses) means 'treat something, generally food, in order to preserve it', e.g. *processed peas*. Process (prə'ses) means 'walk in procession'. (see BACK FORMATION)

programme, program (U.S.) *n., v.*

The latter is used in computer work.

progress (prə'gres) *v.* **progress** ('prougres) *n.*

prohibit *v.*

This verb can be followed either by a noun, e.g. *New laws have been drafted to prohibit people from driving whilst under the influence of alcohol,* or by *from* + participle, e.g. *You will be prohibited from driving,* but not by an infinitive, e.g. [*I prohibit you to drive*] where *forbid* would be better.

proliferation *n.*

This means 'a rapid increase', but it is loosely used for 'a profusion', 'a great quantity'.

prompt *adj.* **promptly** *adv.*

Prompt is used instead of the adverb only when it comes after the time, e.g. *He woke me promptly at six; He woke me at six prompt.*

pronoun

A word used instead of a noun to avoid repetition, to ask a question, or to indicate possession or emphasis. All the unitalicized words in the following passage are pronouns:

*The doctor had breakfast, then he picked up his
gloves, but not those which he usually wore.
"What are you thinking of?" asked his wife as
she saw him doing it, "Both have holes in them.
Are you sure they are yours?" Each started
looking for the other pair.*

It is important to make pronouns equivalent to the words which they replace, both in
number and person. It is a common mistake to
write sentences like *One cannot go there by
[himself]* (oneself), or *Every one of us wished
[themselves]* (himself) *at home when the rain
started.*

prophecy ('profisi) *n.* **prophesy** ('profisai) *v.*
(cf. *advice, licence, practice* etc.)

proportion see PERCENT

proportional, proportionate *adj.*

Both these words mean 'in proportion'. Their
different uses are illustrated in *proportional
representation* and *The work given to each child
should be proportionate to his ability.*

proscribe see PRESCRIBE

protagonist (prə'tægənist) *n.*

This means 'the chief actor or champion of
a cause', so it does not need to be qualified by
chief, e.g. *As the battle in the council chamber
developed, it became obvious that the protagonist
was the member for Woodside.* It is sometimes
confused with *antagonist,* which means

'someone who provokes others into rivalry, an opponent'.

proved, proven ('pru:vən) *past part.*
The second form is used only in Law.

provided that, providing *conj.*
A clause which establishes a condition can be introduced by *provided that* or *providing*, not [*providing that*]. Both are often used where *if* alone would be better style.

provident, providential *adj.*
A *provident* person is thrifty, and provides for the future; a *providential* happening is 'an unexpected stroke of good luck'.

prox. see INST.

ps- see PN-

pseudonym ('sju:dənim) *n.* **pen name, nom de plume** ('nɔmdə'plu:m)
When a writer does not wish to publish a book under his own name he uses a *pseudonym*, *pen name* or *nom de plume*, e.g. Charlotte Brontë wrote under the pen name of Currer Bell. (see ALIAS; INCOGNITO)

pt- see PN-

punctilious, punctual *adj.*
Punctilious means 'strictly attentive to detail' whether of dress, hygiene, speech or conduct; *punctual* describes a similar frame of mind which compels one always to arrive promptly, exactly at the fixed time.

PUNCTUATION AND THE USE OF CAPITAL LETTERS

The purpose of punctuation is to produce clarity and assist ease of reading, and the better it is done the less obtrusive it will be. It serves to divide a passage of writing according to sense, and to define the relationship between the different parts of a sentence. To some extent it reflects the pauses which would be made in reading aloud, but it is also helpful to the eye to have a long passage broken up by stops and spaces. Punctuation is a sufficiently important part of the art of writing to be subject to changes of fashion, and is used by some writers in a highly individual way. Attempts to abolish it have not been successful, and the painful difficulty of trying to extract information from modern texts printed without stops or capital letters is a good illustration of its usefulness. At present the practice is to use stops, exclamation marks, underlinings and capitals very sparingly; they are no longer used by good writers as ornaments or to provide emphasis, which means that the choice of words and their arrangement are of even more importance in conveying meaning.

apostrophe The sign ('). (see POSSESSIVE FORMS)

brackets Brackets serve to isolate part of a sentence (a word, phrase or clause) which could be omitted and still leave an intelligible statement. The previous sentence is an example of this (see PARENTHESIS). Punctuation of the rest of the sentence should run as if the bracketed portion were not there, e.g. *Out of all the people at the meeting only one (a stranger probably) dared to speak* (there is no need for a comma after *one* or before *dared*). At the end of a sentence the full stop usually comes outside the bracket, unless the sense requires it to be inside, e.g. *The answer to this problem appears later in the book (p. 21).* but *The answer to the problem is extremely obscure. (It is discussed further on p. 21.)* Square brackets are used where the author of a passage inserts his own information into a quotation, e.g. *Enter the King [Henry V] with his Court.*

capital letters These are used at the beginning of a sentence or quoted speech, and for proper names and titles of people and organizations, e.g. *Mr. Robertson, Dr. Smith, Princess Anne, The House of Commons, South America, The Prisoner of Zenda, Imperial Chemical Industries.* They are not used when speaking of a general topic like *the position of professors, the study of continents.* If an initial *the* is included in a title it has a capital, as in

237

I have been reading The Pickwick Papers, but not in *I have been reading the Wessex novels of Thomas Hardy*. Outside these categories there is wide variation; the tendency is for as few as possible to be used, and it is only necessary to be consistent.

colons and semicolons In the past there was not always a clear distinction between these two stops, which provide more of a break than a comma, and less than a full stop. At present the *colon* is used to make an abrupt break between two statements which are related. *Your life is in front of you: make the best of it you can.* It is also used to introduce a list, quotation or summary. *I was confronted with this choice: to continue with my work in the hope that it would prove useful, or to give it up and begin something else.* A colon followed by a dash is sometimes used to introduce a list or quotation, not within a sentence but rather where the list will start on a separate line:—

The following authors will be studied next year:—
    Milton, Tennyson, Browning etc.

Semicolons can be used instead of conjunctions to link two sentences or parts of them. *Some of us were envious of his success; others were sure it would not last.* They are also useful in a passage containing long clauses, some of which may have commas within them.

commas 1. These are used to make divisions in sentences, while heavier pauses are marked by semicolons or full stops. A sentence like *The houses were set on fire, and the bridges destroyed* could be written with or without a comma in the middle, according to individual taste or the degree of separation required between the clauses. It would be usual to put a comma in *They were not only neighbours, but good friends as well*, because the second clause introduces a new idea, and does not simply follow the first.

2. There are different opinions about the use of commas to divide the units in a series of adjectives, nouns or phrases such as *He was a tall(,) thin(,) elegant man*; *They were told to bring cups(,) saucers and spoons*. When commas are used, it is usual not to write one after the last adjective, which is inevitably the one most closely attached to the noun, as in *It was a fine, bright, sunny day*. This closeness can be emphasized by omitting the preceding comma, as in *He was an old, sturdy seafaring man*.

3. Commas can be used to mark off a parenthesis, as can dashes and brackets. Commas give the lightest degree of separation, dashes produce a jerky effect—sometimes desirable—and brackets cut off part of a sentence the most firmly, e.g. *He could*

239

not help noticing, in spite of her attempt to con-
ceal it, that she was anxious to get rid of him;
I was told—though I could hardly believe it—that
the firm was closing down; A list of those eligible
for the prize (except those who have already applied)
will be published tomorrow. When two commas
are used in this way it is important not to
forget the second, otherwise there will be
ambiguity, as in *It was the same alligator, which
I had seen asleep yesterday* [ ] *swimming stealthily
towards our boat.*

(see PARENTHESIS)

4. Sometimes commas are used to separate
two clauses instead of a conjunction (or a full
stop and a new sentence), e.g. *I cannot tell
you any more, I have promised not to.* It would be
better style to write *I cannot tell you any more
as I have promised not to* or to make two
sentences.

5. When two phrases are linked by a conjunction a comma is used if there is a contrast, e.g. *I was in good time, but my friend was
late* but not in *I was late and my friend had
already arrived.*

6. Commas are used before and after a
person's name or title when addressing him
or her, e.g. *Now, Mr. Jones, may we have your
opinion?* (for the use of commas with reported
speech see INVERTED COMMAS)

240

dashes These are used like brackets for separating asides from a sentence, but their effect is more abrupt and less formal, e.g. *He has remembered at last—and about time too—to return those books to the library.* A second dash is not necessary when the separated phrase comes at the end of the sentence. (see COMMAS; PARENTHESIS; COLONS)

exclamation marks These should always be used after genuine exclamations, such as *How cold it is today!* but not after statements like *You will be surprised how much he has grown.*

full stops (periods) Normally these appear only at the end of a complete sentence containing a main verb, except in reported speech and where a passage takes the form of an argument, as in *Some people think that we should wait for further information before taking action. Quite wrong.* Some writers like to break up long passages and produce a jerky effect by the use of full stops:—

The house seemed to be everything they were looking for. A south aspect. A big garden. And above all it had a spacious garage. This could just as well be punctuated in the usual way with commas or semicolons.

Full stops are also used after abbreviations and initial letters standing for the whole word

(*Dec.*, *i.e.*, *R.C.*) but there is a growing practice of omitting them after abbreviations which include the first and last letters of the word *Dr*, *Mr*, *regt*, *coy*, *bros*, *Gk* (but *Lat.*), *ft* (but *in.*), and in much-used titles like *BBC*, *ITV*, *NATO*. In titles and announcements, full stops are usually omitted as they serve no purpose:—

OTHELLO
by William Shakespeare

hyphens Compound words, like *lamp-post* or *back stroke*, or words with a prefix, like *unpick*, may or may not contain a hyphen. It is generally used when the compound is new and dropped as it becomes familiar, unless there is an awkward pair of letters at the join which can lead to a wrong pronunciation as in *top-hat*. This does not always happen: *porthole* is written as one word. The hyphen is often also retained where there are two equal accents as in *half-crown*, *farm-hand*. It can be very misleading to write a compound epithet as two separate words when it comes before a noun, as in [*He was a slow moving man*], because unless the *slow* is shown to be attached to *moving* it can equally apply to *man*. There is less danger with a noun compound, so it is usual to write *It is a common-sense suggestion* but *The suggestion shows common sense.* (see also under individual prefixes, e.g. OUT-; PRE-)

inverted commas (quotation marks, quotes) 1. A common mistake is to use these for an indirect version of the words spoken instead of confining their use to direct quotation, e.g. not [*She stopped and asked me, "Was I coming to the meeting?"*] but *She stopped and asked me, "Are you coming to the meeting?".* It is usual to have a comma before a quotation and one after it if the sentence is resumed, e.g. *I said to him, "Please tell me exactly what you mean", but he could not explain.*

2. There is no difference in function between single and double quotation marks, but it is useful to have two forms when there is a title or quotation within a speech, as in *"I am going to tell you a story", said the teacher, "it is called 'Little Red Riding Hood'."* In more formal writing, titles are usually indicated by underlining in manuscript and typescript, and by italics in print.

question marks These are used at the end of direct questions, but not after reported ones: *Why are you late?* but not in *He asked me why I was late.*

purport ('pə:pət) *n.* **purport** (pə'pɔ:t) *v.*

The noun has the straightforward sense of 'apparent meaning', 'intention', but the verb usually implies deception, e.g. *He purports to be an original writer, but most of his ideas are taken from other people.* If *purport* has an animate subject it must be followed by *to be*, e.g. [*He purports to have written many novels*] is wrong.

purposely, purposefully *adv.*
Purposely means 'on purpose', 'intentionally', e.g. *I insulted him purposely to see what would happen.* Purposefully means 'in a determined manner', e.g. *He came purposefully forward to settle the dispute; The police advanced purposefully to break up the gang.*

pygmy *n. adj.*
This spelling is preferred to *pigmy*.

Q

quadroon *n.*
'The offspring of a mulatto and a white person, i.e. one who is one-fourth Negro.' If a quadroon married a white person, their child would be an *octoroon.*

quasi- ('kwaːzi) or ('kweisai) *prefix*
Meaning 'as if', 'not quite', 'apparently', *quasi* is usually derogatory, e.g. *a quasi-Tudor cottage.*

query *v.*
This verb is loosely used for 'question', 'ask,'

but its real meaning is 'to throw doubt on'.

question as to

This is an awkward construction which can often be avoided, either by omitting *as to* or by using a noun instead of a verbal phrase, e.g. *The question as to who would succeed* can be simplified to *the question of the succession* (or *successor*).

question mark see PUNCTUATION

questionnaire *n.*

Usually fully anglicized to (ˌkwestʃəˈnɛə) but sometimes pronounced more like its French original (ˌkestiəˈnɛə). The alternative form *questionary* is not much used.

quick, quicker *adj.* **quickly, more quickly** *adv.*

Quick, quicker are sometimes used instead of the adverbs and are more emphatic, e.g. *Come quick! You get there quicker by bus.*

quiet, quietness, quietude, quietism *n.*

There is some overlapping between these words, of which the first is the most commonly used. *Quiet* is used for 'a temporary lull' or 'freedom from disturbance', e.g. *a few moments' quiet. Quietness* is the one used to describe a personal quality, e.g. *the quietness of her manners*, and *quietude* is archaic and literary; it carries the idea of calm and tranquillity as well as absence of noise.

Quietism is a form of mystic religious doctrine.

quiet, quieten *v.*

Either of these verbs can be used for 'make quiet'. The second is the commoner.

quite *adv.*

A word which is often used redundantly and which has contradictory meanings in different contexts. In *I was quite surprised to hear from him*, it means 'a good deal'; in *It is quite finished* it means 'completely'. The colloquial phrase *I quite like it* means 'only moderately'. *Quite so* is used for sober agreement, rather than the more emphatic *Quite!*

quiz *n. v.*

The verb originally meant 'make fun of', often by asking awkward questions; now used colloquially, especially by the Press, with the meaning 'to ask searching questions'. The noun means 'a general knowledge game', or 'a series of questions to test knowledge', especially on Radio and Television.

Plural *quizzes*.

quotation marks see PUNCTUATION, INVERTED COMMAS

quotations

It is always worth while checking the accuracy of a quotation from a well-known work, as even the most popular lines are often misquoted, e.g. [*But screw your courage to the sticking point*], where the line in *Macbeth* actually reads *sticking-place*. Writers and publishers have different ways of indicating quotations, but it is usual for those in English to be put inside inverted commas, foreign ones going into italics. Long quotations are given a separate paragraph without inverted commas. (see PUNCTUATION)

q.v.

Abbreviation of Latin *quod vide*, literally 'which see'. It is used to refer readers to another part of a book.

R

-r, -rr

(For the spelling of words ending in *r* plus a suffix, see SPELLING, VERBS)

rack and ruin

Often misspelt [*wrack*].

racket, racquet *n.*

The first of these spellings is now generally used for all meanings of the word.

raise, rise *v.*

Raise is transitive, e.g. *The landlord raised the rent*; *rise* is intransitive, e.g. *Fares will rise from tomorrow*. *Raise* is used in the U.S. to mean 'bring up', e.g. *I was raised in Alabama*.

rancour *n.* **rancorous** *adj.*

(cf. *valour, valorous; humour, humorous* etc.)

rapt *adj. past part.*

'Enraptured', 'carried away by', e.g. *The audience listened with rapt attention to his performance.* It is sometimes confused with *wrapped* used in the figurative sense, e.g. *The subject is wrapped* (not *rapt*) *in obscurity.*

raze, rase *v.*

This means 'level to the ground', 'demolish'. The first spelling has become general.

re

The legal term *in re*, 'in the matter of', has given rise to *re* in commercial writing. It can be replaced by *about* or *concerning.*

re- *prefix*

This means 'again' or 'back'. A hyphen is used in compounds:—

1. when the next part of the word begins with *e*, e.g. *re-export*;

2. when it is used for a contrast, e.g. *take* and *re-take*;

3. when the compound has another meaning, e.g. *recreate* and *re-create*.

-re, -er *suffix*

Words ending in *-re* are usually spelt with *-er* in the U.S. (see METER)

reaction *n.*

This means 'reciprocal action', 'opposition',

248

'response to a stimulus'. It is frequently loosely used especially in journalism with the sense of 'effect', 'action', 'response', 'opinion', e.g. *It will certainly have a reaction on the Stock Exchange.* This could mean either *There will be a reaction by the Stock Exchange* or *It will have an effect on the Stock Exchange.*

readable see ILLEGIBLE

real *adj.* **really** *adv.*
Often used in a superfluous way, e.g. *There is a [real] need for further research* where *real* is doing duty for *great* or *strongly felt*. Similarly with *really*, e.g. *You [really] have a lovely voice.* Like *actually*, *definitely* etc. it adds nothing to the sense, but emphasizes the statement.

reason *n.*
Often unnecessarily followed by *because* rather than *that*, as in [*The reason I am late is because there was a traffic-jam*]. (see CAUSE)

receipt (ri'si:t) *n. v.* **recipe** ('resipi) *n.*
The first word (N.B. spelling) is no longer used in cookery instead of *recipe*.

receptive *adj.* **recipient** *adj. n.*
Receptive and *recipient* both mean 'receiving', but *receptive* has the additional meaning of 'quick to receive new ideas and impressions', e.g. *He found them a very receptive audience.* The noun *recipient* has its place in formal and legal writing, e.g. *The recipient of these documents will*

be expected to return them, but it is a pretentious word when used in journalism, e.g. *He was the recipient of* (he received) *hundreds of congratulatory letters.*

reckless see RUTHLESS

re-cover, recover see RE-

re-collect, recollect see RE-

recourse, resource *n.* **resort** *n. v.*

Similar in sound and meaning, these words are often confused and used unidiomatically. Examples of their correct uses are: *Recourse* (noun only) *have recourse to violence*; *without recourse to further measures. Resource* (noun only) *a man of great resource*; *I have no other resources. Resort* (noun and verb) *in the last resort*; *he resorted to cheating.*

rector see VICAR

reduce *v.* **reducible** *adj.*

The verb is followed by a present participle not the infinitive, e.g. *I was reduced to asking* (not ask) *the way. Reducible* is spelt like *inducible* and *deducible.*

reference, testimonial *n.*

A *reference* is 'a letter written to a possible new employer giving information about an applicant for a job', or simply 'the name of someone who might support the application', e.g. *May I use your name as a reference?* A *testimonial* is 'a more formal letter of recommendation which remains in the possession of the applicant', whereas a *reference* does not.

reflection, reflexion *n.*

The distinction between these two spellings has become almost entirely obscured, but strictly *reflection* should be used for all senses of the verb *reflect* ('throw back light, heat or sound', to 'mirror', to 'meditate', 'consider') and *reflexion* should apply to the noun *reflex* as used in botany and biology.

re-form, reform see RE-

refuse ('refju:s) *n.* **refuse** (ri'fju:z), **re-fuse** ('ri:'fju:z) *v.*

regard, consider *v.*

These two verbs have different constructions, e.g. *I regard it as probable*; *I consider it probable*. The phrases *as regards, with regard to* are over-used variants of *about*.

regardless *adj.*

An adjective also used as an adverb, e.g. *They were regardless of the disturbance their appearance was causing*; *He drove on regardless of the falling snow*. It is colloquial to use it by itself in the sense of disregarding expense or consequences, e.g. *On this occasion she was dressed regardless.*

in the region of

Needlessly used for *about*, e.g. *There were in the region of two hundred people there* (cf. *neighbourhood*).

Register (or **Registrar's**) **Office, Registry Office**

In England a *Register Office* (called a *Registrar's Office* in Scotland) is the place for recording births, deaths and marriages. A *Registry Office* is a domestic employment agency. A Registry being the section of a government department where papers are filed.

regretful, regrettable *adj.*

The first means 'full of regret', the second describes the cause of regret.

rehabilitate, repair, restore *v.*

To *rehabilitate* is strictly to 'restore a person to a useful life after an incapacitating illness'. It is also widely used to mean 'restore to proper rights or reputation'. It is inaccurately used instead of *restore*, e.g. [*The building has been rehabilitated after the fire.*] *Repair* and *restore* have many meanings in common, but *repair* is used for 'make usable again' *restore* for 'put back to its original state', e.g. *My car has been repaired, but the paintwork has not been restored.* (see SYNONYM)

relative, relation(s), relationship *n.*

A matter of personal preference, but generally when speaking of members of a family, *relative* implies distance, whereas *relation* can be either distant or close. *Relation* is used in the singular when it refers to the connection between two things, e.g. *the relation between poverty and crime*, but the plural is used for the dealings between people or countries, e.g. *relations between husband and wife*; *Trade relations between Russia and France*. *Relationship* means 'degree of kinship or similarity', e.g. *There is a close relationship between music and mathematics*. It is inaccurately used for *relations*, e.g. [*The manager had a good relationship with the workers.*] (*The manager enjoyed good relations with the workers*).

relative, relevant *adj.*

These words are interchangeable when the meaning is 'pertinent', e.g. *the papers relative (relevant) to the case*, but *relevant* is more often used in the negative, e.g. *Your remarks are not relevant to the argument*. *Relative* has more uses, e.g. *Are the results relative to the cost? Their relative positions were reversed*. It is often used in commercial jargon for *about, concerning* (which are to be preferred), e.g. *relative to our conversation yesterday*. The negative forms are *unrelated, irrelevant*.

relatively *adv.*

Like *comparatively*, this word is often loosely used where there is no comparison, to mean 'fairly' or 'rather', e.g. *I am relatively sure it will not rain*.

remain see LETTER-WRITING

reminisce (remi'nis) *v.*

A back formation from *reminiscence*, still colloquial, but widely used.

remittal, remittance, remission *n.*

Remittal is used when a legal case is sent from one court to another; *remittance* is 'money sent in payment or as an allowance'. *Remission* means 'paying off a debt' 'shortening a prison sentence', or 'forgiveness', e.g. *the remission of sins.*

renaissance *n.*

This is a commoner spelling than *renascence.*

repair see REHABILITATE

repel, repulse *v.*

Both these verbs mean 'drive back'; *repulse* also means 'reject', e.g. *efforts, advances*, while *repel* also means 'disgust', e.g. *His self-righteousness repelled me. Repulsive* is stronger than *repellent. Repellent* (adjective and noun), *repellence* (noun) are the usual spellings, not [*repellant, repellance*].

replace see SUBSTITUTE

reported speech see PUNCTUATION, CAPITAL LETTERS

repulse see REPEL

require *v.*

This is a transitive verb, but it is often used intransitively on the analogy of *need*, e.g. [*You require to get more information*] whereas

254

You require more information is quite correct.
It is also used in DOUBLE PASSIVES (q.v.) and
as a genteel variant of *want*.

resentment *n.*

Followed by *at* or *against*, not *to*.

reset, re-set see RE-

resign *v.*

Can be followed by a direct object, e.g. *He
resigned the Chairmanship*, but one resigns *from*
an organization or Society. In the passive it
is followed by *to*, e.g. *resigned to poverty*.

resin, rosin *n.*

Rosin is the solid form of *resin*, the sticky
substance secreted in plants and trees,
especially firs and pines. It is used on the
bows and strings of musical instruments.

resolution, motion *n.*

These terms are both used to describe something which has been or will be voted upon
at an assembly. A *resolution* can be simply
'an expression of opinion', whereas a *motion*
is intended to lead to action.

resource, resort see RECOURSE

respectable, respectful *adj.*

Respectable means 'worthy of respect', *respectful*
'showing respect', 'courteous'.

respective(ly) *adj. adv.*

These words are often used superfluously,
especially with *each* or *own*, e.g. *They each gave*

their respective answers. They are useful when they relate different pairs of words, e.g. *Jones and Smith came from London and Manchester respectively.* (i.e. Jones from London, Smith from Manchester).

respite (ri'spait) or ('respit) *n.*

Both pronunciations are used, the first more often.

restaurant ('restərɔ̃:ŋ) or ('restərɔnt) *n.*

Both pronunciations are widely used; the second is more common.

restore see REHABILITATE

reverend, reverent, reverential, revered *adj.*

Reverend means 'worthy of veneration'. When it is used as a title for clergymen it can be abbreviated to *Rev.* It is not used with the surname alone, e.g. [*The Rev. Smith*] but with first name or initials or a further title, e.g. *The Rev. Sydney Smith*; *The Rev. Dr. Smith.* *Reverent* means 'feeling or showing reverence', *reverential* and *revered* both imply an exaggerated form of reverence.

review, revue *n.*

A *review* can be 'a formal inspection of troops' etc., 'a survey or revision', or 'a critical assessment of a book, film or play'. A *revue* is 'a theatrical entertainment with songs, sketches and dancing'.

reward see AWARD

rhyme *n. v.* **rime** *n.*

The first spelling is used for the poetical device and is another word for 'verse' or 'poetry'. It is occasionally spelt *rime*, but this spelling is usually reserved for 'hoarfrost'.

rhyming slang see LANGUAGE TERMS

right, rightly *adv.*

Both forms of this adverb are used. The following sentences illustrate their use: *He never gets the answers right*; *This key does not fit right*; *He rightly supposed I would be glad to see him*; *You have acted rightly in refusing to submit to this injustice.*

rime see RHYME

rise, arise *v.*

Rise is used in the literal sense of 'move upwards', *arise* for the figurative sense of 'come into existence', 'occur'. (see RAISE; ROUSE)

road *n.*

Names of roads are written with capitals, thus *Addison Road* not *Addison road*.

root, rout *v.*

Both spellings of the verb are used if the meaning is 'dig up with the snout', 'poke about', 'rummage'. But if it is 'defeat utterly' only *rout* is correct.

rosin see RESIN

rotary, rotatory (rou'teitəri) *adj.*

Both these words are used for 'turning on an axis', e.g. as a wheel. *Rotary* (with a capital R) describes an international system of clubs with a wheel as a badge.

rotten *adj.* **rottenness** *n.*

(cf. *craven, cravenness*)

rouse, arouse *v.*

Rouse can be either transitive or intransitive, literal or figurative, e.g. *to rouse from sleep*; *to rouse anger*; *to rouse to action*. *Arouse* is transitive only, and usually figurative, meaning 'give rise to', e.g. *The sight aroused compassion*; *His action aroused criticism.*

rout *v.* **route** *n. adj.*

The verb *rout*, to 'put to flight', is pronounced (raut) the noun meaning 'course of travel' is pronounced (ru:t). As an adjective it is used in *route march*, one 'undertaken by troops as a training-exercise'.

rural *adj.* **rustic** *adj. n.* **rusticate** *v.*

Rural means 'belonging to the countryside', 'the opposite of *urban*'. *Rustic* suggests 'artificially primitive', e.g. *a rustic seat for the garden*. As a noun it means 'a peasant'. To *rusticate* is to 'retire to or live in the country'. Students can be *rusticated* by a university, in which case it means 'temporarily excluded'.

ruthless, reckless *adj.*

Ruthless means 'unscrupulous', 'merciless', e.g. *His ruthless ambition swept all obstacles from his path.* Reckless means 'careless', 'rash', 'heedless of consequences', e.g. *Many road accidents are caused by reckless drivers.*

S

-s, -ss, -sss

(For compounds involving two or more *s* together, see PUNCTUATION, HYPHENS. For plurals of words ending in *s*, see SPELLING)

Sabbath *n. adj.*

This is a general term for a 'holy day', e.g. Saturday for Jews, Sunday for Christians, and it usually requires a capital.

sabotage ('sæbətɑːʒ) *n. v.*

The strict meaning of this word is 'wilful damage done by workers to their employers' property'. It is used in wartime for 'the destructive activities of members of a resistance or underground movement', and has recently come to mean 'any kind of destructive opposition', e.g. *Lack of co-operation with the government amounted to sabotage of its economic aims.*

sack *n. v.*

This is an accepted informal word for 'dismissal from a job or post'.

said see SPELLING, VERBS

Saint

Can be abbreviated to *St* (without a full stop) or *S.*; plural forms are *Sts* or *SS.*

sake *n.*

The *'s* is omitted after a noun ending in an *s* sound when it precedes *sake*, e.g. *for goodness sake, for conscience sake.*

salubrious (sə'lu:briəs), **salutary** ('sæljutəri) *adj.*

Both these words mean 'beneficial', the first is used in the physical sense of 'good for the health', e.g. *a salubrious climate*, the second has a moral sense, e.g. *a salutary lesson.*

same *n., adj.* **the same**

Both are used instead of the pronouns *it* or *them* in legal and commercial documents, e.g. *The samples ordered have arrived and we find (the) same satisfactory*, but they sound clumsy or archaic in ordinary writing. There is a distinction between *as* and *that* after *same*, e.g. *Your views on the subject are the same as mine. I can hear a cuckoo; I wonder whether it's the same (one) that I heard yesterday?*

sanction *v. n.*

This word is generally used in the sense of

'permit', 'allow' (verb); 'permission', 'consent' (noun), but its original meaning was 'a law or decree and the reward or punishment given in accordance with it'. Consequently there is a contradiction in the modern usage of it: to *sanction the use of force* is to permit it, but to *impose sanctions* on another country is 'to withdraw trade etc. as a punishment for a violation of international law'.

sarcasm

A bitter, cutting remark or scornful utterance, usually implying the opposite of what is said, e.g. "*I expect you remember perfectly everything I told you yesterday?*" or "*What a quite brilliant observation!*" Closely allied to IRONY (q.v.)

sardonic *adj.*

Describes a person's nature or a *smile, laugh, grin* etc. It means 'mocking', 'scornful', but in a passive rather than an active sense. The scorn is often self-mockery, e.g. *He received the news of his failure with a sardonic smile, and returned to his work.* The adverb is *sardonically.*

satiety (sə'taiəti) *n.*

'The feeling of having had too much'. Note the pronunciation of the past participle *satiated* ('sei ʃieitid).

satire

'A method of exposing the evils and injustices of society and individuals by holding them up to ridicule or rendering them absurd', used in literature, journalism and all forms of dramatic entertainment. It ranges from serious moral indictment, as practised by Swift, to light entertainment in the form of mockery of national figures.

satiric, satirical *adj.*

These forms are interchangeable, but the second is becoming commoner, especially when speaking of people and attitudes.

satisfy *v.*

This verb can be used in two senses: to 'please' or to 'convince'. Thus *I was satisfied that his efforts had failed* can have two meanings. The use of *convince* avoids this possibility of confusion.

save *prep.*

Used instead of *except* or *but*, *save* sounds formal and artificial, e.g. *He lost all his belongings save a box of chocolates he had bought for his wife.*

scallop ('skɔləp) or ('skæləp) *n. v.*

Participles *scalloping, scalloped.*

scandal *n.*

Used as journalistic jargon for any case of injustice or mismanagement however unimportant, e.g. *Broken window scandal at Children's Home.* (see LIBEL)

scarce *adj.* **scarcely** *adv.*

Scarce is no longer used as an adverb, e.g.

[*I could scarce believe my ears*]. Scarcely (like *hardly*) is followed by *when*, not *than*, e.g. *Scarcely had I left the room when the phone rang.* It is sometimes clumsily used so that it produces a double negative, e.g. [*I wasn't scarcely out of the room before their arrival*].

scarcity *n.*

This, not [*scarceness*], is the noun from *scarce.*

scarify ('skærifai) *v.*

This word has no connection with *scare*. It means to 'scratch' or 'lacerate', and hence literally or figuratively to 'criticise unmercifully', e.g. *He was scarified by the critics when his book appeared.*

scene see LOCALE

sceptic ('skeptik) *n.* **septic** ('septik) *adj.*

Although these words are pronounced differently, they are sometimes confused. *Sceptic* is a noun meaning 'a sceptical or incredulous person'; *septic* is an adjective meaning 'infected by sepsis', e.g. *the wound turned septic.*

schedule *n.*

Pronounced ('ʃedjuːl) in Britain, and ('skedjuːl) in the U.S.

school, shoal *n.*

Both these forms are used as a collective noun for fish, but *school* is preferred for whales and porpoises.

263

Scot *n.* **Scotch** *adj. n.* **Scots, Scottish** *adj.*

A native of Scotland can be called a *Scot* or a *Scotsman*, but not a [*Scotchman*]. *Scottish* is the usual adjective for 'pertaining to Scotland'; and is used in phrases like the *Scottish Highlands, ancestry* etc., but *Scotch* is used for food and drink, flora and fauna originating in Scotland, e.g. *Scotch* (*whisky*), *beef, broth, tweed, thistle, terrier* etc.

scot-free *adj.*

The original meaning of this phrase was 'free of scot', *scot* being 'a payment for entertainment or a tax'. It now means 'unharmed', 'unhurt', e.g. *He escaped scot-free.*

scream, screech, shriek *n. v.*

These words are interchangeable, except that *screech* emphasises harshness or stridency of sound and is generally the one chosen for inanimate objects, e.g. *the screech of brakes.*

scull, skull *n.*

A *scull* is 'a light one-handed oar'; the *skull* is 'the bony framework of the head'.

seasonable, seasonal, seasoned *adj.*

The first of these means 'appropriate to the time of year', e.g. *seasonable weather*. The second means 'depending on the season', e.g. *He suffered seasonal attacks of hay-fever.* *Seasoned* can mean either 'hardened by use', 'experienced', e.g. *seasoned timber, a seasoned*

traveller, or 'flavoured by spices or herbs', e.g.
a well-seasoned dish.

second *v.*

Pronounced ('sekənd) this verb means to
'support' or 'encourage'. Pronounced (si'kɔnd)
it means 'transfer an officer or official to
temporary duties', e.g. *He was seconded to work
in the flooded area.*

seem *v.*

Negatives are often attached to the auxiliary
verb *seem*, instead of to the main verb, in an
illogical way, e.g. [*I don't seem able to hear what
you are saying*]. (*I seem unable to hear . . .*).
This is because *seem* is used in speech to
convey 'vagueness, confusion or reluctance
to admit something'. Followed by an adjective, e.g. *He doesn't seem happy*, the negative
form does not create this illogicality. (see
CAN)

seize *v.*

This word is one of the exceptions to the rule
that *i* comes before *e*, when the sound is (iː),
except after *c*. Other exceptions are *weird* and
counterfeit. (see SPELLING)

seldom *adv.*

Like *often*, this adverb is unnecessarily used
as an adjective to mean 'infrequent', e.g.
[*His visits were seldom and short*]. It may be
used to qualify a whole phrase, e.g. *When the*

wind is in the east, which is seldom, it never rains.

self- *prefix*

Most compounds made with this prefix have a hyphen, e.g. *self-supporting, self-control.* Some of them are redundant, e.g. [*self-*]*conceit*; [*self-*]*complacent,* because *conceit* and *complacent* already have the idea of *self.* A few words are made without a hyphen, e.g. *selfhood, selfsame.*

-self, -selves *suffix*

Pronouns with these endings are used either reflexively, e.g. *I have hurt myself,* or for emphasis, e.g. *You can do it yourself.* Other uses are generally poetic, archaic, jocular or commercial, e.g. *Myself I heard the awful sound*; the Irish idiom *It was himself that told me*; *I will keep your good-selves informed*; *The other directors and myself think the plan a good one.*

semi- *prefix*

Makes most compounds with a hyphen, e.g. *semi-detached, semi-retired,* but there are some exceptions such as *semicolon* and musical terms like *semitone, semibreve.*

semicolon see PUNCTUATION

senior see THAN

sensible, sensitive *adj.*

Sensible corresponds to the noun *sense,* in its meaning of 'common sense', and means 'wise', 'practical' except when it is followed

266

by *of*, when it means 'conscious', e.g. *She was sensible of a change in his manner towards her.* *Sensitive* can correspond to the noun *sensibility* and mean 'easily affected by', e.g. *He was particularly sensitive to criticism.* It has also a physical application in which it corresponds to *sensitivity*, e.g. *A sensitive film is affected by light.*

sensual, sensuous *adj.*

Both these words refer to 'the pleasures derived from the senses', but *sensual* is generally used to mean 'dissolute', 'licentious', e.g. *He was a grossly sensual man.* *Sensuous* means 'received through the senses' or 'alive to the pleasures derived from the senses', as in *The moonlit garden has an unusual sensuous quality*; *Respighi was a sensuous rather than an intellectual composer.*

sentence

A group of words which is complete in itself. It can take the following forms:—

1. a statement *It is cold.*

2. a question *Is it cold?*

3. a command *Keep still.*

4. an exclamation *What a pity!*

5. a comment, greeting or announcement *Hardly*; *Not at all*; *Good morning*; *Fire!*; *Cars at ten-thirty.*

Longer sentences are built up of CLAUSES and PHRASES (q.v.) They can be arranged in many different ways and their arrangement plays a large part in a writer's style. A series of consecutive statements makes for dullness, and the careful arrangement of clauses can both relieve this and indicate where the emphasis lies. The two most emphatic places in a sentence are the beginning and the end, but a well-balanced sentence can be produced by starting and ending with a less important clause or phrase and making the main statement in the middle, e.g. *Without knowing more of the subject he was unwilling to give an opinion, but he thought the first speaker was probably right.* It is not advisable to pile up too many clauses at the beginning of a sentence, as the reader becomes lost if he has to wait too long for the subject and the main statement. Moreover the writer is in danger of losing the subject himself. A sentence is unsuccessful if it has to be read twice before its sense can be discovered.

Some of the ways in which the placing of words can obscure meaning are given under ADVERBS and NEGATIVES.

sentiment, sentimentality *n.*

Sentiment is 'feeling', 'emotion'; *sentimentality* is 'false or exaggerated feeling'.

sentinel, sentry *n.*

These words are generally interchangeable, but *sentinel* is the more general and literary term, *sentry* the more precise and military one.

separate ('sepərət) *adj.* ('sepəreit) *v.*

Always spelt with two *a*s and two *e*s.

sergeant, serjeant *n.*

The first spelling is used for the non-commissioned officer in the army and police. The second is used for a *Serjeant-at-Law*, formerly a barrister of the highest rank, also in the titles of certain court officers.

service *v.*

A recently formed variant of *serve* with the specialised meaning of 'overhaul machinery, motor-cars etc.'

serviette see NAPKIN

session, sitting *n.*

A *session* of Parliament is 'the period of the year from its opening to the prorogation'; a *sitting* is 'a single day's work'.

sew, sow *v.*

To *sew* (past tense *sewed*, past participle *sewn*) is to 'use a needle and thread'; to *sow* (past tense *sowed*, past participle *sown*) is to 'plant seeds', with the figurative sense to 'spread', e.g. *to sow doubts*

sewage, sewerage *n.*

Sewage is 'waste material that goes through a

269

sewer'; the whole pipeline system for its disposal is known as the *sewerage*.

shade, shadow *n.*

Shade is a more general word for 'partial darkness' than *shadow*, which describes 'an area from which light has been excluded'. In figurative use the distinction has lapsed.

Shakespearian *adj.*

Scholars are divided on the spelling of this word, partly because of doubts about the spelling of the poet's name itself, which may have been *Shakspere*, for which the adjective would be *Shakspberian*. The forms *Shakespeare*, *Shakespearian* are most widely accepted.

shall see WILL

shambles *n.*

Originally this word meant 'slaughterhouse', and by extension 'a scene of bloodshed', but it is now widely used for any scene of confusion or destruction.

sharp, sharply *adv.*

Sharp is used as an adverb especially when referring to time, e.g. *I shall be there at ten sharp*, direction, e.g. *turn sharp left*, and musical pitch, e.g. *the violins were playing sharp*. But for movements and manner of speech *sharply* is used, e.g. *I spoke to him sharply*; *He turned round sharply* etc.

shear *n. v.*

Past tense *sheared*, past participle *sheared* or *shorn*.

sheath (ʃiːθ) *n.* **sheathe** (ʃiːð) *v.*

(cf. *wreath, wreathe*; *teeth, teethe*; *grief, grieve*)

shew, show *v.*

Shew is now obsolete and *show* is the accepted spelling. Past tense *showed*, past participle *shown*.

shoal see SCHOOL

should see WILL

shriek see SCREAM

shrink *v.*

This verb has past tense *shrank*, past participle *shrunk* or *shrunken*. *Shrunken* is preferred for the adjectival use, e.g. *a shrunken head*.

(see DRINK)

shy *adj. v.*

The adjective has forms *shyer, shyest*; the verb has past tense and past participle *shied*, present participle *shying*.

sic

Latin, 'so', 'thus'. Used in brackets after a word or statement in a passage being quoted, either to question its accuracy or to reassure the reader that the writer is quoting correctly, e.g. *The Second World War, which began in 1938* [*sic*], *lasted until 1945*, where the date (1938) is a matter of argument.

sick *adj.*

Sick, meaning 'unwell', is often replaced by *ill* except in the U.S. or Scotland. It can also mean 'vomit', e.g. *I am going to be sick.* *To be sick of* means to 'be disgusted with or vexed at'. In many expressions it cannot be replaced by *ill*, e.g. *sick benefit, sick leave, sick list, the chronic sick, to report sick* (in army), *Hospital for Sick Children* etc. When used to describe humour or jokes it means 'macabre', 'bitter'.

signal, single out *v.*

Confusion arises in sentences like *He was [signalled] out for punishment* where *singled out* is meant.

similar *adj.*

Sometimes used with clumsy effect instead of the adverb *similarly* to mean 'like' or 'the same as', e.g. [*I always vote similar to my husband*] (*like my husband does*).

simulate, assimilate *v.*

To simulate is 'to pretend', 'to appear to be', e.g. *He simulated illness in order to avoid conscription.* *To assimilate* means to 'take in', 'absorb' or 'become like', and can be used literally or figuratively, e.g. *He could only take food which was easily assimilated; The book was full of new ideas, but some of them were difficult to assimilate.*

since see AGO

single out see SIGNAL

sink *v.*

Past tense *sank*, rarely *sunk*. Where it is the result of an action, the past participle is *sunk*, e.g. *Six destroyers have been sunk*; where the action is intransitive or metaphorical it is *sunken*, e.g. *sunken cheeks*. (see DRINK)

sitting see SESSION

ski *n. v.*

The pronunciation (ski:) is now more general than (ʃi:).

skilful *adj.*

Spelt *skillful* in the U.S. (cf. WILFUL)

slander see LIBEL

slant *n. v.*

In journalists' jargon the noun is used to mean 'a point of view', 'prejudice', the verb to mean 'distort'.

slatternly, slovenly *adj.*

Both these words are adjectives. The accepted adverbial form is the phrase *in a slovenly way* etc., although the *-ly* form is sometimes used adverbially in poetic diction. (cf. *leisurely*)

slough *n. v.*

The noun meaning 'bog' or 'morass' is pronounced (slau); the verb meaning 'cast off (usually an outer skin)' is pronounced (slʌf).

slovenly see SLATTERNLY

slow v.

This verb can be transitive or intransitive, e.g. *Rheumatism slowed his movements*; *Slow down as you approach the crossroads.*

slow adj. **slowly** adv.

Slow is acceptable as an adverb where brevity is required, e.g. *Go slow*, or where it is emphasized in the sentence, especially in comparative and superlative forms, e.g. *The train went slower and slower until it stopped.*

sly adj.

The adjectival forms are spelt *slyer, slyest*; the adverbs are *slily* or *slyly*.

so adv.

1. Theoretically, *so* cannot be used before an adjective with an absolute meaning, e.g. *so unique, so perfectly done*, since there cannot be degrees of uniqueness or perfection. However, this usage is widespread.

2. To *do so* is used to avoid repetition of a previous verb. However, it is unacceptable to make it replace a passive verb, as in *He was told he must be examined by a doctor, but [forgot to do so]. Forgot to have it done* would be better, or *forgot (to be)*.

so as, so that conj.

A clause conveying purpose is introduced by *so that* rather than by *so*, e.g. *I went to both performances, so that I could compare them in my review. So as is followed by an infinitive, e.g. He went nearer so as to see better.*

so called, so-called

These words are hyphenated when used as a compound adjective, e.g. *your so-called liberal views*, but not when *so* is used adverbially, e.g. *The Red Dean was so called because of his left-wing opinions.*

soliloquy see MONOLOGUE

sort see KIND

Soviet ('souviǝt) or ('sɔviǝt) *adj. n.*

sow see SEW

specially see ESPECIALLY

spectacular *adj.*

Sometimes misspelt [*spectactular*]. This word should strictly be used to describe 'a fine show', e.g. *a spectacular exhibition of chrysanthemums*, but is often metaphorically used where there is no visual element, e.g. *He is making spectacular progress.*

SPELLING

A book of this size cannot hope to cover all the difficulties which may arise in spelling or to answer all the questions which even a large dictionary leaves unanswered. Some of the words which give trouble are subject to rules, others are exceptions, and the most elusive are often those words which have added a suffix, such as *chirruping, blameable*.

verbs The usual way TO FORM THE PAST TENSE AND PAST PARTICIPLE of a verb is to add *ed* to the present: *I walk, I walked, I have walked*. Where the infinitive form ends in *e* this letter is dropped when *ed* is added (*I hoped*). *-y* is changed to *-i* after a consonant (*imply, implied*) but retained after a vowel (*play, played*). *Paid* and *said* are exceptions. A final consonant is doubled when it is in an accented syllable and preceded by a single vowel (*stop, stopped; regret, regretted*) but not where there are two vowels (*heap, heaped*) or the syllable is unaccented (*gallop, galloped*). A final *-l* is usually doubled irrespective of accent (*tunnel, tunnelled*) except where there are two vowels before it, or a vowel and a consonant (*initial, initialed; reveal, revealed; furl, furled*). *Paralleled* is an exception.

The same rules apply generally when adding *-ing* to the verb TO MAKE THE PRESENT PARTICIPLE (*hoping, stopping, regretting, heaping, galloping, tunnelling, revealing, furling, initialing, paralleling*). *y* is retained (*playing, implying*) and *ie* becomes *y* (*tying, dying*). *Singeing* and *dyeing* are thus spelt to avoid confusion with *singing* and *dying*. Others which may cause difficulty are *ageing, awing, cringing, hoeing,* *icing, impinging, picknicking, shoeing, swingeing* ('forcible, huge') and *tingeing*.

With VERBS ENDING IN -ISE OR -IZE, -*ize* is the commoner spelling and is used when new words are formed with this ending, such as *computerize*. *Televise* is an exception and has this form because it is made from a noun with an -*s* already in it, *television*. Others which end in -*ise* are *advertise, advise, affranchise, apprise* ('inform') *chastise, comprise, despise, devise, disguise, enfranchise, excise, exercise, improvise, incise, prise* ('lever open'), *supervise, surmise, surprise*. (For different spellings in the U.S. see AMERICAN USAGE)

nouns Plural forms end in *es* rather than *s* when a word ends in *ch, s, sh, ss,* or *x* (*beaches, crocuses, radishes, misses, foxes*). (see below for *ex, ix*)

WHEN Y FOLLOWS A CONSONANT at the end of a word the plural form is *ies* (*cities, ladies*) except in proper names (*the three Marys, my friends the Parrys*). When *y* follows a vowel, an *s* is added (*keys, plays*).

Some words have both SINGULAR AND PLURAL FORMS ENDING IN -S (*corps, mews, mumps*). Those ending in *ex* or *ix* sometimes retain the Latin plural (*matrix, matrices*) and sometimes add *es* (*apexes, annexes*) or use either according to whether they are being used generally or in a technical sense (*appendixes* or *appendices*).

A similar distinction appears in the plural forms of NOUNS ENDING IN O. The more familiar words and those of one syllable have plurals in *oes* (*banjoes, buffaloes, cargoes, echoes, haloes, heroes, mottoes, Negroes, tomatoes, volcanoes*). Where there is a vowel before the *o*, where the word is unfamiliar or foreign, has four or more syllables, or is a shortened form of a compound word, the plural is *os* (*altos, archipelagos, armadillos, avocados, autos, cameos, dynamos, folios, photos, quartos, ratios*).

WORDS ENDING IN F form their plural either by adding *s* (*chiefs, cliffs, dwarfs, hand-kerchiefs*), or by turning *f* into *v* and adding *es*, which is the usual form when there is an *l* before the *f* (*calves, elves, leaves, loaves, sheaves, thieves, themselves*). *Staffs* is the usual plural of *staff*, but in music they are spelt *staves*. *Wharfs* and *wharves* are both used. *Is* becomes *es* in the plural (*analyses, antitheses, axes, bases, crises*) but *iris* has plural *irises*. A few words ending in *on* have a plural with *a*, such as *criteria, phenomena*, but most add *s*, as in *lexicons*.

Some NOUNS WHICH END IN UM always have the plural with *a* (*agenda, corrigenda, dicta, errata, strata*). Others which have *a* in formal or scientific writing (*aquaria, gymnasia, media, memoranda, sanatoria*) otherwise add *s* (*aquari-ums* etc.). Similarly *focus, nucleus* and *radius* in technical writing have plurals *foci, nuclei, radii*, and this form is also used in such common words as *cacti, fungi, gladioli, narcissi*. *Corpus, genus* and *opus* have plurals *corpora, genera, opera*. When the plural is made by adding *s*, the first one is not doubled (*circuses, crocuses*).

A few NOUNS ENDING IN A have the Latin plural form ending in *ae* (*algae, formulae, larvae*) but most are like *petunias*. The French ending *eau* retains the plural *eaux* in a few cases, e.g. *beaux, chateaux, plateaux, tableaux*.

adjectives COMPARATIVES AND SUPERLA-TIVES. Adjectives of one syllable, and those of two syllables, either ending in *er, le, ow* and *y* or with the accent on the second syllable, add (*e*)*r* and (*e*)*st* to make the comparative and superlative *sweeter, cleverer, abler, shallow-est, prettiest, remotest*. Their negative forms are similar (*ignobler*). Others use *more* and *most*, as do those which can be used to describe the subject of a sentence (*afraid, alone*) and those which are really past participles (*refined, tired*). There are many exceptions, some accounted for by frequency of use, others by pleasantness of sound (*commoner, pleasanter, handsomer, more eager, more bizarre, most correct*). When there is a doubt it is better to use *more* and *most*, though some writers try to enliven their style with forms like *excitingest*. A single consonant at the end of a monosyllabic adjective is doubled if it comes after the short vowels *a*, *e*, *i*, *o*, *u* (*fatter*, *wetter*, *biggest*) but otherwise remains single (*dearer*, *neatest*, *shortest*).

ADJECTIVES MADE WITH -ABLE, -EABLE, AND -IBLE. These suffixes may be used to make an adjective from any transitive verb and some nouns. If the word ends with a silent *e* this is kept where necessary for pronunciation (*serviceable*, *manageable* but *debatable*, *usable*). *Blameable*, *rateable* and *giveable* are exceptions. When a word ends with a consonant followed by *y*, the *y* becomes *i* (*pitiable*, *reliable*) but if there is a vowel before the *y* it is retained (*payable*, *destroyable*). Many words have the ending *-ible* because of their form in Latin. The commonest are *accessible, admissible, audible, collapsible, comprehensible, controvertible, credible, discernible, edible, eligible, feasible, flexible, forcible, gullible, incorruptible, incredible, indefensible, indelible, indestructible, indigestible, inflexible, intangible, intelligible, irresistible, legible, negligible, ostensible, permissible, plausible, reprehensible, reversible, tangible, visible*. (see -OR)

NEGATIVE FORMS WITH IN-, UN-, OR NON-. There is no infallible rule about the choice of a prefix for negative forms, but words of Latin origin more often start with *in*, (or *il*, *imm* or *irr* where the *n* has been dropped), e.g. *inestimable, illegible, immaterial, irregular*. Words ending in *ed* (except *inexperienced*) usually start with *un* (*unconcealed, unsupported*) as do those ending in *ing* (*unseeing, unbelieving*). Words ending in *ible* and *ent* more often have *in* (*inexhaustible, indecent*). The prefix *non*, usually spelt with a hyphen in recent formations (*non-resident, non-combatant*) and without in older words (*nonconformist, nondescript*), is sometimes used to make a new word where the older one has lost its purely negative sense, e.g. *non-moral* meaning 'outside morality', while *immoral* means 'contrary to moral law'.

adverbs see ADVERB

ei, ie When the sound of these letters is (i:) as in *chief*, *i* precedes *e* except after *c* (*field, relief, receive, ceiling*). Exceptions are *seize, counterfeit, plebeian, weird*.

(For the use of hyphens, capital letters, and the spelling of contracted forms such as *Dr* see PUNCTUATION)

spiritual, spirituous adj.

Spiritual means 'connected with the mind, spirit or soul', the opposite of *bodily, secular*, e.g. *The vicar took over the spiritual direction of the parish. Spirituous* means 'containing alcohol', as in *spirituous liquors.*

split infinitive

The term used when an adverb comes between *to* and its verb, e.g. *to fully expect.* Sometimes it is more natural and less ambiguous to place the adverb in this position, e.g. *I expect to nearly finish it by Thursday* is better than [*I expect nearly to finish it by Thursday*]; *He asked them to kindly stop talking* is less ambiguous than [*He asked them kindly to stop talking*]. In most cases, however, it is better to put the adverb before or after the infinitive phrase. *He expects to be soundly beaten* is not a split infinitive, since the infinitive phrase is *to be* not *to be beaten.*

spoiled, spoilt *past part. past t.*

These forms are more or less interchangeable, although *spoilt* is more commonly used in its adjectival sense of 'pampered', 'over-indulged', e.g. *She has always been a spoilt child.* As the past tense and past participle of *spoil,* either form is used, e.g. *You spoilt your good record by arriving late today*; *The garden party was spoiled by a cloudburst half an hour after the opening.*

-spoken *past part.*

Most compounds formed with this past participle of *speak* are hyphenated, e.g. *well-*

spoken, soft-spoken. Outspoken is an exception
(see OUT-). *Spoken* in these compounds is used
in the active sense of 'speaking' rather than
'spoken of'.

sponge *n. v.*

Adjectives *spongeable* and *spongy.*

spoonful *n.*

The plural form is *spoonfuls.* (see -FUL)

sprain, strain *n.*

These words are often used for bodily
injuries as if they had the same meaning, but
strictly a *sprain* is 'a sudden wrench', a *strain*
'prolonged muscular exertion'.

squalor *n.*

Sometimes misspelt [*squalour*].

staffs, staves see SPELLING, NOUNS

stalactite, stalagmite *n.*

A *stalactite* is formed by water containing
calcium carbonate dripping from the roof
of a cave; it hangs like an icicle. A *stalagmite*
is formed in the same way, but it rises from
the floor of the cave.

stalk, stem, trunk *n.*

In botany, *stem* is only used for the main
stem of a plant, *stalk* for the individual stem
of a leaf or flower. The stem of a tree is the
trunk.

In ordinary usage *stalk* and *stem* are often
used as if interchangeable.

283

stanch, staunch *v.* **staunch** *adj.*

The verb means 'stop or check a flow of blood'; the adjective 'constant', 'loyal', 'trustworthy'.

Standard English see LANGUAGE TERMS

start see BEGIN

starve *v.*

To *starve* in the sense of 'suffer from cold', rather than 'from hunger', is now only used in dialect.

stationary *adj.* **stationery** *n.*

The first of these words means 'not moving', e.g. *a stationary vehicle*; the second means 'goods sold by a stationer', e.g. writing materials (paper, pens, etc.).

stay, stop *v.*

To *stop* is to 'cease moving', to *stay* is 'to remain'. *Stop* is loosely used in *He stopped in London for several months*, but useful where the emphasis is on the interruption of movement, e.g. *I shall stop here till you come back. Stay put*, i.e. 'don't move', is colloquial usage.

stem see STALK

sterile *adj.*

Usually pronounced ('sterail), sometimes ('sterəl) as in U.S.

sterling *adj. n.* **Stirling** *n.*

Stirling is the Scottish town. *Sterling* is British money and the adjective from it, e.g. *sterling silver* which is also used figuratively in the sense of 'having good moral qualities', e.g. *He showed his sterling character in these difficult times.*

stile, style n.

Stile is used for 'a set of steps or other device for crossing a wall or fence', as in *turnstile*. The pin on the face of a sun-dial can be *stile* or *style*. *Style* is used for 'fashion' or 'manner'.

still see YET

stimulant, stimulus n. **stimulate** v.

Stimulant is used to describe 'a drink or drug which produces activity', e.g. *He gave the patient a stimulant to revive the action of the heart. Stimulus* is used more figuratively, e.g. *The sight of so much poverty was a stimulus to action.* To *stimulate* is to 'rouse' or 'excite', e.g. *Even before she began to sing, I was stimulated by her presence on the stage.*

Stirling see STERLING

stop see STAY

storey, story n.

Storey (plural *storeys* or *stories*) is the usual spelling for 'a floor of a building' (see FLOOR). *Story*, with no *e*, means 'a narrative'.

strain see SPRAIN

strait, straight adj.

The first of these means 'narrow', 'difficult', and in modern usage appears only in compounds such as *strait-laced*, *strait-jacket*, and the past participle *straitened*, meaning 'impoverished', e.g. *in straitened circumstances*. (see STRAIT *n*.)

strait *n*.

In the sense of 'a narrow channel of water connecting two seas' this can be either singular or plural, e.g. *Magellan's Strait*, *the Straits of Dover*. Where it means difficulty it is usually plural, e.g. *I hear you are in financial straits*.

strategy see TACTICS

stratum ('strɑːtəm) *n*.

The plural form is *strata* ('strɑːtə), very occasionally *stratums*. (see SPELLING, NOUNS)

streamlined *adj. past part.*

Properly used, this word describes 'a building or vehicle which is designed to offer the least possible resistance to air or water'; it is widely used for anything made simpler or more efficient, e.g. *The procedure for making claims has been streamlined so that there is less delay*, and it has recently become a vogue word with various meanings having little connection with efficiency, e.g. 'up-to-date', 'graceful', 'slim' etc.

stringed, strung *past part.*

Strung is the usual form, except in *stringed instruments*.

stupefy *v.*

Sometimes misspelt [*stupify*].

sty, stye *n.*

Sty (plural *sties*) means 'place for pigs', *sty* or *stye* (plural *sties* or *styes*) means 'inflammation of the eyelids'.

style see STILE

STYLE

It is worse than useless to be dogmatic about style, because so much depends on the purpose for which the language is being used. There are various kinds of jargon which are referred to in this book in a way which is not intended to recommend them: journalese, official and bureaucratic jargon, technical words used by politicians, critics and others whose aims should be to make their meaning clear. Of course most groups of people have and indeed need their special vocabulary and style of usage, and there is no need to complain when journalists, for instance, condense their material to make it fit into headlines such as *Star Weds Fan*, or politicians invent words and phrases to describe new situations and movements. There are, however, three dangers which arise out of these specialized forms of speech. One is the use of words to make a situation appear more complicated and obscure than it really is. This is common in political speeches, and increases the sense of distance between the reader or listener and the man in control of events. It can be used to give the impression that something important is being revealed when there is really no substance in the speech, or to be deliberately misleading without committing oneself to what can afterwards be proved to be false. Television has added to the effectiveness of this habit, for it is much easier to stop reading an article in a newspaper if it becomes dull and meaningless than it is to switch off a speaker in full flood.

Even more pernicious perhaps is another widespread misuse of language, official jargon. Confronted with forms, letters or instructions which he cannot understand, a member of the public pursuing his legitimate enquiries is often reduced to impotence and despair; and unnecessary antagonism is set up between the citizen and his government, the agencies which may be trying to help him, or the firm with whom he is trying to deal. This form of obscurity would be very more general without the work of the late Sir Ernest Gowers, whose books on the subject were collected under the title *The Complete Plain Words* (Pelican 1962). His object was "to help officials in their use of written English as a tool of their trade".

Thirdly there is the danger of words being taken over from the specialist and becoming so fashionable that they lose their freshness and precision. Writers of books on usage often classify these as "vogue words", but this seems to imply that they will pass out of common use, and who is to decide whether a word like *escalation*, much overused at present, will pass out of the language, or come to be as accepted as *teenage* has been? A rapidly-changing and inventive generation needs many new words, and the danger comes from using them merely because they are fashionable, in letting them become predictable and boring, and saving oneself the trouble of thinking afresh. Fowler's *Modern English Usage* (Oxford, 1965) includes in this category *iron curtain* and *wind of change*, which already seem less like tiresome catch-phrases and more like those favourites of the history books, *the Yellow Peril*, *the White Man's Burden*, and "*the Sick Man of Europe*" (Turkish Empire). Another class of word which Fowler's readers are warned to use with care he calls *Popularized Technicalities*, and this includes words from the arts and sciences, especially psychology, such as *allergic, blueprint, per-*

centage, the subconscious. Where their origins are borne in mind these can be appropriate, but they are often used as slick substitutes for simpler expressions.

Writing would be very dull without the use of *metaphor*, which means the expression of an idea, or the description of an object or action, in terms of something more concrete which it resembles, often in one characteristic only. It is used unconsciously in many phrases which have become fixed in the language, such as a *biting wind*, a *split second, turn the other cheek.* Other metaphorical expressions have not been so closely absorbed and produce staleness instead of liveliness. They are known as clichés and include *Wild horses would not drag me there; food for thought; bloated capitalist; cut-throat competition; when it comes to the crunch.* Not all clichés are metaphorical, sometimes an adjective becomes glued to a noun, as in *tender mercies; agonizing reappraisal.* Some writers try too hard to escape the charge of using hackneyed phrases by adapting or adding to them, as in *She collected not only lame but also blind and elderly ducks.* A useful image can be spoilt by using it too literally. Another constant danger in the use of metaphor is that of mixing two or more images, as in the newspaper headline:

Electrical Bid Battle Hinging on Credibility Gap.

Metaphor is valuable where it makes for clarity and liveliness, which are the two most desirable qualities in writing; liveliness, while it is essential where pleasure or persuasion are concerned, should perhaps come second to brevity in business letters and official communications of all kinds. There is nothing duller than a letter padded out with meaningless politeness and the unhelpful jargon of the sender, especially if it is in the old-fashioned obsequious style of *Trusting to be favoured with your esteemed order* . . .

The object of this book is to assist clarity by providing an easy method of reference to the accepted forms and the current meaning of certain difficult words, and to the ways words can be put together without ambiguity or waywardness. Nothing is final in language or usage, and there is no ultimate authority; we can only recommend, not prescribe.

(see also AMERICAN USAGE)

stylish, stylized ('stailaizd) *adj.*

Stylish means 'fashionable', 'smart', 'showy', e.g. *I thought her hat was extremely stylish.* *Stylized* means 'in conformity with a certain style', 'not naturalistic', and is used in describing the arts, e.g. *He gave a stylized performance as Figaro.*

subconscious(ly), unconscious(ly) *adj. adv. n.*
These words overlap when they are used in the sense for which *subconscious* has been borrowed from psychology, to describe 'thoughts, feelings and motives which influence a person's behaviour without his being aware of them'. *He sub* (or *un*)*consciously accepted his teacher's point of view. Unconscious* has the additional meanings of 'not knowing', 'unaware' and 'without consciousness through accident or illness'. The noun here is *unconsciousness*, whereas *the subconscious* and *the unconscious* are short for the *sub* (or *un*)*conscious mind.*

subject
In grammar, the subject of a sentence is the word or group of words which dictate the number and person of a verb. The unitalicised words in the following are examples:

The daffodils *were yellow.*
Have you *seen the new postman?*
Has the new postman *seen you?*
No one *will ever come.*
Crying *never did anyone any good.*
Who *said that?*

subject (*n.* and *v.*) see OBJECT
subjective see OBJECTIVE
substitute (for), replace (by) *v.*
These verbs are not interchangeable though

292

they are sometimes used as if they were. *Substitute* means 'put in the place of' and is followed by *for*, e.g. *During the game, Manchester United had to substitute Smith for Lawson.* *Replace* means 'take the place of', and is either followed by *by*, as in *The ten shilling note will be replaced by a 50 pence coin in the new currency*, or written without a preposition as in *A 50 pence coin will replace the old ten shilling note.*

such *adj. pro.*

[*Many have been found guilty and it is probable that such will commit another crime*]. This is not an accepted use of *such*, and it should be replaced by *they* or *such as they*. Clauses beginning with *such* should come immediately after the noun they qualify to avoid the ambiguity of a sentence like *After the first bus left, the visitors wandered round the ruins, such of them as remained.* Here it is doubtful whether *ruins* or *visitors* remained, and the sentence would be better running: *After the bus left, the visitors, such of them as remained, wandered round the ruins.*

such as, such that *conj.*

Both these phrases mean 'of a kind that', but *such that* implies a consequence. cf. *There were animals on the island such as I had never seen before; The abundance of fruit was such that we could hardly eat it all.*

suffer *v.*

This should be followed by *from* rather than *with*. It is colloquial to say *He suffers with his legs.*

sufficient *adj.* **enough** *adj. n.*

Enough can be a noun, unlike *sufficient* which is only used alone if the noun which should follow is clearly understood, e.g. *Will you need more men? No, ten will be sufficient. Sufficient* is often used in official or deliberately genteel language.

suffix

The grammatical term to describe 'a group of letters added to the end of a word to make a new word'. They usually imply the part of speech of the new word, e.g. *-ible* for an adjective, *-hood* for a noun, *-ly* for an adverb. Verbal endings and possessive forms are also suffixes, e.g. *hat*ing, *hat*ed, *hat*es, *yours*, *Jim*'s. (see SPELLING, ADJECTIVES and VERBS)

suit (su:t), **suite** (swi:t) *n.*

Suit is used for clothes, cards (hence *follow suit*), armour, a lawsuit or an attempt to win a woman in marriage; *suite* for a set of rooms or furniture, a retinue and a series of pieces in music.

summary see PARAPHRASE

summon, summons *v. n.*

The verb form is *summon* where it has the usual

sense of 'call', 'send for', e.g. *My father was summoned to a meeting*; *summons* where it is strictly a legal term, meaning 'serve with a summons', e.g. *He was summonsed for libel, and summoned to appear in court*. The noun is always *summons*, e.g. *The bell rang a summons to lunch*. It takes a singular verb.

sunk, sunken see SINK

superior *adj.*

Strictly this comparative form is not used with *more* or *most*. It is followed by *to* not *than*.

superlatives see SPELLING, ADJECTIVES

supplement ('sʌplimənt) *n.* (sʌpli'ment) *v.*

complement *v.*

To *supplement* is to 'make necessary additions to something', e.g. *They supplemented the prison food with the contents of the parcels which were sent to them*. To *complement* is to 'make complete', e.g. *Now that you have arrived we have complemented our numbers*. Sometimes confused with COMPLIMENT (q.v.)

suppose, supposing *conj.*

There is very little distinction in the use of these two forms when they mean 'if'. *Suppose* is more likely to be used in a straight question such as *Suppose you find you have been wrong, what will you do?* *Supposing* is more often used where there is an indication that something is likely or unlikely, e.g. *Supposing the work will*

*be finished in time, we shall move in next week;
Supposing it was too far to walk to the village we
could turn back.*

surprise, surprised *v.*

The double negative form (e.g. *I shouldn't be
surprised if it doesn't rain tomorrow*) appears
regularly in speech but is often ambiguous,
and not acceptable in writing. *Surprised by*
implies more sudden shock and less moral
disapproval than *surprised at*, e.g. *surprised by
an attack*; *by the turn of events*; *surprised at finding*
(or *to find*) *you still in bed*.

susceptible (sə'septəbl) *adj.*

Susceptible of means 'allowing', 'capable of',
e.g. *susceptible of only one interpretation*. *Susceptible to* means 'easily affected by', e.g. *susceptible
to flattery, chilblains*. It is loosely used for
prone to, liable to, e.g. *susceptible to being mis-
understood*.

swap, swop *v.*

Both spellings are used for this verb, meaning
'exchange', which is still largely colloquial.

swat, swot *v.*

To *swat* is to 'hit something', usually an insect
or a ball; to *swot* is to 'work hard' in school-
children's idiom.

swell *v.*

The past tense of this verb is *swelled*; the
past participle is *swelled* if it means simply

'increased', *swollen* if it means 'harmfully increased', e.g. *The number of boys in the choir has been swelled for the occasion; The river has swollen till it has burst its banks.* Note: *A swelled head* (from conceit), *a swollen head* (from injury).

swim *v.*

The past tense of this verb is *swam*; the past participle is *swum*.

sympathy *n.* **sympathize** *v.* **sympathetic** *adj.*
To have sympathy *for* usually implies some detachment, e.g. *I have every sympathy for those who have suffered in the accident.* To feel or be in sympathy *with* implies understanding as well as good will, e.g. *I have sympathy with you in your difficulties.* Sympathize is always followed by *with*. The adjective *sympathetic*, besides its usual meaning of 'showing sympathy', can be used to mean 'pleasing', 'congenial', like the French *sympathique* and Italian *simpatico*.

synonym
'Two words with approximately the same meaning' are known as *synonyms*. But it is very rarely true that any two words are interchangeable in every one of their senses, e.g. *repair* and *mend*; either could be used for a pair of shoes, but an engine would be *repaired*, and a broken cup *mended*.

(see also HOMONYM)

T

tactics, strategy *n.*

Strategy is 'the overall plan of a campaign', *tactics* 'the art of manoeuvring one's forces', or figuratively 'the adroit management of any situation'.

talent, genius *n.*

Talent is 'the innate ability to do something well'; *genius* is 'an exceptional degree of talent', involving original perception beyond most people's power. This word is frequently debased by being incorrectly used as in [*He has a genius for getting things to work*] or [*He has a genius for doing the wrong thing*].

tall see HIGH

target *n.*

An overworked and mis-used metaphor for 'an objective', e.g. *We hope to double our target next year.* It is liable, too, to produce a mixed metaphor, e.g. *The Committee has set a target of £1000 and will pursue it with vigour.* (see STYLE)

tartan see PLAID

tautology (tɔ:ˈtɒlədʒi)

This term describes 'the unnecessary repetition of an idea in the same sentence', e.g. *There was one more [extra] guest than we expec-*

ted, so we added a[n additional] chair or *This shop-keeper has the [sole] monopoly to sell waterproofs.*

tax *n.*

This is the general term for 'money which has to be paid to the state'. As well as *income tax* there are other forms such as *rates*, which are based on the rateable value of property and paid to the local authority; *customs duties* paid on articles imported from abroad; *purchase tax*, a percentage tax added to the retail price of certain articles; *dues*, which are paid for the use of harbours etc.; *excise*, paid on manufactures such as liquor; and *toll*, a charge made for the use of a road or bridge.

teach-in *n.*

An American phrase for 'an informal large-scale debate bringing together the best available exponents of divergent views on a chosen subject'.

teaspoonful *n.*

Plural *teaspoonfuls*

teenager *n.*

An accepted word (which does not need a hyphen) meaning 'a young person between thirteen and nineteen years of age'.

teens *n.*

No longer spelt ['*teens*] with an apostrophe. (cf. *bus, plane*)

televise *v.*

This is a back formation from *television* so it must be spelt *ise* not [*ize*]. (see SPELLING, VERBS)

tell see ACQUAINT

temporal, temporary *adj.*

Temporal means 'having to do with time', or 'relating to this life'; one of its opposites is *eternal*, another *spiritual*. *Temporary* means 'lasting only for a certain time', 'fleeting', and is the opposite of *permanent*.

tendency see TREND

tepid see TORPID

terminal, terminus *n.*

Both these words refer to traffic and mean 'a point of arrival and departure', especially in a town. *Terminal* is generally used for air traffic, *terminus* (plural *terminuses* or *termini*) for trains and buses.

testimonial see REFERENCE

than *conj.*

Than is used after most comparative adjectives and adverbs except *superior* and *inferior*, *junior* and *senior*, which are followed by *to*. Where a clause is implied after *than*, e.g. *You reached the top of the hill faster than I* (*reached the top of the hill*), it is usual to repeat the verb or substitute *do* (*faster than I did*). It would be colloquial in this case to say *faster than me*, but

acceptable with such verbs as *be, become, seem,*
e.g. *You seem younger than me.*

that *(adj.)* see THOSE

that *relative pro. conj.*

1. In the majority of cases *that* can be used
instead of *which* or *who* in a sentence like
This is the book that I enjoyed most. (Or it could
be omitted altogether.)

2. However, where the relative clause is
between commas, *who* or *which* must be used,
e.g. *The book, which I very much enjoyed, was too
large to bring in my handbag; The old gentleman,
who had put on his deerstalker to keep out the cold,
told me the history of the castle.*

3. Used after a comparative, *that* is
redundant: *The sooner* [*that*] *we do it the better.*

4. *I need you that badly* is colloquial. It would
be more formal to use *so.*

the *definite article*

1. *The* is used before the noun when it
denotes a generic class rather than a plain
singular, e.g. *The thrush is my favourite bird.*

2. *The* is only repeated before the second
of two nouns when they are thought of separately, e.g. *I measured the length and breadth of
the table,* but *I chose the wallpaper and the furniture.* After *both,* and when *or* is used, *the* must
appear before both nouns.

3. *There are two books on this subject, but I am*

not sure which is the better. The definite article
is used here to show that another noun (*book*)
is to be understood after *better.*

4. *The* is used before a comparative when
it is followed by *because*, e.g. *He was the more
frightened because the sounds appeared to be coming
from the deserted west wing of the house.* (For the
use of *the* before titles, see PUNCTUATION,
CAPITALS; ITALICS)

their see THEY

theirs *personal pro.*

Spelt without an apostrophe.

them see THEY

there *pro.*

In sentences like *There are three people living
next door*, where *there* is used as an impersonal
pronoun followed by the verb and then the real
subject of the sentence, doubts can arise
about the number of the verb. It usually
agrees with the subject following it, but it is
singular when the subject is a number or
group, e.g. *There is a family of three people living
next door*, or when two or more nouns are
usually treated as one, e.g. *There was a good
deal of fuss and bother before it was done.* It is also
singular before a series of nouns, e.g. *There is
water, gas and electricity on the premises.*

therefore *adv. conj.* **therefor** *adv.*

Therefore is only followed by a comma when

it is in parenthesis in the middle of a clause, e.g. *The French, therefore, felt unable to welcome Great Britain into the Common Market.* It has no following comma when it is used to introduce or connect a clause, e.g. *It was here yesterday, therefore it cannot be lost. Therefor,* now archaic, used to mean 'for that'.

they, them *pro.* **their** *adj.*

They and *them* are often carelessly used without making it clear what nouns they refer to, e.g. [*I heard from the Browns that the Jones' were leaving, when they complained they had not said goodbye to them*]. It is better to repeat the nouns in these cases. *Their* is often used instead of a third person singular pronoun, because there is no one word which conveys *his* and *hers* together, e.g. *Everyone learnt to their dismay that the school was about to close.* In writing, *his* is more often used in such cases.

think *v.*

Think does not need to be followed by *that. Think to* is colloquial when it is used to mean 'remember' or 'think of', e.g. *Did you think to try the Lost Property Office?* instead of *Did you think of trying the Lost Property Office?* but is acceptable usage in the sense of 'expect', e.g. *He never thought to see New York again.*

those *adj.*

Sometimes loosely and clumsily used instead

of *that* in phrases like [*those sort*], [*those kind*].

though *conj.*

As though is followed by *were*, *had*, rather than *was*, *has*, e.g. *He spoke as though he were a foreigner*. (see ALTHOUGH; IF)

thrash, thresh *v.*

These are basically the same word, but *thresh* is now only used for 'separating the grain from the chaff of grain'; *thrash* for the general meaning of 'beat', and in the figurative sense, e.g. *thrashing out a problem*.

through *prep.*

To be through with meaning 'to be finished' is colloquial. *Monday through Friday*, meaning *from Monday to Friday inclusive*, is an Americanism.

thus *adv.*

This word is often carelessly used before a present participle, leaving it doubtful to what the participle refers, e.g. [*He made a long speech, which was stiff with formality and delivered in a low, dull voice, thus driving his audience to distraction*]. It is better omitted in these cases. (see SENTENCE)

tie *n. v.*

Present participle *tying*, past participle and past tense *tied*.

tight, tightly *adv.*

Tight can be used as an adverb as well as

tightly, and is more appropriate where the result rather than the manner is to be emphasised, e.g. *Fasten it tight* but *He screwed it tightly into place.* (cf. *sharp*)

till, until *prep. conj.*

The choice between these two forms is dictated by sound; *until* is generally used at the beginning of a sentence. (cf. *though, although*)

time(s) *n.*

In the time of is used where it refers to a specific person, e.g. *in the time of Julius Caesar*, but the plural is used for more general expressions such as *in times gone by*; *keep up with the times.*

-tion *suffix*

A sentence containing too many abstract nouns is likely to have the ugly sound resulting from a succession of words ending in *tion* (ʃən), e.g. *I shall demand a consultation in connection with the position we have reached in the accommodation situation.* (see SENTENCE)

tire see TYRE

titillate, titivate *v.*

To *titillate* is to 'stimulate the mind by excitement or curiosity', e.g. *He gave me some titillating hints but would not tell me the whole story.* To *titivate* is a familiar term and means 'dress up smartly', 'tidy oneself', e.g. *How much longer will you be titivating in front of the mirror?*

titles

These are quoted in italics in print, and underlined in handwriting and typed manuscripts. Inverted commas are sometimes used, but are better reserved for subtitles etc., e.g. I found what I wanted in *The Encyclopedia Britannica* under the entry "Clocks". *A* and *The* are usually included in the title, but sometimes omitted for the sake of brevity or where the book is very well known. (See ITALICS)

today, tomorrow, tonight *n.*

These are written without a hyphen.

toll see TAX

ton, tun *n.*

A *ton* is 'a measure of weight equivalent to twenty hundredweight in British avoirdupois measure'; a *tun* is 'a cask for beer or wine'.

tongs *n.*

This is a plural noun which has no singular form.

too *adv.*

Too is used before a passive past participle when it is adjectival, e.g. *He was too drunk to stand.* Strictly, when the participle is used as a verb, *too much* is required, e.g. *They were too much concerned with the future to notice the present.* (cf. *very*). As *too* is often used for understatements like *He was not too pleased with the results* it can cause ambiguity in a sentence such as [*We cannot take his plans too seriously*], which could mean either *They are too serious to be ignored* or *They are not worth taking seriously*.

top- *prefix*

Compounds made with *top-* usually have a hyphen, e.g. *top-coat*, *top-secret*, *top-soil*. Exceptions are *topless*, *topmost* and nautical terms such as *topmast*, *topside*.

torpid, tepid ('tepid) *adj.*

Torpid means 'inactive', 'sluggish'; *tepid* used literally means 'slightly warm', figuratively 'half-hearted'.

tortuous ('tɔ:tju:əs), **torturous** ('tɔ:tjurəs) *adj.*

Tortuous means 'twisting', 'not straightforward', e.g. *a tortuous path up a mountain*, *a tortuous argument*. *Torturous* means 'causing torture', 'cruel', e.g. *The enemy inflicted torturous punishments on the prisoners*. It is not in wide use.

toward(s) *prep.*

Towards is more generally used.

trade union

The plural form is *trade unions*, except in *Trades Union Congress*.

traffic *n. v.*

Present participle *trafficking*, past participle *trafficked*.

trait *n.*

This word, meaning 'characteristic' is generally pronounced (treit), but occasionally as in French (trei).

tranquil *adj-*

The nouns are spelt *tranquillizer* and *tranquillity*.

transient, transitional, transitory *adj.*

The first two words have roughly the same meaning of 'fleeting', 'not lasting'. They are most commonly used of emotions and impressions. *Transitional* means 'belonging to a state or age of transition', 'intermediate', e.g. *There will have to be a transitional stage while decimal coinage is introduced* (or *before the introduction of decimal coinage*).

transitive verbs see VERB

transpire *v.*

This word is popularly used to mean 'happen', 'turn out', e.g. [*I saw it all transpire as I passed your window*]. Its correct meaning is 'become gradually known', 'come to light', e.g. *It transpired many years later that the pair had been happily married since the beginning of the century.*

transport ('trɑːnspɔːt) *n.* (trɑːns'pɔːt) *v.*

travel *v.*

This verb always doubles the *l* before a suffix, as in *travelled, travelling, traveller.* (cf. *grovel, revel, drivel*) (See SPELLING, VERBS)

traverse *n. v. adj.* ('trævəs; trə'vəːs)

treble, triple *adj. v. n.*

    Treble is the more usual form for the noun and verb, *triple* for the adjective. *Treble* means 'three times as much or as many', *triple* means 'threefold' or 'of three kinds', e.g. *I paid treble as much as I expected*; *There were triple locks on the door.* *Treble* also describes the highest male voice in choral singing.

trend *v. n.* **tendency** *n.*

    The verb is not much used and is being replaced by *tend*. The noun has a similar meaning to *tendency*, but implies something more long-lasting, e.g. *There is a trend towards shorter working hours in all industrialised countries*; *Some countries show a tendency to distrust sterling.*

triple see TREBLE

triumphant, triumphal *adj.*

    Triumphant is the general word for 'victorious' or 'having a feeling of triumph'; *triumphal* is only used of occasions such as processions, e.g. *a triumphal march.*

trunk see STEM

try and

    Used in the present tense only, this is an accepted variant of *try to* and is more persuasive, e.g. *Do try and be in time.*

-t, -tt

    (see SPELLING, VERBS for final doubling of *t*)

turf *n.*
Plural *turfs* or *turves*; the second form is always used for 'blocks of peat'.

twenties, thirties etc.
These words do not require an apostrophe where *nineteen* is understood.

twopence see PENCE

tycoon *n.*
This U.S. term, Japanese in origin, for 'a business magnate' is now accepted usage in Britain.

tyrannize ('tirənaiz) *v.*
This verb is followed by *over*, but the analogy of *terrorize* sometimes leads to its omission.

tyre, tire *n.*
The first spelling is generally used for 'the inflated rubber rim surrounding a wheel'.

tzar, tsar see CZAR

U

un- *prefix*
Un is not usually joined to the rest of the word by a hyphen, except where it is followed by a capital, e.g. *un-American*. Confusion may be caused if an adjective such as *unknown* is used with the same value as *not known* in a sentence, e.g. [*I was told that chestnut trees were unknown,*

but oak trees were (i.e. *known*)]. (For other negative prefixes such as *in-*, *non-* see SPELLING, ADJECTIVES)

unanimous (juːˈnænɪməs) *adj.*

If voting is *unanimous* it means that 'everyone present is in agreement'; if any abstain from voting, the motion is carried not *unanimously* but *nem. con.* (Latin *nemine contradicente*), i.e. 'nobody speaking against it'.

unashamed (ˈʌnəˈʃeɪmd) *adj.* **unashamedly** (ˈʌnəˈʃeɪmɪdli) *adv.*

unaware *adj.* **unawares** *adv.*

E.g. *He was unaware that he was being watched* but *Coming so early in the morning, you have caught me unawares* (i.e. 'inadvertently').

unconscious(ly) see SUBCONSCIOUS(LY)

unconsolable see INCONSOLABLE

under see BELOW

under- *prefix*

As with *un*, compounds made with *under* only have a hyphen when the second half of the word has a capital, e.g. *Under-Secretary*, though there are a few exceptions such as *under-expose*, *under-belly* (figuratively 'a vulnerable area').

underline *v.*

This word is inaccurately used instead of *emphasize*, e.g. *He underlined some of his points by quoting figures.*

undue *adj.* **unduly** *adv.*

 Through clichés like *undue haste, undue optimism, unduly alarmed*, the meaning of 'more than is necessary' is shifting to 'ill-judged' or 'misconceived'.

uninterested see DISINTERESTED

unique (juː'niːk) *adj.*

 This means 'the only one of its kind', so it may be used with *almost* or *nearly*, but not with *very, more* or *most*. (see ABSOLUTES)

unlawful see ILLEGAL

unloose *v.*

 This archaic term means the same as *loose*, e.g. *Whose shoes' latchet I am not worthy to unloose* (St. John).

unpractical see IMPRACTICABLE

unreadable see ILLEGIBLE

unrelated participle see PARTICIPLES

unstable *adj.*

 The noun form is *instability*. (cf. *unable*)

until see TILL

unto *prep.*

 Archaic.

up to date, up-to-date

 Hyphens are used only when this is used as a compound adjective, e.g. *the most up-to-date styles*, not in *See that the files are brought up to date*.

-us

 (For plural of nouns ending in *us* see SPELLING)

usage (′juːsidʒ) *n.*

This word does not mean the same as *use*, but is 'a manner of use established by custom'. It is usually applied to language, but is sometimes loosely applied as in the following sentence: *During that very cold winter there was a heavy usage of coal.* (see IDIOM; STYLE)

use *n.*

Of is usually dropped before *use* in sentences like *It is no use thinking things will improve*, but retained in *Would this coat be of any use to you?* (cf. *value, advantage*)

used, used to *v.*

1. *Used* (juːzd) is the past form of to *use*. It forms the interrogative and negative in the conventional way, e.g. *I used hair cream; I didn't use hair cream; Did I use hair cream?*

2. When meaning 'accustomed to', *used to* (′juːsttu) is followed by a present participle, pronoun or noun, e.g. *She was used to (tolerating) (him) and (his ways).* The interrogative and negative are formed by using the auxiliary *be*, e.g. *I am used to working hard; Am I used to working hard?*

3. *Used to* (′juːsttu) meaning 'did (habitually)', has alternative interrogative and negative forms with or without *did(n't)*, e.g. *Did you use to go there?* or *Used you to go there?; I didn't use to like it* or *I used not to like it.* The

313

forms with *did(n't)* are more informal (cf.
have to, ought to)

utilize *v.*

This word has a narrower meaning than *use*,
though it is often substituted for it in official
and political writing. It means 'make profit-
able use of', and implies that something has
not been fully used before, e.g. *These are highly
trained men, and their skill is not being utilized.*

V

v.

This abbreviation which appears mostly
between the names of opposing teams, is
short for Latin *versus* meaning 'against', and is
pronounced in full, e.g. *France versus Germany.*
It also has other meanings as an abbreviation.
(see Appendix)

vainglory *n.*

Written as one word, as is *vainglorious.*

valet ('vælit) or ('vælei) *n.* ('vælit) *v.*

Present participle *valeting*, past participle
valeted.

valour *n.* **valorous** *adj.*

(cf. *humour, vigour* etc.)

value *n.*

Unlike USE (q.v.), this word requires *of* when

following *to be*, e.g. *It is of no value*; not [*What value will it be?*] but *Of what value will it be?* *Values* has recently become a popular word for 'ethical standards or opinions', e.g. *He has all the wrong values.*

valueless *adj.*

This means *of no value*, but is sometimes loosely used to mean 'extremely valuable' on the analogy of *priceless*.

Van Dyck

Generally anglicised to *Vandyke*, e.g. *a Vandyke beard, Vandyke brown.*

vanity *n.*

This is the usual noun from *vain*; *vainness* is rarely used.

vantage see ADVANTAGE

variance ('vɛəriəns) *n.*

Followed by *with* not *from*, e.g. *My views are at variance with his.*

various *adj.*

There is a tendency to use *various* as a pronoun followed by *of*, as in *Various of my hopes have been disappointed*; but it is still regarded as correct to say *my various hopes* or *several of my hopes.*

vast *adj.* **vastly** *adv.*

These words are properly used to mean 'great in size', 'by a great deal' respectively, e.g. *a vast hall, a vast crowd, a vastly increased population,* but they are colloquial where there is no sense of size or comparison, e.g. *There was a vast amount of talking going on; I was vastly surprised to see you.*

veld, veldt (velt) or (felt) *n.*

The more general spelling is *veld,* as in *veldschoen,* 'shoes made of untanned hide'.

venal ('viːnəl), **venial** ('viːnɪəl) *adj.*

Venal means 'corruptible', 'mercenary', e.g. *His conduct became venal as he charged his tenants higher rents. Venial* is applied to 'errors of omission or commission', 'trivial faults' and means 'pardonable', e.g. *venial sins.*

venue ('venjuː) *n.*

This word has become popularly used for 'a place or scene', without necessarily being given its proper sense of 'a meeting-place'.

veranda, verandah *n.*

Both spellings are used.

verb

The *tense* of a verb indicates present, past or future (*I walk, I walked, I shall walk*).

Person is the term used to indicate who performs the action described by the verb. In English, only the third person singular has a different form to indicate person (*I, you, we they rise, he rises*), except *to be* with three different forms for denoting person. (See also WILL and SHALL, WOULD and SHOULD)

Active and *Passive Voice* are the terms used to distinguish between an action performed by the subject of the verb: He broke *the glass* (active), and something which it undergoes: *The glass* was broken (passive).

An *Auxiliary Verb* is one which is used with another verb for one of the following purposes:—

To indicate the tense: *I* shall *come, We* have *been.*

To make a passive: *He* has *been* killed.

To add emphasis: *I* do *hope you will come.*

To turn the sentence into a question: Do *you see that tall man?*

To make a negative: *He knows the way, but I* do *not know it.*

To substitute for another verb: *He knows the way—but I* don't.

Some verbs can be used as either main verbs or auxiliaries, e.g. *I have a book* (main verb), *I have come* (auxiliary). Others are only used as auxiliaries and have only one form, e.g. *can, may, might, must, shall.* (see NEED; DARE)

A *Reflexive Verb* describes an action in which the object is the same as the subject and is expressed by a pronoun, e.g. *The dog shook itself.*

A *Transitive Verb* has a direct object (*He broke the cup*). An *intransitive* one can have an indirect object introduced by a preposition (*We talked about our work*) or none at all (*The old man spat*). Some verbs can be used in any of these ways: *He drove the car*; *He drove down the street*; *He drove fast*. (see PREPOSITION)

The *Infinitive* can take the place of a noun and become the subject or object of a sentence, e.g. To expect more *would be a mistake* (subject); *I was never taught* to read (object).

verbal *adj.*

This means 'expressed in words' and can apply to speech or writing. When spoken words are intended, ORAL (q.v.) is clearer, e.g. *We made an oral agreement*. It is also the adjective from the noun *verb*. Note that the adjective from *adverb* is *adverbial*.

verify see CORROBORATE

veritable *adj.* **veritably** *adv.*

These words are often used without much meaning merely to provide emphasis and forestall disbelief, e.g. *I veritably believe that there is real cream in this cake.* (cf. *actually*, *really*)

vermin *n.*

A collective noun with no plural form.

very, very much see MUCH

via ('vaɪə) *prep.*

Latin for 'a way', 'hence', 'by way of'. This is used of a place but not of a means of transport, e.g. *The train goes via Crewe* but *We sent the goods by* (not *via*) *British Road Services*. (SEE PER)

viable ('vaiəbl) *adj.*

This is a medical team meaning 'born alive' and therefore 'capable of leading a separate existence'. It has become a fashionable word loosely used to mean 'practicable', 'feasible', 'effective', 'lasting', e.g. *His plan is not a viable proposition at this time.*

vicar, rector *n.*

Both are 'parish priests in the Church of England'. The difference is historical and concerns the payment of tithes. A *rector* received *all* tithes, a *vicar* was given a salary out of tithes appropriated by an institution, religious corporation, or layman.

vicious, rector ('viʃəs), **viscous** ('viskəs) *adj.*

Vicious means 'wicked', 'very ill-tempered', 'spiteful'; *viscous* describes 'liquids which are thick and treacly in consistency'. A *vicious circle* or *spiral* is a series of difficulties, each of which makes the next one inevitable, e.g. *Poverty produces hunger, which leads to sickness, which reduces earning power, which therefore means worse poverty.* The phrase is loosely used for 'an argument which leads back to its beginning'.

vide ('vi:dei)

Latin for 'see', used for cross references in books, e.g. *For further discussion on this point vide* (or *v.*) *p. 40. Vide* is loosely used as if it meant 'for example look at', e.g. *The country is in a state of decline, vide the coal industry.*

view *n.*

With a view to and with the view of both express purpose and are followed by a noun or verbal noun, not an infinitive, e.g. *I am going to France with the view of buying a house there*; *He is learning Russian with a view to a post as an interpreter.* In view of means 'in consideration of', and is followed by a noun or pronoun, e.g. *In view of his age the old man decided not to move house.*

view, viewpoint, point of view

Viewpoint is used in the U.S. where British English uses *point of view.* Both are often used instead of the simpler *view(s), opinion(s)* (as is the more recent word *angle*), e.g. *The chairman was asked for his (point of) view on the proposals.* The stricter use is illustrated in *From our point of view the new plans seemed excellent, but the architect was far from satisfied.* (see SLANT)

vigour *n.* **vigorous** *adj.*

(Cf. *humour, rigour* etc.)

villain ('vilən), **villein** ('vilin) *n.*

Villain (adjective *villainous*) means 'scoundrel'; *villein* means 'feudal serf'. The abstract nouns are *villainy* and *villeinage.*

violoncello (.vi:ələn'tʃelou) *n.*

Often misspelt [*violoncello*]. Usually abbreviated to '*cello* or *cello*

virtual, virtuous *adj.*

Virtual describes something 'which exists unrecognised, unacknowledged or potentially', e.g. *It was virtual war between the two countries.* It can also mean 'for all practical purposes', e.g. *It is a virtual certainty that we shall win in the end.* (see LITERALLY) *Virtuous* means 'having virtue', 'upright', 'blameless', 'chaste'.

visit, visitation *n.*

Visitation has a narrower range of meanings than *visit*; it can mean either 'a formal visit of inspection', e.g. *the annual visitation of the governing body,* or 'an affliction or favour thought to be sent by God'.

viz.

This is an abbreviation of the Latin *videlicet* and means 'namely'. It is used to introduce the enumeration of some things which have been before referred to as a whole, e.g. *I have visited the main European capitals, viz. Rome, Berlin, Paris and London,* or to specify something previously described in general terms, e.g. *We must now consider the most important people in agriculture, viz. the farmers.*

vogue words see STYLE

W

wagon, waggon *n.*

The first spelling is now more general.

wait, await *v.*

Wait is now generally used for the intransitive verb, e.g. *I am waiting for your answer*; *await* for the transitive, e.g. *I await your answer*.

waive, wave *v.*

These are quite separate words, *waive* having the meaning 'abandon', 'relinquish', 'forgo', 'dispense with', e.g. *Let us waive ceremony*; *The eldest son waived his right to the title*. *Wave*, however, implies physical motion, e.g. *The man in the car ahead waved us on*. They are sometimes confused, e.g. *The publisher [waived] aside my objections*.

waltz (wɔ:lts), **valse** (vɑ:ls) *n.*

The first of these forms is generally used.

want see REQUIRE

-ward, -wards *suffix.*

The final *s* is added to this suffix when it makes adverbs, e.g. *We march onwards*, but not for adjectives, e.g. *the onward march*.

warp, woof *n.*

The vertical threads in weaving are the *warp*, the horizontal ones the *woof* (or *weft*).

waste, wastage *n.*

Wastage means 'what is lost by waste', e.g. *There was a considerable wastage of water because of a leaking pipe.* It is commonly misused as if it meant simply 'waste', e.g. [*To use highly skilled men where untrained workers could do the job means a great wastage of manpower*]. Here *waste* would be better.

watch *v.*

Watch does not need to be followed by *out* as *look* does when used in the same sense, e.g. *Look out for ice on the roads* but *Watch for ice on the roads.*

watershed *n.*

This term describes 'the high ground dividing the flow of rivers and streams into different basins', e.g. *the Pennine Range* in England, the *Great Continental Divide* in America. It is loosely used in this country and accepted in the U.S. for 'a drainage or catchment area'. It is figuratively used in history and journalism for 'a decisive period' such as the 1914–18 war.

wave see WAIVE

way, weigh *n.*

Way is the term used for a ship in motion, e.g. *When we had got under way.* There is sometimes confusion in spelling because of the phrase *to weigh anchor.*

-ways see -WISE

we-_pro._

We is used instead of *I* by monarchs and editors of newspapers, also by writers not wishing to commit themselves to full responsibility for their statements. It is often called the *royal* or *editorial we.* (see ONE)

wed, marry *v.*

Marry is the general term, *wed* is literary but also used by journalists for brevity. The past tense and past participle are *wed*, except in the figurative use, e.g. *wedded to an idea*. Wedding and marriage are both used for the ceremony, but only *marriage* for 'the state of matrimony'.

Wedgwood *adj. n.*

The name of this pottery is often misspelt [*Wedgewood*].

weigh see WAY

Welch, Welsh *adj.* **welch, welsh** *v.*

The adjective form *Welch* is only used in the names of certain regiments, e.g. *The Royal Welch Fusiliers.* The adjective meaning 'from Wales' is *Welsh*. To *welsh* or *welch* is 'the action of a bookmaker who runs off from a racecourse without settling bets'.

well-, good-; ill-, bad- *prefix*

Compound adjectives are more often made with *well* and *ill* than *good* and *bad*, though

324

there are some exceptions such as *good-humoured*; *good-natured*; *good-looking*. They are hyphenated rather than written as one word, but written separately without a hyphen when they complete the verb, e.g. *I found him a well- (or ill-) informed boy*; *The neighbours were well (or ill) disposed towards the newcomers*.

well-nigh *adv.*

An uncommon and literary adverb meaning 'very nearly', sometimes ungrammatically used as if it meant 'near', e.g. [*He came well-nigh to tears*] instead of *He well-nigh came to tears*. It always has a hyphen.

Welsh see WELCH

were, had *v.*

As subjunctives in *if* clauses, *were* and *had* occur only where there is a hypothesis concerning the present or future, e.g. *If our house were (or were to be) demolished, would the Council re-house us? Was* and *had* are used in similar clauses in the past, e.g. *If he was there I should have seen him.* (see ALTHOUGH; IF; THOUGH)

wharf (wɔːf) *n.*

Plural *wharfs* or *wharves*. (cf. *scarf*)

what *pro.*

The number of the verb to be used with *what* can cause difficulty. When it means 'that which' the verb is singular, e.g. *I do not always believe what I am told*; when it means 'those which' it is plural, e.g. *We have a great many apples this year and what we cannot eat are to be given away.* (For *what* in questions see WHICH)

whence, whither *adv.*

Though slightly archaic these are useful and concise forms of 'from where' and 'to where'. *Whence* is sometimes used with a redundant *from*, e.g. [*From whence came the stranger?*].

where-

Compounds made from *where* are written as one word, e.g. *wherein*, except *where ever*, in which *ever* is emphatic, e.g. *Where ever have you put my dictionary?* (SEE EVER)

whereabouts *n.*

This is always treated as singular, e.g. *The whereabouts of the documents is a mystery.*

wherewithal *adv. n.*

This is no longer much used as an adverb equivalent to *wherewith*, but is employed colloquially as a noun meaning 'the money or other resources needed to do something', e.g. *He has no longer the wherewithal to keep up the estate.*

whether see IF

which *adj. pro.*

1. *Which* as an interrogative adjective is more precise than *what*, *who*. It implies a specific choice, e.g. *Which book shall I buy?*

(from among certain possibilities); *What book shall I buy?* (from an unlimited number). Similarly, it is used instead of *who* when there is a choice to be made from among a few, e.g. *Which of you saw him go?*

2. *Which* as a relative pronoun is sometimes omitted when it needs to be repeated, especially at the beginning of a second clause which has a different form of verb, e.g. [*The council pursued a policy which was unsuccessful and was seen to be causing distress*] (*and which was seen*).

3. *And which* and *but which* only introduce clauses of the same kind, e.g. *the house they bought which was built in 1800 and which was exactly what they wanted* not [*the house they bought which was built in 1800 and which living in seemed ideal*].

4. *That* and *which* can be used to introduce parallel clauses, e.g. *the dress that I bought yesterday, and which I like very much.*

while, whilst *conj.*

While can mean either 'during the time that', e.g. *While we were waiting for the train a woman came and spoke to us*, or 'although', 'but' with a sense of comparison, e.g. *My sister is older than I am, while my brother is younger.* In some sentences it is not clear which is meant, as for example: *Her husband looked after the children*

327

while she did nothing. A comma after *children*, or *but* instead of *while*, would make it clear that a comparison was intended. The form *whilst* is infrequently used.

while *v.* **wile** *v. n.*

The first spelling is used for 'while away the time' whereas *wile* is used for 'trick', 'entice', e.g. *She did not mean to tell me, but I wiled the secret out of her.*

while *conj.*

In Yorkshire and other regional speech *while* can mean 'until'. This can be confusing as in the case of the ambiguous directions on an unmanned railway crossing: *Do not cross line while lights flash.*

whilom ('wiləm) *adj. adv.*

An archaic word meaning *former, formerly,* e.g. *a whilom Harley Street specialist.*

whisky, whiskey *n.*

The second spelling is used only for Irish whiskey.

whiz, whizz *n. v.*

Both spellings are used. The verb has participles *whizzing, whizzed.*

who, whom *pro.*

Generally *who, whom* are used of people or things; but *who* is often used for animals and of nations when they are regarded as people. The choice between *who* and *whom* gives constant trouble. In speech it is unusual and would sound very formal to use *whom* in questions like *Who were you talking to?* and *I don't know who it is for*; but it is usual to write *The doctor whom I mentioned in my letter*. In a sentence such as [*The prisoner, whom I hear escaped through the window, was soon recaptured*] *who* should have been used because it is the subject of *escaped*, not the object of *hear*.

whodunnit *n.*

A popular term for a crime or detective novel which is now accepted by literary critics.

whoever, who ever, whosoever *pro.*

When *whosoever* is used as the object in a sentence it becomes *whomsoever*, but *whoever* remains the same. (see EVER)

wholly *adv.*

Pronounced ('houlli).

whose *pro.*

This is the possessive form of both the pronouns *who* and *which*, though very formal writers prefer *of which*, e.g. *the old house, of which I knew the history well* rather than *the old house, whose history I knew well*.

why *n.*

As a noun meaning 'reason' or 'cause', *why* has the plural form *whys*, e.g. *whys and wherefores*.

wide see BROAD

wide awake, wide-awake, wideawake

These forms are used as follows:— *I shook him till he was wide awake*; *He had a wide-awake look in his eyes*; *He was wearing a wideawake hat.*

wile see WHILE

wilful *adj.*

Sometimes misspelt [*willful*] or [*wilfull*]. (cf. *skilful*)

will, shall; would, should *auxiliary v.*

1. When expressing a simple future the forms are:— *I* and *we shall*, *he*, *you*, and *they will*, e.g. *I shall go back tomorrow*; *He will come home tonight*. When they are used to express determination, the forms are reversed, e.g. *I will manage to get there somehow*; *You shall do what I tell you.*

2. In the conditional, *should* is the same for all persons, e.g. *if I should forget*; *if you should happen to see him*; *if they should arrive unexpectedly.*

3. *Would* is also the same throughout the tense (a) when it conveys choice or consent, e.g. *If only you and Mary would stop quarrelling, I could get on with my work*; *We would accept your offer if we could* (b) when it means 'used to', e.g. *Every morning I would get up at sunrise*; *He would often forget his latchkey* (c) when it expresses determination, e.g. *You would have it your own way.*

4. *Will* is used throughout the tense when it denotes capacity, e.g. *This jug will hold three pints*, or agreement, e.g. *I will join the club if you will, and we will go together.*

In Scotland, Ireland and the U.S. less distinction is made between *will* and *shall*.

will *v.*

Besides being the auxiliary verb used to make a future tense or express determination *will* has the two meanings of 'leave something in one's will', e.g. *He willed his house to his daughter*, or 'exercise will power', 'influence events by doing so', e.g. *He willed her to open the door; She willed that he should come home safely.*

wind *v.*

There are three separate verbs. To *wind* (waind), the commonest, has the past participle *wound* and means 'twist', the second has the past participle *winded* or *wound* and means 'sound the horn'. To *wind* (wind) is 'render breathless' or 'catch a scent in hunting' and has the past participle *winded*.

-wise, -ways *suffix*

In the few cases where both forms do exist, e.g. *lengthwise* and *lengthways*, *wise* is generally used.

wishful *adj.*

This word had become rare but has been revived in the phrase *wishful thinking*.

with *prep.*

With is sometimes used where *of* would be more appropriate, e.g. *With Physics, as with Chemistry, we know a great deal more than our grandfathers.* Also, *with* is sometimes used after *concern*, e.g. *He was not concerned [with] the robbery*, where *in* gives the meaning intended. (SEE PREPOSITIONS)

with- *prefix*

Words made with this prefix, which means 'away', 'back', 'against', have no hyphen, e.g. *withdraw, withstand. Withhold* is often misspelt [*withold*].

without *adv.*

Used either as adverb or preposition to mean 'outside', 'out of doors', this word is archaic, e.g. *Can you hear knocking without?*; *without the gates. Without hardly* is often written with the meaning of 'with hardly' or 'almost without', e.g. [*He bore the pain without hardly a cry*]. In speech *without* is occasionally used for 'unless', e.g. *He will not come without you ask him.*

womankind, womenkind *n.*

Womankind means 'women in general'; *womenkind* is used in this sense, but can also mean 'female relations'.

wonder *v.*

Used in the sense of 'ask oneself' followed by an indirect question without a question mark,

332

e.g. *I wonder where he has gone*, unless it is purely polite, e.g. *I wonder whether you would help me?* Illogical double negatives often occur especially in speech, e.g. [*I shouldn't wonder if it doesn't rain*].

wont *adj. n.*

The pronunciation is (wount) in the adjective meaning 'accustomed' and the noun meaning 'custom'; the adjective *wonted* is pronounced (wountid).

woof see WARP

wool *n.*

The adjectives are *woollen*, *woolly* in Great Britain; *woolen*, *wooly* in the U.S.

work *v.* **worked** *past part.* **wrought** (rɔːt) *adj. past part.*

The usual past participle is *worked*, but *wrought* is used of metals, e.g. *wrought iron.*

worth while, worth-while

A hyphen is only used when a compound adjective is made, e.g. *a worth-while occupation*, not as in *His work was worth while*. *While* is not needed after *be worth* when it already has an object in the form of a participle, e.g. *It is not worth [while] waiting for the bus.*

would see WILL

I wouldn't know

A colloquial expression for 'I don't know'.

wrapped see RAPT

wrong, wrongly *adv.*

Like *quick*, *sharp* and other adjectives, *wrong* is often used adverbially, e.g. *You must have heard me wrong.*

wrought see WORK

X

-x

Words taken from French and ending in *eu* or *eau* usually form the plural by adding *x*, which is pronounced, if at all, as (z), e.g. *gateaux* ('gætou) or ('gætouz). (see SPELLING, NOUNS)

Xmas

A commercial abbreviation of *Christmas*, not used in speech and generally unacceptable if pronounced ('eksməs).

Y

-y, -ey, -ie

(see SPELLING for the use of these suffixes in making adjectives)

yankee *adj. n.*

A term used originally in the American Civil War for the armies of the North. It is loosely used for any citizen of the U.S.A.

ye *definite article pro.*

An archaic form of the definite article (based originally on error), pronounced (ðə) or (ði), e.g. *Ye Olde Tea-shoppe.* It is in common use pronounced (ji:). Also when it is the archaic plural of *you* its pronunciation is (ji:), as in *Ye gods!*

year's, years' see POSSESSIVES

yes

Plural *yeses.*

yet *adv.*

Ambiguity can arise over the use of *yet* in the sense of 'still', owing to differences in local usage. In Scotland and Ireland *Is your Father here yet?* can mean 'Is he still here?'. In Standard English it means 'Has he come yet?'

Yiddish

The language used by some Jews in Europe and America. It is a form of dialectal German and corrupt Hebrew written in Hebrew characters.

yodel

Past tense *yodelled,* present participle *yodelling.*

yours *personal pro.*

Spelt without an apostrophe.

youth (ju:θ), **youths** (ju:ðz) *n.*

Youth can be used as a collective plural without the final *s,* e.g. *The youth of the country are up in arms.*

Z

z

The American name for this letter is *zee*, not *zed* as in British English.

zigzag

Past tense *zigzagged*, present participle *zigzagging*

APPENDICES

1. INDEX OF PROPER ADJECTIVES

This list contains some unusual adjectives made from the names of people, towns, countries, rivers, mountains and gods. These are all exceptions to the general method of making an adjective from a proper noun, i.e. adding the suffix *–ian*, as in *Shakespearian, Edwardian, Italian* etc. (or, in the case of French words, adding *–ais*, as in *Lyonnais* from Lyon, or *–ese* to Italian words, as in *Milanese* from Milan, or *–er* to German words, as in *Berliner* from Berlin).

Names are also listed which have the same form for noun and adjective, e.g. *Maori*. The list may also be useful in distinguishing between proper nouns which are spelt in a similar way, e.g. *Augustan, Augustinian*; *Jacobin, Jacobite*; *Laurentian, Lawrencian* etc.

The left-hand column contains the nouns and the right-hand column the adjectives, but some particularly eccentric adjective forms have been put in the left-hand column in italics for ease of reference. The cross-references in capitals refer the reader back to entries in the dictionary proper.

Aaron   Aaronical
Aberdeen   Aberdonian
Achilles   Achillean
Adam   Adamite, Adamitic
Aestival   of Summer
Afghanistan   Afghan (*native* Afghan)
Afrikaans   see AFRICAN
Aldus Manutius   Aldine
Alexander the Great   Alexandrine
Alexandria (Egypt)   Alexandrian
Alhambra (Granada)   Alhambraic
Anacreon   Anacreontic
Anjou (France)   Angevin
Antipodes   Antipodean, Antipodal
St. Thomas Aquinas   Thomist
Apollo   Apollonian, Pythian
Apostle   Apostolic
Arabia   Arabian, Arabic (of language and
   numerals only) (*native* Arab)
Archimedes   Archimedean
Argentina   Argentine (*native* Argentine)
Argos (Greece)   Argive
Aristophanes   Aristophanic
Aristotle   Aristotelian
St. Augustine   Augustinian, Austin
Emperor Augustus   Augustan
Jane Austen   Jan(e)ite
Autumn   Autumnal
Aztec   Aztec

Bacchus   Bacchic
St. Benedict   Benedictine
Bengal (India)   Bengali
Jeremy Bentham   Benthamite
St. Bernard   Bernardine
Birmingham   Brummagem
The Black Sea   Pontic
Bordeaux   Bordelais
Brumal   of Winter
Burma   Burmese
I. of Bute   Brandane
Byron   Byronic
Byzantium (Constantinople)   Byzantine
Cadmus   Cadmean
Julius Caesar   Julian, Caesarean
Caledonian   Scottish
Calvin   Calvinist, Calvinistic
Cambrian   Welsh
Cambridge   Cantabrigian
Canaan   Canaanite
Carlovingian, Carolingian   of Charlemagne
Cartesian   of Descartes
Carthage (N. Africa)   Carthaginian, Punic
Carthusian   of Chartreuse, of Charterhouse
   School
Castile (Spain)   Castilian
Catalonia (Spain)   Catalan
Caucasus Mts.   Caucasian
Celt   Celtic

Ceylon Cingalese, Singhalese
Charlemagne Carlovingian, Carolingian
King Charles Caroline
Charterhouse School, Chartreuse (France)
   Carthusian
China Chinese, Sinic, Seric
Cicero Ciceronian, Tullian
Cingalese of Ceylon
Cîteaux (France) Cistercian
Copernicus Copernican
Cordoba (Spain) Cordovan
Cornwall Cornish, Cornubian (*native* Cor-
   nishman)
Cumberland Cumbrian
Cymric Welsh
Cyprus Cyprian, Cypriot
Czechoslovakia Czech, Czechoslovak,
   Czechoslovakian, Czechish
Dante Alighieri Dantean, Dantesque
Delphi (Greece) Delphian, Delphic
Demosthenes Demosthenic
Derby Derbeian
René Descartes Cartesian
The Devil Diabolic
Diluvian of the Flood
Divine of God
St. Dominic Dominican
Druid Druidical
Dundee Dundonian

Easter (Passover)   Paschal
Eire   Eireann
Elysium   Elysian
Epicurus   Epicurean
Erastus   Erastian
Estival   of Summer
Etruria (Roman province)   Etrurian, Etruscan, Tyrrhenian
Euclid   Euclidean
The Fall   Lapsarian
Faroe Is.   Faroese
Flanders   Flemish (*native* Fleming)
The Flood   Diluvian
Florence   Florentine
St. Francis   Franciscan
Friesland   Fri(e)sian
Galilee (Israel)   Galilean
Gallic   of France, Gaul
Galloway   Gallovidian
Gaul   Gallic, Gaulish
King George, Georgia (U.S. and U.S.S.R.)   Georgian
Gilbert and Sullivan   Savoyard
Glasgow   Glaswegian
Gloucester   Glostonian
God   Divine
Goth   Gothic
Greece   Greek, Hellenic
Pope Gregory   Gregorian

Grimsby Grimbarian
Hebrew Hebraic
Hebrides Hebridean
Hellenic Greek
Helvetian, Helvetic Swiss
Heracles, Hercules Heraclean, Herculean
Hermes Hermetic
Hibernian Irish
Hiemal of Winter
Hippocrates Hippocratic
Hispanic Spanish
Hitler Hitlerian
Thomas Hobbes Hobbesian
Holland Dutch (*native* Dutchman, Hollander)
Homer Homeric
Q. Horatius Flaccus (Horace) Horatian
Hudibras Hudibrastic
Hull Hullensian
Hun Hunnish
Hungary Hungarian, Magyar
John Huss Hussite
Hymen (Gk. God of Marriage) Hymeneal
Iceland Icelandic (*native* Icelander)
Inca Inca
Iraq, Irak Iraqui, Iraki
Ireland Irish, Hibernian, Milesian
Islam Islamic, Islamitic
Israel Israeli

Jacobite a follower of the Old or Young
   Pretender
Monastery of St. Jacques Jacobin
King James Jacobean
Jan(e)ite of Jane Austen
Japheth Japhetic
Java Javanese
Jehova Jehovistic
Jew Jewish, Judaic, Semitic
St. John Johannine
Julian of Julius Caesar
Kent Kentish (see KENT)
The Koran Koranic
Lacedaemonian, Laconian Spartan
Joseph Lancaster Lancasterian
Lancaster, Lancashire Lancastrian
Laos Laotian
Lapsarian of The Fall of Man
Latvia Latvian, Lettish
St. Lawrence River Laurentian
D. H. Lawrence, T. E. Lawrence
   Lawrencian
Lebanon Lebanese
Leeds Leodiensian
Leicester Leicestrian
Lenin Leninist
Lettic, Lettish of Lithuania
The Levant Levantine
Lithuania Lettic

Liverpool   Liverpudlian, Scouse
John Locke   Lockian
Lutetian   Parisian
Luther   Lutheran
Magyar   Hungarian
Malaya   Malay, Malayan
Malta   Maltese
I. of Man   Manx
Manchester   Mancunian
Maori   Maori
Christopher Marlowe   Marlovian
Mars   Martian
Karl Marx   Marxian, Marxist
Queen Mary   Marian
The Virgin Mary   Marian
the Medici   Medicean
Messiah   Messianic
Milesian   Irish
John Milton   Miltonic
Minos (Crete)   Minoan
Mohammed (Mahomet)   Mohammedan
   (Mahomedan), Moslem (Muslim)
Montenegro (Yugoslavia)   Montenegrin
Moor   Moorish, Moresque (architecture)
Morpheus (God of Sleep)   Morphean,
   Morphetic
Moscow   Muscovite
Moses   Mosaic
The Nine Muses   Pierian

Mycenae (Greece)   Mycenaean
Naples   Neapolitan
Nazareth   Nazarene
Negro   Negro negroid
Emperor Nero   Neronian
New Zealand   Zelanian
Nicaea (Asia Minor)   Nicene
River Nile   Nilotic
Norse   Scandinavian
Odysseus   Odyssean
Olympia (Greece)   Olympic
Mt. Olympus   Olympian
Orkney Is.   Orcadian
Ottoman   Turkish
Oxford   Oxonian
Pakistan   Pakistani
Pan (God of Flocks)   Pandean
Panama   Panamanian
Paris   Parisian, Lutetian (*poetic*)
Parma (Italy)   Parmesan
The Passover   Paschal
St. Paul   Pauline
The Pentecost   Pentecostal
Pericles   Periclean
Peru   Peruvian
Pharaoh   Pharaonic
Pharisee   Pharisaic
Philippine Is.   Filipino (*native m.* Filipino,
  f. Filipina)

Pierian of the Muses
Plato   Platonic
Poland   Polish, Polack (*native* Pole, Polack)
Pollokshaws   Pollokshavian
Pompeii (Italy)   Pompeian
Alexander Pope   Popian
The Pope   Papal, Popish (*derogatory*)
Portugal   Portuguese
the Old or Young Pretender   Jacobite
Provence (France)   Provençal
Ptolemy   Ptolemaic
Punic Carthaginian
Pyrrho   Pyrrhonic
Pyrrhus   Pyrrhic
Pythagoras   Pythagorean
Pythian Apollonian, Delphic
Quaker   Quakerish, Quakerly
The Quattrocento   Quattrocentist
Don Quixote   Quixotic
Raphael   Raphaelesque
Rembrandt   Rembrandtesque
River Rhine   Rhenish
I. of Rhodes   Rhodian
Rhodesia   Rhodesian
Rugby   Rugbeian
Russia   Russian, Muscovite
Sabbath   Sabbatic
Sadducee   Sadducean
Salopian of Shropshire

Samaria   Samaritan
Satan   Satanic, Satanical
Savoy, Savoyard of Gilbert and Sullivan
Scandinavia   Scandinavian, Norse
Scilly Is.   Scillonian
Scotland   Scottish, Scots, Caledonian (see SCOT)
Semitic Jewish (properly includes Arabs, Syrians, Phoenicians, Assyrians)
September   Septembral
Seric of China
George Bernard Shaw   Shavian
Shrewsbury, Shropshire   Salopian
Sibyl   Sibylline
Sicily   Sicilian, Trinacrian (*poetic*)
Sienna (Italy)   Sienese
Mt. Sinai   Sinaitic
Singhalese of Ceylon
Sinic Chinese
Sioux Indians   Siouan
Sistine   Pope Sixtus
Solihull   Silhillian
Solomon   Solomonic
Spain   Spanish, Hispanic
Sparta   Spartan, Lacedaemonian, Laconian
Spring   Vernal
Strasbourg   Strasbourgeois
Strathaven   Stravonian

Summer   (A)estival
Switzerland   Swiss, Helvetian, Helvetic
Tangiers   Tangerine
Thebes (Greece)   Theban
Theocritus   Theocritean
Thespis   Thespian
Thomist   St. Thomas Aquinas
Thrace (Greece)   Thracian
Titian   Titianesque
Abbey of La Trappe   Trappist
Council of Trent   Tridentine
Trinacrian   Sicilian
The Trinity   Trinitarian
Troy   Trojan
Tullian   Ciceronian
Turkey   Turkish, Ottoman
Tuscany (Italy)   Tuscan
Austrian Tyrol   Tyrolean, Tyrolese
Tyrrhenian   Etrurian
St. Ursula   Ursuline
Vandemonian   of Tasmania
Venice   Venetian
Vernal   of Spring
Vesta (Goddess of the Hearth)   Vestal
Mt. Vesuvius   Vesuvian
Vienna   Viennese
St. Vincent   Vincential, Vincentian
Wales   Welsh, Cambrian, Cymric (*natives*
  Welshmen, Cymri)

W. Australia   Westralian
Whig   Whiggish
Winchester College   Wykehamist
Winter   Brumal, Hiemal
Wolverhampton   Wulfrunian
Wycliffe   Wycliffite
House of York   Yorkist
York   Eborian
Zanzibar   Zanzibari
Zelanian   of New Zealand
Emile Zola   Zolaesque, Zolaist

2. AMERICAN WORDS AND PHRASES

N.B. Pure differences in spelling are not included. For further information on usage see AMERICAN USAGE in the dictionary.

American	*English*
absorbent cotton	cotton wool
acclimate	acclimatize
adhesive tape	sticking plaster
admit to the bar (*law*)	call to the bar
airplane	aeroplane
airfield	aerodrome
aluminum	aluminium
apartment	flat (cf. *flat* in American list)
apartment-hotel	service flats
artsy-craftsy	arty-crafty
ashcan	ashbin, dustbin
automobile	car
baby carriage *or* buggy	perambulator (pram) *or* baby coach
baggage car	luggage van
baseboard	skirting (board)
bath (*noun* as in *sea bath*)	bathe
bathrobe	dressing gown
beet	beetroot
bellboy, bellhop	page, buttons

352

bill	banknote, note
billboard	hoarding
billfold	wallet, notecase
billion	milliard
biscuit	scone, teacake
blank (*noun*)	form
boner	howler
boxcar	goods van
braid	plait
broiled (meat)	grilled
bughouse (*coll*)	nut house, loony bin (*coll*)
bulletin board	notice board
burglarize	burgle
burlap	hessian
business suit	lounge suit
caboose (railroad)	brake van
cab stand	cab rank, taxi rank
calaboose	clink (*coll*)
campground	camping ground
can (container)	tin
candy	sweets
cane	stick
car (railway passenger)	coach
check	bill, cheque
checkers	draughts
checkroom	left-luggage office or cloakroom

cigar store	tobacconist's shop
clerk	shop assistant
clothespin	clothespeg
coal oil, kerosene	paraffin
collar button	collar stud, back stud
comfort station	public lavatory
common stock	ordinary shares
commuter's ticket, commutation ticket	season ticket
concertmaster	leader (of symphony orchestra)
conductor (*rail*)	guard
confidence game	confidence trick
cookbook	cookery book
cookie	biscuit
copyreader (*newspaper*)	sub-editor
cotton candy	candy floss
corn	maize ('cattle food')
corporation	limited liability company
creamer	cream jug
cuff (of pants)	turn-up
deck (of cards)	pack
deliveryman (e.g. of milk or bread)	roundsman
Department of State	Foreign Office
derby	bowler

detour (*road*)	road diversion, traffic diversion, or loopway
diaper	napkin, nappy
dining car, diner	restaurant car
dinner pail	lunch box
dirt (*gardening*)	soil
dishpan	washing-up bowl
distributor (of merchandise)	stockist
district attorney or state's attorney	public prosecutor
domestic mails	inland mails
dove	dived
druggist	chemist
dry-goods store	draper's shop
dumbwaiter	service lift
editorial (*noun*)	leading article, leader
electric heater	radiator (*this word used for hot water or steam heat*), electric fire
elevator	lift
express company	carrier
extension courses	extramural studies
extension wire	flex
eyeglasses	spectacles
fall	autumn

faucet	tap
fender	wing, mudguard
finishing nails	panel pins
fink	blackleg
fire department	fire brigade
first balcony	dress circle
first floor	ground floor
fixtures	fittings
flashlight	torch
flat	puncture
flophouse	doss house
footpath	pavement
freight car	goods waggon, goods van
French fries	chips
game (of football)	match
garbage can	dustbin
garbageman	dustman
garter (men's)	sock suspender
garter belt	suspender belt
gas	petrol
gearshift	gear-lever
general delivery (*post office*)	poste restante
generator	dynamo
girl scout	girl guide
given name, first name	Christian name
grab bag	lucky dip

grade (*noun*, e.g. of a road)	gradient
grade (*school*)	form, standard, class
grade crossing (*rail*)	level crossing
grippe	influenza
grocery	grocer's shop, grocer's
ground wire	earth wire
handicart	truck
highboy	tallboy
hood (of car)	bonnet
hoosegow	prison
hot-water heater	geyser
icebox	refrigerator
identification tag	identity disk
installment plan	hire-purchase system, hire system, 'never-never'
internal revenue	inland revenue
janitor	caretaker, porter
lifeguard	lifesaver
life preserver	life belt
line up (*verb*)	queue up
lost-and-found department	lost property office
lumber	timber
mad	angry
mail car, railway post office	postal van

mailman	postman
master of ceremonies	compère
mean	unpleasant, evil
mineral oil	liquid paraffin
mortician	undertaker
movies	cinema, films, flick(er)s
muffler	silencer
newsstand	kiosk
notions	haberdashery
oarlock	rowlock
oatmeal (boiled)	porridge
office (doctor's or dentist's)	surgery
oil pan	sump
one-way ticket	single ticket
operating cost	running cost, working expense
orchestra seat	stall
pacifier	dummy
paid-in	paid-up
package	parcel
pants	trousers
parking lot	car park
patrolman (*police*)	constable
pavement	paved surface, road, paving
pay station	public telephone
penitentiary	prison

penpoint	nib
personal (*business*)	private
phonograph	gramophone, record player
pie (fruit)	tart
pit	stone (of fruit)
pocketbook	handbag, purse, wallet
polyethylene	polythene
poolroom	billiards saloon, hall
potato chip	crisp
potpie	meat pie, stew
preferred stock	preference shares
public comfort station	public convenience
publisher (newspaper)	proprietor
purse	handbag
Quonset (*trademark*)	Nissen hut (*approx.*)
race track	race course
railroad	railway
raise (in pay)	rise
realtor	estate agent
recess (school)	break
rooming house	boarding house
round-trip ticket	return ticket
rube	country bumpkin
run (in stocking)	ladder
saloon keeper	publican

schoolbag	satchel
scratchpad	scribbling block
scrubwoman	charwoman
sedan	saloon car
sidewalk	pavement
silent partner (in business)	sleeping partner
slingshot	catapult
smoked herring	kipper
soda biscuit, cracker	cream cracker
spark plug	sparking plug
spool (of thread)	reel (of cotton)
sporting goods	sports requisites, sports goods
spread-eagleism	jingoism
squash	vegetable marrow
state's evidence	King's or Queen's evidence
stenographer	shorthand writer
stock (in public company)	share
stone-broke	stony-broke
stop-and-go	stop-go
store	shop
straight (of a drink)	neat
streetcar	tram, trolley
subway	underground
surplus (corporation)	reserve
suspenders	braces

taffy	toffee
tax-exempt	tax-free
taxicab stand	taxi rank
temblor	earth tremor
thumbtack	drawing pin
ticket agent (*rail*)	booking clerk
ticket office (*rail*)	booking office
tie (*rail*)	sleeper
tie-up	hold-up
tire	tyre
track (*rail*)	platform
traffic circle	roundabout
trash can	dustbin
trolley, streetcar	tram, tramcar
trot (in school)	crib
truck	lorry
truck farm, garden	market garden
truck line	road haulier
trunk	box, boot (of car)
tube	wireless valve
unemployment compensation	unemployment benefit
union suit	combinations
vacationist	holidaymaker
vacuum bottle, thermos bottle	thermos flask
valance	pelmet
vaudeville	variety
vaudeville theater	music hall

vest	waistcoat
veterinarian	veterinary surgeon
washday	washing day
washrag	face flannel
weather bureau	meteorological office
windshield	windscreen
wiretapping	phonetapping
withholding tax	P.A.Y.E. (*approx.*)
witness stand	witness box
yard	garden
zee (the letter)	zed
zip code	postal code
zipper	zip, zip fastener

3. INDEX OF ABBREVIATIONS AND FOREIGN WORDS AND PHRASES COMMONLY USED IN ENGLISH

Included in this list are (a) abbreviations for: commercial terms; military ranks and units; naturally occurring elements; academic honours; military and civil honours; the books of the Bible; the British counties which have an abbreviated form approved by the G.P.O.; the American states; international organizations; international car registration letters; legal terms; weights and measures; bibliographical and grammatical apparatus etc. (b) words and phrases commonly used in spoken and written English either in their original form or anglicized slightly. These terms occur in cookery, music, politics, legal English and in many quotations from Latin and spoken languages. (For information on using these terms see FOREIGN WORDS AND PHRASES)

A

A argon; adult (motion picture certificate); (*international registration*) Austria.

A. anna; answer; (with other initials) Academy, Acting, Amateur, American, Assistant, Associate, Association.

a. acre; aged; accepted; afternoon; (*mus.*) alto; before (L. *ante*).

A.A. anti-aircraft; Associate in Arts; Automobile Association; Alcoholics Anonymous.

A.A.A. Amateur Athletic Association.

A.A.C. in the year before Christ (L. *anno ante Christum*).

A. & M. (Hymns) Ancient and Modern.

A.B. able seaman; see **B.A.**

à bas (F.) down with.

abbatoir (F.) slaughterhouse.

abbr., abbrev. abbreviation.

abd. abdicated.

Abend (G.) evening.

ab extra (L.) from without.

ab initio (L.) (**ab init.**) from the beginning.

ab intra (L.) from within.

abl. ablative.

A.B.P. Associated Book Publishers.

Abp. Archbishop.

abr. abridged, abridgement.

A.B.S. American Bible Society; American Bureau of Shipping.

abs., absol. absolutely.

abs., abstr. abstract.

abs. re. the defender being absent (L. *absente reo*).

A.B.T.A. Association of British Travel Agents.

A.C. Aero Club; Athletic Club; Alternating Current; Appeal Court; aircraftman; before Christ (L. *ante Christum*); in the year of Christ (L. *anno Christi*).

Ac actinium.

a/c account.

A.C.C. Army Catering Corps.

acc., accus. accusative.

A.C.G.B. Arts Council of Great Britain.

à cheval (F.) on horseback.

Achtung (G.) look out; beware.

A.C.M. Air Chief-Marshal.

actionnaire (F.) a shareholder.

A.D. in the year of our Lord (L. *anno Domini*).

adagio (*mus.*) slow(ly).

ad astra (L.) to the stars.

A.D.C. aide-de-camp; Amateur Dramatic Club.

add. addendum.

addio (It.) good-bye.

ad finem (L.) (**ad fin.**) to the end.

ad hoc (L.) 'for this special purpose.'

ad hominem (L.) to the man.

ad infinitum (L.) (**ad infin.**) to infinity, for ever.

ad interim (L.) (**ad int.**) in the meanwhile.

adiós (Sp.) good-bye.

adj. adjective.

Adj., Adjt. Adjutant.

ad libitum (L.) (**ad lib.**) 'at pleasure,' freely.

ad locum (L.) (**ad loc.**) at the place.

Adm. Admiral, Admiralty.

ad majorem Dei gloriam (L.) 'to the greater glory of God.'

ad nauseam (L.) 'to the point of disgust'; enough to make one sick.

ad referendum (L.) for consideration.

ad rem (L.) to the point.

à droite (**gauche**) (F.) to the right (left).

adsum (L.) 'I am here'; present!

ad unguem factus (L.) 'done to the nail'; finished to the last detail.

adv. adverb; against (L. *adversus*).

ad valorem (L.) (**ad val.**) according to the value.

advert., advt. advertisement.

aegrotat (L.) a note certifying that a student is ill and unable to attend lectures.

aet., aetat. aged (so many years) (L. *aetatis*).

A.E.U. Amalgamated Engineering Union.

A.F.A. Amateur Football Association.

affaire de coeur (F.) 'affair of the heart.'

affaire d'honneur (F.) 'an affair of honour,' i.e. a duel.

affiche (F.) poster, placard.

Afgh. Afghanistan.

à fond (F.) 'to the bottom'; thoroughly.

a fortiori (L.) with stronger reason.

Ag silver (L. *argentum*).

agent provocateur (F.) a police or secret service spy.

A.G.M. Annual General Meeting.

A.H. in the year of the Hegira, i.e. dating from A.D. 622 (L. *anno Hegirae*).

à haute voix (F.) loudly, aloud.

A.I.D. Artificial Insemination by Donor.

AL (*international registration*) Albania.

Al aluminium.

Ala. Alabama.

à la belle étoile (F.) in the open air.

à la bonne heure (F.) well and good; that's fine.

à la carte (F.) choosing from the bill of fare; *see* **table d'hôte**.

à la française (F.) in the French style.

à la mode (F.) in fashion.

Alas. Alaska.

Alba (Gael.) Scotland.

Albannach (Gael.) a Scot.

Ald. Alderman.

al fresco (It.) in the open air.

alg. algebra.

allegro (*mus.*) quickly.

allez-vous-en (F.) go away!

alma mater (L.) 'benign mother' (used by former students with reference to their university).

alt. alternate; altitude; (*mus.*) alto.

Alta. Alberta.

alter ego (L.) 'another self,' i.e. a close friend.

alter idem (L.) another exactly the same.

A.M. Air Ministry; Albert Medal; Hail Mary (L. *Ave Maria*); see **M.A.** (L. *Magister Artium*).

A.-M. Alpes-Maritimes, a department of France.

a.m. before noon (L. *ante meridiem*).

amen (Heb.) 'so be it'.

amende honorable (F.) apology, honourable reparation.

amor patriae (L.) love of one's country.

amor vincit omnia (L.) 'love overcomes all things.'

amour-propre (F.) self-esteem.

A.M.S. Army Medical Staff.

amt. amount.

anal. analysis; analogy.

ananas (F.) pineapple.

anat. anatomy.

ancien régime (F.) the old order (used especially of France before 1789).

AND (*international registration*) Andorra.

anglice (L.) in English.

anno aetatis suae (L.) 'in the year of his/her age'; at the age of.

anno Domini (L.) (**A.D.**) 'in the year of our Lord', i.e. so many years after the birth of Christ.

anno urbis conditae (L.) (**A.U.C.**) 'in the year from the building of the city', i.e. so many years after the building of Rome.

annus mirabilis (L.) year of wonder.

anon. anonymous.

A.N.S. Army Nursing Service.

an e meridiem *see* **a.m.**

A.N.Z.A.C. Australian and New Zealand Army Corps.

A.O. Army Order.

A.O.C. Air Officer Commanding.

A.O.D. Army Ordnance Department.

à outrance (F.) to the utmost.

Ap., Apr. April.

ap. in the works of (L. *apud*).

A.P.D. Army Pay Department.

a posteriori (L.) from effect to cause; by experiment.

app. appendix.

appartement (F.) suite of rooms, flat.

appro. approbation, approval; **on appro.** on approval.

approx. approximate(ly).

après-midi (F.) afternoon.

a priori (L.) from cause to effect.

à propos (F.) to the point; **à propos de** concerning.

aqua vitae (L.) 'water of life,' brandy.

A.R. in the year of the reign (L. *anno regni*).

arbiter elegantiarum (or **elegantiae**) (L.) a judge in matters of taste.

Archd. Archdeacon.

archit. architecture.

aria (*mus.*) a melodic set-piece in opera; *see* **recitative**.

Ariz. Arizona.

Ark. Arkansas.

arpeggio (*mus.*) the notes of a chord played in rapid succession.

arr. arrives.

arrière-pensée (F.) mental reservation.

ars longa vita brevis (L.) 'art is long, life short', i.e. work of art can survive the death of the artist.

A.S. Anglo-Saxon.

As Arsenic.

A.S.R. Air-Sea Rescue.

assiette (F.) plate.

Assoc. Associate; Association.

Asst. Assistant.

astr., astron. astronomer, astronomy.

astrol. astrology.

A.T.C. Air Training Corps.

atelier (F.) workshop, studio.

à tort et à travers (F.) at random.

Att. Attorney.

A.U. Ångström unit.

Au gold (L. *aurum*).

A.U.C. *see* **anno urbis conditae.**

au courant (F.) fully acquainted (with).

au fait (F.) well-informed, knowledgeable.

auf Wiedersehen (Ger.) goodbye, till we meet again.

Aug. August.

au pis aller (F.) 'if the worst comes to worst.'

au revoir (F.) goodbye till we meet again.

AUS (*international registration*) Australia, Norfolk Island.

auto da fé (Port.) 'act of faith'; public burning of heretics.

autres temps, autres mœurs (F.) 'other times, other customs.'

aut vincere aut mori (L.) victory or death.

A.V. Authorised Version (of the Bible).

av. average.

avant-garde (F.) the vanguard of an army; those with the latest ideas.

avant-propos (F.) preliminary matter, preface.

A.V.C. Army Veterinary Corps.

avdp., avoir. avoirdupois.

Ave. Avenue.

ave Maria (L.) hail Mary.

A.V.M. Air Vice-Marshal.

a vostra salute (It.) Your health!

à votre santé (F.) Your health!

A.W. Atomic Weight; all-widths (of cut timber).

ax. axiom.

B

B boron, black (of pencil-lead); (*international registration*) Belgium.

B. (*mus.*) bass; (with other initials) British, Bachelor, Blessed (L. *beatus, beata.*)

b. born; book; bowled (by); brother.

B.A. Bachelor of Arts (L. *Baccalaureus Artium*); British Academy.

Ba barium.

Baccalauréat (F.) school-leaving certificate in France.

bain-marie (F.) a double saucepan.

bal. balance.

ballade (*mus.*) either a medieval song with refrain or an instrumental piece of a lyrical or romantic nature.

B.A.O.R. British Army of the Rhine.

Bap., Bapt. Baptist.

bap., bapt. baptised.

Bar. barrister.

bar. barometer (–tric); barrel.

barcarolle (*mus.*) originally a boating-song, hence any music with a persistent but relaxed rhythm.

Bart., Bt. Baronet.

Bart's St. Bartholomew's Hospital.

basta! (It.) enough!

batt. battery; battalion.

Bav. Bavaria(n).

B.B. Boys' Brigade.

BB double black (of pencil-lead); **BBB** treble black.

B.B.C. British Broadcasting Corporation.

B.C. Before Christ; British Columbia; British Council; Board of Control; battery commander; bomber command; battle cruiser; Boat Club; Bowling Club.

B.D. Bachelor of Divinity.

Bd. Board.

Bde. Brigade.

Bdg. Building.

Bdr. Bombardier.

BDS (*international registration*) Barbados.

B/E bill of exchange.

Be beryllium.

B.E.A. British European Airways.

beatae memoriae (L.) of blessed memory.

beau idéal (F.) ideal excellence, imagined state of perfection.

beau monde (F.) fashionable world.

béchamel (F.) white sauce.

Beds Bedfordshire.

bel canto (*mus.*) 'fine singing'; a florid style of singing at its most popular in the eighteenth century.

bel esprit (F.) a man of wit.

belles-lettres (F.) literature; learning.

Belg. Belgium, Belgian.

B.E.M. British Empire Medal.

benvenuti (It.) welcome.

berceuse (*mus.*) 'cradle song,' or any music which suggests this.

Berks Berkshire.

bête noire (F.) an object of special detestation, a pet aversion.

bêtise (F.) a stupid action or remark.

b/f brought forward.

b.f. bloody fool.

B.F.I. British Film Institute.

B.F.P.O. British Forces Post Office.

BG (*international registration*) Bulgaria.

BH (*international registration*) British Honduras.

B'ham Birmingham.

B'head Birkenhead.

B. Hond. British Honduras.

b.h.p. brake horse-power.

Bi bismuth.

Bib. Bible, Biblical.

B.I.F. British Industries Fair.

biftek (F.) beef-steak.

billet(s) doux (F.) love-letter(s).

biog. biography (–ical).

biol. biology (–ical).

bistecca (It.) beef-steak.

bitte (G.) please; excuse me.

bk. book.

bkg. banking.

bkrpt. bankrupt.

bkt. basket.

BL (*international registration*) Basutoland.

bl. barrel; bale.

blanquette (F.) stew of white meat, esp. veal, rabbit.

bldg. building.

B. Litt. (L.) Bachelor of Letters.

Blitzkrieg (G.) 'lightning war', i.e. a war intended to be short and decisive.

blvd. boulevard.

B.M. British Museum; Brigade-Major; of blessed memory; bench mark.

B.M.A. British Medical Association.

Bn. Baron.

b.o. buyer's option; branch office; body odour.

B.O.A.C. British Overseas Airways Corporation.

boeuf à la mode (F.) stewed steak and vegetables.

B. of E. Bank of England; Board of Education.

B. of H. Band of Hope

Bol. Bolivia(n).

bona fide (L.) in good faith.

bonhomie (F.) good nature.

bonjour (F.) good day, good morning.

bon marché (F.) cheaply.

bon mot (F.) a witty saying, an aphorism.

bonne-bouche (F.) a delicious titbit.

bonsoir (F.) good evening, goodnight.

bon ton (F.) good breeding, good taste.

bon vivant (F.) epicure; good companion.

bon voyage (F.) a pleasant journey!

bor. borough.

bot. botany, botanical; bought.

B.O.T. Board of Trade.

boutique (F.) shop, esp. a fashion shop.

BP (*international registration*) Bechuanaland.

Bp. Bishop.

b.p. birthplace; bills payable; boiling-point;
below proof.

B.Q. 'may he/she rest well' (L. *bene quiescat*).

BR (*international registration*) Brazil.

Br bromine.

Br., Bro. brother. (*pl.* **Bros.**)

bravo (It.) well done! splendid!

bravura (*mus.*) technical or vocal virtuosity in
music.

Braz. Brazil(ian).

breveté(e) (F.) patented.

BRG (*international registration*) British Guiana.

Brig. Brigade; Brigadier.

Brit. Britain; Britannia; Briton; British.

Britt Omn. (on coins) 'of all the Britains'

BRN (*international registration*) Bahrain.

Bro(s). Brother(s).

brom bromide.

BRU (*international registration*) Brunei.

B/S Bill of Sale.

BS (*international registration*) Bahamas.

B.Sc. Bachelor of Science.

B.S.I. British Standards Institution.

Bt. Baronet.

bt. bought.

Btu. British Thermal Unit.

Bucks Buckinghamshire.

Bulg. Bulgaria(n).

BUR (*international registration*) Burma.

B.V.M. The Blessed Virgin Mary (L. *Beata Virgo Maria*).

B.W.I. British West Indies.

C

C carbon; (*international registration*) Cuba.

C. centigrade; Cape; Conservative; 100; (with other initials) Catholic, Central, Commander, Companion, Consul.

c. cent; centigram; centime; centimetre; century; chapter; cubic; about, approximately (L. *circa*); (in cricket) caught.

Ca calcium.

cadenza (*mus.*) virtuoso piece for solo instrument in a concerto.

Cal. California.

Cambs Cambridgeshire.

campanile (It.) bell-tower (of a cathedral, usually separate from the main building).

campo santo (It.) a burial ground.

canapé d'anchois (F.) anchovy on toast.

Cantab. of Cambridge (L. *Cantabrigiensis*).

Cantuar. of Canterbury (L. *Cantuariensis*).

cap. capital letter; chapter (L. *caput*).

Capo d'Anno (It.) New Year's Day.

capolavoro (It.) a masterpiece.

Capt. Captain.

car. carat.

Card. Cardinal.

carême (F.) Lent.

Carms Carmarthenshire.

carpe diem (L.) sieze the opportunity.

carte blanche (F.) full powers.

casus belli (L.) something which leads to war.

Cath. Catholic.

cath. cathode.

cause célèbre (F.) law case that attracts much attention.

Cav. Cavalry.

ça va sans dire (F.) that is a matter of course.

cave canem (L.) beware of the dog.

C.B. Companion of the order of the Bath; Common Bench; confined to barracks; County Borough.

C.B.C. Canadian Broadcasting Company.

C.B.E. Commander of the Order of the British Empire.

C.B.I. Confederation of British Industries.

C.B.S. Columbia Broadcasting System; Confraternity of the Blessed Sacrament.

C.C. Chamber of Commerce; Circuit Court; Civil Court; Corpus Christi; County Council; County Councillor; County Court; Cricket Club; Cycling Club.

c.c. cubic centimetre.

cc. chapters.

C.C.C. Central Criminal Court; Corpus Christi College.

C.C.P. Court of Common Pleas.

C.D. Chancery Division, Civil Defence; contagious diseases; Corps Diplomatique.

Cd cadmium.

CDN (*international registration*) Canada.

C.E. Church of England (sometimes C. of E.); Civil Engineer.

Ce cerium.

Céilidh (Gael.) a social evening with songs and story-telling.

Cels. Celsius (thermometer).

Cent. Centigrade.

C.E.M.A. Council for the Encouragement of Music and the Arts.

cent. a hundred; central; century.

cert. certificate; certificated; certified.

Cestr. of Chester (L. *Cestrensis*).

cetera desunt (L.) 'the rest is lacking.'

ceteris paribus (L.) (**cet. par.**) 'other things being equal.'

cf. compare (L. *confer*); (in binding) calf.

c/f carried forward.

c.f.i. cost, freight and insurance.

C.G. Captain-General; Captain of the Guard; Coastguard; Coldstream Guards; Commissary-General; Consul-General; Croix de Guerre (French military decoration).

cg. centigram.

C.G.M. Conspicuous Gallantry Medal.

CGO (*international registration*) Congo.

CH (*international registration*) Switzerland.

C.H. Companion of Honour; Court-House; Custom-House.

Ch. Church.

ch. chapter.

chaconne (*mus.*) stately music, orig. for a dance, in triple time (also called *passacaglia*).

chacun à son goût (F.) everyone to his taste.

Chap. Chaplain; chapter.

charlotte russe (F.) custard and sponge cake.

Chas. Charles.

chef d'orchestre (*mus.*) leader of the orchestra.

chef-d'oeuvre (F.) masterpiece.

cherchez la femme (F.) 'look for the woman,' i.e. there is a woman at the bottom of the business.

che sarà, sarà (It.) what will be, will be.

chicanerie (F.) trickery, quibbling.

chq. cheque.

Chron. Chronicles (O.T.)

chron. chronological; chronology.

CI (*international registration*) Ivory Coast.

C.I. Channel Islands; Chief Inspector.

Cicestr. of Chichester (L. *Cicestrensis*).

C.I.A. Central Intelligence Agency (U.S.)

ciaò (It.) hello, goodbye.

C.I.D. Criminal Investigation Department.

ci-devant (F.) former.

Cie. Company (F. *Compagnie*).

c.i.f.c. cost, insurance, freight and commission

C.-in-C. Commander-in-Chief.

C.I.R. Committee for Industrial Relations.

cir. about (L. *circa, circiter*).

cit. citation; cited; citizen.

civ. civic; civil; civilian.

C.J. Chief Justice.

CL (*international registration*) Ceylon.

Cl chlorine.

cl. centilitre; class; clause; closed.

C.M. Master of Surgery (L. *Chirurgiae Magister*); (*mus.*) common metre; Corresponding Member.

cm. centimetre.

c.m. by reason of death (L. *causa mortis*).

C.M.G. Companion of the Order of St. Michael and St. George.

CNB (*international registration*) North Borneo.

CO (*international registration*) Colombia.

C.N.D. Campaign for Nuclear Disarmament.

C.O. Colonial Office; Commanding Officer; conscientious objector; Criminal Office; Crown Office.

Co cobalt.

Co. company; county.

c/o care of.

C.O.D. cash on delivery.

coda (*mus.*) 'tail', i.e. the end of a movement which restates the main themes.

C. of E. Church of England.

C. of S. Church of Scotland.

coiffeur (F.) hairdresser; **coiffure** way the hair is dressed.

Col. Colonel; Colossians (N.T.).

col. colour; column.

Coll. College.

coll. collected; colloquial (sometimes **colloq.**).

Colo. Colorado.

coloratura (*mus.*) extreme, often improvised ornamentation of the **v**ocal line.

Com. Commander; Commissioner; Committee; Commodore; Commonwealth; Communist.

com. commentary; commission; common.

Comdr. Commander.

Comdt. Commandant.

Cominform Communist Information Bureau.

Comintern Communist International.

comme il faut (F.) as it should be.

Commr. Commissioner.

communiqué (F.) official report.

comp. comparative; compositor; compound.

compos mentis (L.) of sound mind; sane.

compte rendu (F.) a report (of meeting etc.)

Con(**s**). Consul; Conservative.

con. against (L. *contra*).

con amore (It.) 'with love,' i.e. earnestly, passionately.

con brio (*mus.*) 'with vigour.'

concierge (F.) porter or doorkeeper.

concours (F.) a competition.

conf. conference; confederated; confederation.

confrère (F.) fellow-member of profession, club, etc.

con fuoco (*mus.*) 'with fire.'

Cong. Congress.

congé see **P.P.C.**

conj. conjugation; conjunction.

Conn. Connecticut.

consommé (F.) clear soup.

constr. construction.

cont. continued.

contretemps (F.) untoward event, snag.

conversazione (It.) a meeting to discuss intellectual topics; a social gathering.

Co-op Co-operative Society.

Cor. Corinthians (N.T.); Coroner.

coram populo (L.) 'in the presence of the people,' i.e. openly, manifestly.

cordon bleu (F.) 'blue ribbon', used of someone of outstanding merit in some occupation, especially cooking.

Corp. Corporation; Corporal.

corpus delicti (L.) 'the body of the crime,' i.e. the substance of the offence.

corrigenda (L.) things to be corrected.

cos. cosine.

cosec. cosecant.

così fan tutte (It.) 'so do all (women).'

cot. cotangent.

coup d'état (L.) a sudden, often revolutionary political move; an abuse of authority.

coup de grâce (F.) a finishing blow.

coup d'oeil (F.) a glance.

coup de théâtre (F.) a theatrical effect, a dramatic and unforeseen happening.

384

coûte que coûte (F.) at any price.

C.P. carriage paid; Charter Party; Clerk of the Peace; Communist Party; Common Pleas; College of Preceptors.

c.p. candle-power.

cp. compare.

Cpl. Corporal.

C.P.O. Chief Petty Officer.

C.P.R. Canadian Pacific Railway.

CR (*international registration*) Costa Rica.

C.R. Keeper of the Rolls (L. *Custos Rotulorum*); King Charles (L. *Carolus Rex*).

Cr chromium.

cr. credit; creditor; crown.

C.R.A. Commander Royal Artillery.

C.R.E. Commander Royal Engineers.

crème de la crème (F.) the very best.

Cres. Crescent (as an address).

cresc. (*mus.*) growing louder (It. *crescendo*).

croquette (F.) rissole.

c.r.t. cathode-ray tube.

CS (*international registration*) Czechoslovakia.

C.S. Chemical Society; Civil Service; Clerk to the Signet; (*cinema*) close shot; Common Serjeant; Court of Session; Keeper of the Seal (L. *Custos Sigilli*).

Cs caesium.

C.S.C. Civil Service Commission.

C.S.M. Company Sergeant Major.

Ct. Court.

ct. carat; cent; caught.

C.U. Cambridge University *or* Union; (*cinema*) close-up.

Cu copper (L. *cuprum*).

cub. cubic.

cui bono? (L.) who gains by it? to whose advantage is it?

cul-de-sac (F.) a blind alley.

cum grano salis (L.) with a grain of salt, with reservation.

C.U.P. Cambridge University Press.

curt. current.

C.V.O. Commander of the (Royal) Victorian Order.

C.W.O. cash with order.

C.W.S. Co-operative Wholesale Society.

cwt. hundredweight.

CY (*international registration*) Cyprus.

D

D (*international registration*) Federal Republic of Germany.

D. (with other initials) Dame; Deputy; Doctor.

d. date; daughter; died *or* deceased; departs; dime; penny (L. *denarius*); diameter; delete.

D.A. days after acceptance; deposit account; Diploma of Art; District Attorney.

da capo (*mus.*) *see* **D.C.**

d'accord (F.) agreed, O.K.

dag. decagramme.

Dak. Dakota.

dal. decalitre.

dam. decametre.

Dan. Daniel (O.T.); Danish.

Danke! (Ger.) Thanks!

D.A.R. Daughters of the American Revolution.

dat. dative.

d.b. (*tailoring*) double-breasted; decibel.

D.B.E. Dame Commander of the Order of the British Empire.

D.C. District of Columbia; District Court; Direct Current; (*mus.*) repeat from the beginning (It. *da capo*).

d.c. decontamination; double column.

D.C.M. Distinguished Conduct Medal.

D.D. Doctor of Divinity; given as a gift (L. *dono dedit*).

D/D demand draft.

D.D.D. gives, devotes and dedicates (L. *dat dicat dedicat*).

D.D.T. dichloro-diphenyl-trichloro-ethane (an insecticide).

deb débutante; debenture.

début (F.) a first appearance in society or as a performer.

Dec. December.

dec. deceased; declination; decorated.

decl. declension.

déclassé(e) (F.) one who has gone down in the world.

décolleté(e) (F.) low-necked, leaving the shoulders bare.

de die in diem (L.) from day to day.

def. defendant; definition; deficiency; deficit.

de facto (L.) actually, in fact.

défense de fumer (F.) no smoking.

deg. degree.

Dei gratia (L.) by the grace of God.

de jure (L.) in law, by right.

Del. Delaware.

Delicatessen (G.) savoury cooked dishes; a shop which sells these.

de luxe (F.) luxurious, sumptuous.

Dem. Democrat.

démarche (F.) a diplomatic step.

demi-monde (F.) the world of prostitutes.

démodé(e) (F.) out of fashion.

de mortuis nil nisi bonum (L.) '(say) nothing but good about the dead.'

denom. denomination.

dénouement (F.) 'the untying,' i.e. the eventual outcome of a story or situation.

de novo (L.) anew, again.

dent. dental.

deoch an doruis (Gael.) 'a drink at the door,' i.e. one for the road.

Deo gratias (L.) thanks be to God.

Deo volente (L.) (**D.V.**) God willing.

dep. departs; deputy.

de profundis (L.) 'out of the depths' (the first words of Ps. 130 in Latin).

dept. department; deponent.

de rigueur (F.) indispensable; obligatory.

deriv. derivation; derived.

dernier cri (F.) the last word; the most up-to-date.

détente (F.) relaxing of diplomatic tension.

Det. Insp. Detective Inspector.

de trop (F.) superfluous, intrusive.

deus ex machina (L.) 'a god out of the (theatrical) machine,' i.e. a too obvious device in the plot of a play or story.

Deus vobiscum (L.) 'God (be) with you.'

Deut. Deuteronomy (O.T.)

D.F. Defender of the Faith; Dean of the Faculty; direction-finder.

D.F.C. Distinguished Flying Cross.

D.F.M. Distinguished Flying Medal.

D.G. Director-General; see **Dei gratia.**

Dg. decagram.

dg. decigram.

diam. diameter.

dies irae (L.) day of wrath.

dies non (L.) a day on which judges do not sit.

Dieu et mon droit (F.) 'God and my right'.

dim. (*mus.*) growing softer (It. *diminuendo*).

Dioc. Diocese; Diocesan.

Dir. Director.

Dist. District.

dist. distance; distant; distinction.

distingué(e) (F.) of distinguished appearance.

distrait(e) (F.) absent-minded.

Div. Division.

div. dividend.

divertissement (F.) entertainment.

D.J. Dinner Jacket; Disc Jockey.

DK (*international registration*) Denmark and Faroe Is.

Dl. decalitre.

dl. decilitre.

D. Litt. Doctor of Letters.

D.L.O. Dead Letter Office.

D.M. Deputy Master; Doctor of Medicine.

Dm. decametre.

dm. decimetre.

D.N.A. Deoxyribonucleic acid.

do. ditto, the same.

dolce far niente (It.) sweet idleness.

DOM (*international registration*) Dominican Republic.

Dom. Lord; Master (L. *Dominus*); Dominion.

dom. domestic.

D.O.M. to God the Best, the Greatest (L. *Deo optimo maximo*).

double entente (F.) (often **double entendre**) double meaning, one of which is sometimes improper.

douceur (F.) tip, present.

doyen (F.) champion (*fem.* **doyenne**).

D.Ph., D.Phil., Ph.D. Doctor of Philosophy.

D.P.P. Director of Public Prosecutions.

Dr Doctor; debtor.

dramatis personae (L.) (**dram. pers.**) the characters in a play.

D.S. Dental Surgeon; (*mus.*) repeat from point indicated (It. *dal segno*.)

D.S.C. Distinguished Service Cross.

D.S.M. Distinguished Service Medal.

D.T.(s) Delirium Tremens.

dum spiro, spero (L.) 'while I live, I hope.'

Dunelm. of Durham (L. *Dunelmensis*).

duvet (F.) stuffed quilt; eiderdown.

D.V. 'God Willing' (L. *Deo volente*).

d.v.p. died during father's lifetime (L. *decessit vita patris*).

dwt. pennyweight.

DY (*international registration*) Dahomey.

Dy dysprosium.

DZ (*international registration*) Algeria.

E

E (*international registration*) Spain, Balearic Is., Canary Is., Sp. Guinea, Sp. Sahara.

E. East; Eastern; (with other initials) English.

EAK (*international registration*) Kenya.

EAT (*international registration*) Tanganyika.

EAU (*international registration*) Uganda.

EAZ (*international regsitration*) Zanzibar.

ea. each.

E. and O.E. errors and omissions excepted.

eau de nil (F.) a shade of pale green.

Ebor. of York (L. *Eboracensis*).

EC (*international registration*) Ecuador.

E.C. East Central (postal district); Education Committee.

ecce homo (L.) 'behold the man' (spoken by Pilate: St. John c.19 v.5).

Eccl., Eccles. Ecclesiastes (O.T.); ecclesiastical.

Ecclus. Ecclasiasticus.

éclat. (F.) splendour; renown.

Ed. editor.

ed., edit. edited; edition.

Edin. Edinburgh.

éditeur (F.) publisher.

edn. edition.

E.E.C. European Economic Community.

E.F.T.A. European Free Trade Area.

e.g. for example (L. *exempli gratia*).

E.I. East Indies.

eisteddfod (Welsh) 'assembly,' particularly of Welsh bards competing for title.

ejusd. 'of the same' (L. *ejusdem*).

élan (F.) vivaciousness; infectious gaiety.

embarras de richesses (F.) perplexing choice; infinite variety.

emeritus (L.) honourably retired from office (esp. of a Professor).

e.m.f. electromotive force.

eminence grise (F.) the power behind the throne.

E.M.U. electro-magnetic unit(s).

encore (F.) again.

en déshabille (F.) not dressed for receiving company.

E.N.E. East-North-East.

en famille (F.) at home; informally.

enfants perdus (F.) a forlorn hope.

enfant terrible (F.) 'a terrible child,' i.e. a person who is embarrasingly unpredictable and impetuous.

en fête (F.) on holiday, in a holiday mood.

Eng. England; English.

eng. engineer; engineering.

engr. engraved; engraving.

en grande tenue (F.) in full military dress.

en masse (F.) in a body.

ennui (F.) boredom; world weariness.

en passant (F.) 'in passing,' by the way.

en rapport (F.) in sympathy, in touch (with).

en règle (F.) in due order.

en route (F.) on the way; march!

entente cordiale (F.) friendly understanding between two nations.

en train (F.) in progress.

entre nous (F.) between ourselves.

entrepôt (F.) Commercial centre, esp. for collection and distribution of goods.

Ent. Sta. Hall Entered at Stationers' Hall.

Ep. Epistle.

Eph. Ephesians (N.T.)

Epiph. Epiphany.

episc. episcopal.

e pluribus unum (L.) 'many made one' (motto of the U.S.A.)

E.P.N.S. Electro-plated Nickel Silver.

eq. equal.

equiv. equivalent.

E.R. King Edward (L. *Edwardus Rex*); Queen Elizabeth (L. *Elizabetha Regina*); East Riding (of Yorkshire).

Er erbium.

E.R.N.I.E. Electronic Random Number Indicator Equipment (used for selecting winning numbers in Premium Bonds Scheme).

erratum (L.) (*pl.* **errata**) error.

ersatz (G.) a substitute; used as an adjective to mean 'synthetic.'

E.S.E. East-South-East.

E.S.P. extra-sensory perception.

Esp. Esperanto.

esp. especially.

esprit de corps (F.) team-spirit.

Esq. Esquire.

est. established.,

Esth. Esther (O.T.)

E.S.U. electrostatic unit; English Speaking Union.

ET (*international registration*) Egypt.

et. al. and others (L. *et alia, et alii*); elsewhere (L. *et alibi*).

etc. and the rest (L. *et cetera*).

et seq., et seqq., et sq., et sqq. and the following (L. *et sequentes, et sequentia*).

E.T.U. Electrical Trades Union.

étude (*mus.*) a piece of music orig. designed to give practice in technique (Fr. study).

Eu europium.

Eur. Europe; European.

Euratom European Atomic Energy Commission.

eureka! (Gk.) (**heureka!**) 'I have found it!' (said by Archimedes).

ex. example; exception; export; executive; examined.

ex cathedra (L.) 'from the chair of office,' i.e. with authority.

exc. except; engraved by (L. *excudit*).

exeat (L.) 'let him go out,' i.e. formal leave of absence.

exit (L.) 'goes out.'

ex libris (L.) from the books (of).

ex officio (L.) 'by virtue of office,' i.e. officially.

Exon. of Exeter (L. *Exoniensis*).

exor. executor.

ex parte (L.) on one side, biased.

exposé (F.) an explanatory summary; a sensationally full account.

exrx. executrix.

Ez. Ezra (O.T.)

Ezek. Ezekiel (O.T.).

F

F fluorine; (*international registration*) France.

F. Fahrenheit; Friday; Father (R.C.); (with other initials) Fellow, *French*.

f. farthing; fathom; following (page); foot; filly; franc; folio; (*mus.*) loudly (It. *forte*).

F.A. Football Association; Fine Arts.

facile princeps (L.) easily first.

fac(s). facsimile.

Fahr. Fahrenheit.

fait accompli (F.) 'an accomplished fact.'

fam. familiar

fannullone (It.) idler, lounger, ne'er-do-well.

f.a.q. fair average quantity.

farci (F.) stuffed.

f.a.s. free alongside ship.

faute de mieux (F.) for want of anything better.

fauteuil (F.) stalls (in theatre); armchair.

faux pas (F.) a false step, a mistake.

F.B.I. Federal Bureau of Investigation.

fcap., fcp. foolscap.

Fe iron (L. *ferrum*).

Feb. February.

fec. made by (L. *fecit*).

fed. federal; federated.

felo de se (L.) 'a felon of himself,' i.e. a suicide.

fem. feminine.

festa (It.) festival, holiday.

festina lente (L.) hasten slowly.

Festspiel (G.) festival of music.

fête champêtre (F.) a country festival.

feu de joie (F.) a bonfire.

feuilleton (F.) literary article or instalment of a serial printed on the lower part of a newspaper page.

ff. following (pages); folios; (*mus.*) very loudly (It. *fortissimo*).

fff. (*mus.*) as loudly as possible (It. *fortississimo*).

F.H. fire hydrant.

fiat lux (L.) let there be light.

Fid. Def. Defender of the Faith (L. *Fidei Defensor*).

fiesta (Sp.) festival, holiday.

fig. figure; figurative.

fin. at the end (L. *finis*); financial.

fin de siècle (F.) end of the 19th century; decadent.

FL (*international registration*) Liechtenstein.

fl. florin; fluid; flourished.

Fla. Florida.

flagrante delicto (L.) in the very act; red-handed.

flamenco (Sp.) lit. 'Flemish.' Describes a variety of gipsy music esp. popular in Andalusia.

flâneur (F.) an idler, lounger.

Fleisch (G.) meat.

Flt. Lt. Flight-Lieutenant.

F.M. Field-Marshal; frequency modulations.

fm. fathom; from.

F.O. Foreign Office; Field Officer; Flying-Officer.

f.o. firm offer.

fo., fol. folio.

f.o.b. free on board.

fons et origo (L.) 'the source and origin.'

f.o.r. free on rail.

force majeure (F.) irresistible compulsion.

F.P. fire-plug; former pupil; field punishment.

Fr. Father (R.C.); Frau; French; Friday.

fr. fragment; franc; from.

F.R.A.M. Fellow of the Royal Academy of Music.

frappé (F.) iced.

F.R.C.M. Fellow of the Royal College of Music.

Fri. Friday.

Frl. Fräulein.

ft. foot; feet; fort; fortification.

fugue (*mus.*) interweaving of melodic strands which begin successively.

fur. furlong.

fut. future.

f.v. on the back of the page (L. *folio verso*).

G

G. (with other initials) General, Grand; *German*.

g. gauge; genitive; gramme; guinea.

Ga gallium

Ga. Georgia.

G.A. General Assembly.

Gael. *Gaelic*.

Gal. Galatians (N.T.)

gal. gallon(s).

galliard (F.) gay tune in triple time, used in contrast to the **pavane**.

gasconnade (F.) bragging, boastfulness.

gâteau (F.) cake.

G.A.T.T. General Agreement on Tariffs and Trade (1947).

gaudeamus igitur (L.) let us then rejoice.

GB (*international registration*) Great Britain.

G.B. Great Britain.

GBA (*international registration*) Alderney.

G.B.E. Grand Cross of the British Empire.

GBG (*international registration*) Guernsey.

G.B.H. Grievous Bodily Harm.

GBJ (*international registration*) Jersey.

GBM (*international registration*) I. of Man.

G.B.S. George Bernard Shaw.

GBY (*international registration*) Malta, Gozo.

GBZ (*international registration*) Gibraltar.

G.C. George Cross.

GCA (*international registration*) Guatemala.

G. (or **Gr.**) **Capt.** (R.A.F.) Group Captain

G.C.B. Grand Cross of the Bath.

G.C.E. General Certificate of Education.

G.C.F. greatest common factor.

G.C.M. General Court Martial; greatest common measure.

G.C.M.G. Grand Cross of St. Michael and St. George.

G.C.V.O. Grand Cross of the Victorian Order.

Gd gadolinum.

Ge germanium.

Gen. General; Genesis (O.T.)

gen. gender; genitive; general.

gendarme (F.) one of the gendarmerie, a body of armed police in France.

genre (F.) style or variety of art.

genus (L.) a race; a variety.

GH (*international registration*) Ghana.

G.I. American private soldier.

gigot (F.) leg of mutton.

Gk. Greek.

Gl glucinium.

Glam Glamorganshire.

glissando (*mus.*) a series of adjacent notes played so that they merge into each other.

Glos Gloucestershire.

gm. gramme.

G.M. George Medal; Grand Master.

G.M.T. Greenwich Mean Time.

G.O.M. Grand Old Man (originally used of W. E. Gladstone).

gourmand, gourmet see Dictionary.

Gov. Governor.

Govt. Government.

G.P. General Practitioner.

G.P.O. General Post Office.

G.P.U., Ogpu Soviet Russian Secret Police.

GR (*international registration*) Greece, Crete, Dodecanese Is.

G.R. King George (L. *Georgius Rex*).

Gr. Gunner.

gr. grain; gross.

gradus ad Parnassum (L.) a step towards greater learning.

Graf (G.) Count.

graffito (It.) (*pl.* **graffiti**) writing or drawing on wall or building.

gram. grammar; grammatical; gramophone.

G.S. general service; General Staff.

G.T. Gran Turismo.

G.T.C. Girls' Training Corps.

guerre à outrance (F.) 'war to the uttermost.'

G.W.R. Great Western Railway.

H

H hydrogen; (*international registration*) Hungary.

H. hard (of pencil-lead).

h. hour.

Hab. Habakkuk (O.T.).

hab. he lives (L. *habitat*).

habanera (Sp.) rhythmic Cuban dance also popular in Spain.

h. & c. hot and cold water.

hachis (F.) mincemeat.

Hag. Haggai (O.T.).

Hants Hampshire.

haricot (F.) thick stew.

haricots verts (F.) French beans.

hauteur (F.) haughtiness, arrogance.

haut ton (F.) the fashionable world.

HB. hard black (of pencil-lead).

H.B.M. His/Her Britannic Majesty.

H.C. House of Commons.

H.C.F. highest common factor.

hdqrs. headquarters.

H.E. high-explosive; His Eminence; His/Her Excellency.

He helium.

Heb. Hebrews (N.T.); Hebrew.

hectog. hectogramme.

hectol. hectolitre.

hectom. hectometre.

Heil! (G.) Hail!

Herts Hertfordshire.

H.F. High Frequency.

Hf hafnium.

hf. half.

H.G. His Grace; Home Guard; Horse Guards.

Hg mercury (L. *hydrargyrum*).

hg. hectogramme.

H.H. His/Her Highness; His Holiness (the Pope).

hhd. hogshead.

hic jacet (sepultus) (L.) **(H.J.S.)** 'here lies (buried).'

HK (*international registration*) Hong Kong.

H.K. House of Keys (Isle of Man).

H.L. House of Lords.

hl. hectolitre.

H.M. His/Her Majesty.

hm. hectometre.

H.M.C. His/Her Majesty's Customs.

H.M.I.S. His/Her Majesty's Inspector of Schools.

H.M.S. His/Her Majesty's Ship.

H.M.S.O. His/Her Majesty's Stationery Office.

H.O. Home Office.

Ho holmium.

ho. house.

Hoch! (G.) Your health!

homme d'affaires (F.) a business man; an agent.

homo sapiens (L.) Man the thinker; Man as a species.

Hon. Honorary; Honourable.

honi soit qui mal y pense (Old F.) 'evil be to him who thinks evil' (motto of the Order of the Garter).

honoris causa (L.) as a mark of honour, honorary.

Hon. Sec. Honorary Secretary.

hor. horizon.

horribile dictu (L.) horrible to relate.

hors de combat (F.) out of condition to fight.

hors d'oeuvre (F.) appetiser comprising first course of a meal.

hort. horticulture; horticultural.

Hos. Hosea (O.T.)

Hôtel de Ville (F.) Town Hall.

H.P. Houses of Parliament; High Priest.

h.p. horse-power; hire purchase; high-pressure.

H.Q. headquarters.

H.R. House of Representatives; Home Rule.

h.r. high resistance.

hr. hour.

H.R.E. Holy Roman Empire; Holy Roman Emperor.

H.R.H. His/Her Royal Highness.

H.S.R. His/Her Serene Highness.

H.T. high tension.

hubris (Gk.) spiritual pride.

H.W.M. High Water Mark.

h.w., ht. wkt. hit wicket.

Hy. Henry.

I

I iodine; (*international registration*) Italy, Sardinia, Sicily.

I. Island; ionic strength; moment of inertia (in engineering).

Ia. Iowa.

ib., ibid. in the same place (L. *ibidem*).

i/c in charge (of).

ich dien (G.) 'I serve' (the motto of the Prince of Wales until World War I when the English version was substituted).

Ice., Icel. Iceland; Icelandic.

I.C.I. Imperial Chemical Industries.

ici on parle français (F.) French is spoken here.

id. the same (L. *idem*).

Ida. Idaho.

I.D.B. illicit diamond-buying.

idée-fixe (F.) an obsession.

i.e. that is (L. *id est*).

I.F., i.f. (radio) intermediate frequency.

I.F.S. Irish Free State (Eire).

I.F.T.U. International Federation of Trade Unions.

I.-G., Insp.-Gen. Inspector-General.

ign. unknown (L. *ignotus*).

ignis fatuus (L.) a will o' the wisp.

IHS (L.) *Iesus Hominum Salvator;* Jesus Saviour of Mankind.

IL (*international registration*) Israel.

Il illinium.

ill. illustrated; illustration.

Ill. Illinois.

I.L.O. International Labour Organisation.

i.l.o. in lieu of, in place of.

I.L.S. Instrumental Landing System (for aircraft).

I.M.F. International Monetary Fund.

Imp. Emperor (L. *imperator*); imperial.

imp. imperative; imperfect; let it be printed (L. *imprimatur*); import; imported.

impasse (F.) a dead end; an impossible difficulty; stalemate.

impedimenta (L.) baggage.

imprimatur (L.) licence to print a book.

In indium.

in. inch(es).

in articulo mortis (L.) at the point of death.

in bocca al lupo (It.) 'in the wolf's mouth,' i.e. good luck! (refers to fable of Romulus and Remus).

Inc., Incorp. incorporated.

in camera (L.) 'in a private room,' i.e. of a trial where neither the public nor the Press is admitted.

incl. including; inclusive.

incog. unknown (L. *incognitus*).

IND (*international registration*) India.

Ind. Indiana; India; Independent.

ind. index.

ind., indic. indicative.

indef. indefinite.

in esse (L.) in being; actual.

in extremis (L.) at the point of death.

inf. below (L. *infra*); infinitive; infantry.

infra dig. below one's dignity (L. *infra dignitatem*).

ingénue (F.) innocent and artless young girl.

init. at the beginning (L. *initio*).

in lim. on the threshold (L. *in limine*).

in loc. cit. in the place cited (L. *in loco citato*).

in loco parentis (L.) 'in the place of a parent'; as a parent-figure.

in medias res (L.) 'into the midst of things,'
i.e. to begin something directly, with no introduction.

in memoriam (L.) (**i.m.**) to the memory of.

in posse (L.) possible, potential.

in propria persona (L.) 'in one's own person'; without disguise or affectation.

I.N.R.I. Jesus of Nazareth, King of the Jews
(L. *Iesus Nazarenus Rex Iudaeorum*).

in re (L.) in the matter of.

in situ (L.) in its original position.

insouciance (F.) careless indifference.

Inst. Institute.

inst. instant, of the present month.

in statu pupillari (L.) in the state of wardship.

in statu quo (L.) in the former state; as it was.

instr. instructor; instrument.

int. interest.

inter alia (L.) among other things.

inter alios (L.) among other people.

interj. interjection.

intermezzo (It.) a short piece of music connecting the acts of an opera or tragedy, or
the movements of a symphony.

interr., interrog. interrogative.

in toto (L.) entirely.

intr., intrans. intransitive.

in trans. in transit (L. *in transitu*).

intro., introd. introduction; introduced.

Inv. invoice; 'he designed, invented it' (L. *invenit*).

in vino veritas (L.) wine brings out the truth.

Io ionium.

I.O.M. Isle of Man.

Ion. Ionic.

I.O.U. 'I owe you' (memorandum of debt signed by borrower).

I.O.W. Isle of Wight.

ipse dixit (L.) 'he himself said it', i.e. a dogmatic statement.

ipsissima verba (L.) the very words.

ipso facto (L.) by the fact itself, automatically.

I.Q. Intelligence Quotient.

i.q. the same as (L. *idem quod*).

IR (*international registration*) Iran.

I.R. Inland Revenue.

Ir iridium.

Ir. Ireland; Irish.

I.R.A. Irish Republican Army.

I.R.C. International Red Cross.

IRL (*international registration*) Republic of Ireland.

IRQ (*international registration*) Iraq.

irreg. irregular.

IS (*international registration*) Iceland.

Is. island(s).

Is., Isa. Isaiah (O.T.); Isabella.

I.S.M. Imperial Service Medal.

It. Italy; Italian.

I.T.A. Independent Television Authority.

ital. italics.

I.T.B. Industrial Training Board.

I.U. International Unit.

I.W.G.C. Imperial War Graves Commission.

I.W.T. Inland Water Transport.

I.W.W. Industrial Workers of the World.

I.Y. Imperial Yeomanry.

J

J (*international registration*) Japan.

J. Judge; Justice.

JA (*international registration*) Jamaica.

J.A. Judge Advocate.

J/A Joint Account.

Jam. James (N.T.); Jamaica(n).

Jan. January.

Jas. James.

je ne sais quoi (F.) 'I don't know what', something one cannot remember the name of.

Jer. Jeremiah (O.T.)

jeu d'esprit (F.) a witticism.

jeunesse dorée (F.) 'gilded youth,' i.e. smart
young men of society; fops.

JJ. Justices.

J.M.B. Joint Matriculation Board.

jn. junction.

Jno. John; St. John (N.T.)

Jo. Joel (O.T.)

joie de vivre (F.) delight in life.

Jon. Jonathan.

JOR (*international registration*) Jordan.

Josh. Joshua (O.T.)

jour de l'an (F.) New Year's Day.

J.P. Justice of the Peace.

jr. junior.

Jud. Judith (Apocrypha); judicial.

Judg. Judges (O.T.)

Jul. July.

julienne (F.) clear soup.

Jun. June; Junior.

Jupiter Pluvius (L.) 'rain-bringing Jupiter,' i.e. wet weather.

jus gentium (L.) law of nations.

K

K potassium; (*international registration*) Cambodia.

K. King; (with other initials) King's, Knight.

Kal. Kalends.

Kan., Kans. Kansas.

Kapellmeister (G.) orig. a choirmaster, but now used for an orchestral conductor.

Kaput (G.) broken, out of order.

K.B. Knight of the Bath; King's Bench.

K.B.E. Knight Commander (of the Order) of the British Empire.

K.C. King's Counsel.

kc. kilocycle.

K.C.B., K.C.M.G., K.C.S.I., K.C.V.O. Knight Commander (of the Order) of the Bath, St. Michael and St. George, the Star of India, the Royal Victorian Order.

Ken. Kentucky.

K.G. Knight of the Garter.

kg. kilogramme.

K.G.C. Knight of the Grand Cross.

K.G.F. Knight of the Golden Fleece.

kil., kilom. kilometre.

kilo. kilogramme.

K.K.K. Ku Klux Klan.

kl. kilolitre.

K.L.M. Royal Aviation Company (Dutch *Koninklijke Luchtvaart Maatschappij*).

Km. Kingdom.

km. kilometre.

K.O. knock-out.

K.O.S.B. King's Own Scottish Borderers.

K.O.Y.L.I. King's Own Yorkshire Light Infantry.

K.P. Knight of St. Patrick.

Ks. Kansas.

K.T. Knight Templar; Knight of the Thistle.

Kt. Knight.

Kümmel (G.) liqueur flavoured with cumin and caraway seeds.

kw. kilowatt.

KWT (*international registration*) Kuwait.

Ky. Kentucky.

Kyrie (Gk.) Usually first part of the Requiem Mass, which begins *Kyrie eleison* ('Lord have mercy').

L

L (*international registration*) Luxembourg.

L. Lake; *Latin*; Late; Law; Learner; Liberal; Lord; Low; 50; lire; (with other initials) Licentiate, London.

l. land; left; litre.

L.A. Legislative Assembly; Library Association; Law Agent.

La lanthanum.

La. Louisiana.

Lab. Labour; Labrador.

lab. laboratory; labial.

labore et honore (L.) with work and honour.

lacrimae Christi (L.) a sweet wine from Vesuvius and Sicily, literally 'the tears of Christ.'

laissez-faire (F.) policy of inaction and complacency.

Lam. Lamentations (O.T.)

Lancs Lancashire.

LAO (*international registration*) Laos.

lapsus linguae (L.) a slip of the tongue.

lares et penates (L.) household gods.

largo (*mus.*) 'broad', i.e. dignified and stately.

Lat. Latin.

lat. latitude.

Laus Deo (L.) 'Praise be to God.'

L.B. Bachelor of Letters.

l.b. leg bye.

lb. pound (L. *libra*).

l.b.w. leg before wicket.

L.C. Lord Chancellor; Lord Chamberlain.

l.c. (*print*) lower case; (*stage*) left centre.

l.c.d. lowest common denominator.

l.c.f. least common factor.

L.C.J. Lord Chief Justice.

l.c.m. least common multiple.

L.Cpl. Lance-Corporal.

L.D. Doctor of Letters.

Ld. Lord.

legato (*mus.*) 'bound', i.e. smoothly, limpidly.

Leics Leicestershire.

lento (*mus.*) slow(ly).

leitmotif (G.) a theme used to indicate a person, an idea, etc. constantly recurring in a composition, esp. opera.

lèse-majesté (F.) high treason.

l'état, c'est moi (F.) 'The state—I am the state' (Louis XIV).

lettre de cachet (F.) a sealed letter; a royal warrant for imprisonment.

Lev. Leviticus (O.T.)

lex non scripta (L.) 'unwritten law,' i.e. common law.

lex scripta (L.) 'written law,' i.e. statute law.

L.F. Low Frequency.

L.G. Life Guard; Low German; large grain.

L.H.A. Lord High Admiral.

L.H.C. Lord High Chancellor.

l.h.d. left-hand drive.

L.I. Long Island; Light Infantry.

Li lithium.

liaison (F.) secret meeting for amorous purposes; contact between two military units.

Lib. Library; librarian; Liberal.

libretto (It.) 'little book', i.e. the words of an opera or musical; book (U.S.)

liceo (It.) Italian State secondary school (*see* **lycée**).

Lied (*mus.*) (*pl.* **Lieder**) short lyric set to music.

Lieut. Lieutenant.

Lincs Lincolnshire.

lingua franca (It.) 'free language', a foreign language common to two or more speakers who do not speak each other's language.

lit. literal(ly); literary; literature; litre.

literati (L.) learned men; men of letters.

Litt. D. Doctor of Letters (L. *Literarum Doctor*).

L.J. Lord Justice (*pl.* **L.JJ.**).

L.L. Lord Lieutenant; Low Latin; Late Latin.

ll. lines.

LL.B., LL.D., LL.M. Bachelor, Doctor, Master of Laws.

loc. cit. in the place cited (L. *loco citato*).

locum tenens (L.) a deputy or substitute.

locus classicus (L.) the authoritative passage on a subject.

locus standi (L.) recognised position, right to interfere.

log. logarithm.

Lon(d). London.

long. longitude.

loq. he speaks (L. *loquitur*).

LP. long-playing record.

L.P. Labour Party; Lord Provost.

l.p. low pressure; (*print*) long primer.

L.P.O. London Philharmonic Orchestra.

L.P.S. Lord Privy Seal.

L.S. (*stage*) left side; (*cinema*) long shot; the place of the seal (L. *locus sigilli*).

L.S.D. lysergic acid diethylamide; Lightermen, Stevedores and Dockers; (see **£.s.d.**).

£.s.d. pounds, shillings and pence (L. *librae, solidi, denarii*).

L.S.O. London Symphony Orchestra.

LT (*international registration*) Libya.

Lt. Lieutenant.

L.T.A. Lawn Tennis Association; London Teacher's Association.

Ltd. Limited.

Lu lutecium.

L.V. Luncheon Voucher; Licensed Victuallers.

L.W.L. Load Water Line.

L.W.M. Low Water Mark.

LXX. Septuagint Version.

lycée (F.) secondary or grammar school in France.

M

M. Monsieur; Monday; 1,000; (with other initials) Master, Majesty, Marshal, Member.

m. married; metres; miles; minutes; (G.) mark; (*cricket*) maiden over; masculine; (*mech.*) mass; medium; meridian; (*mus.*) mezzo; middle; month; mount(ain).

MA (*international registration*) Morocco.

M.A. Master of Arts.

macédoine (F.) dish of mixed fruit or vegetables; miscellany of literary extracts.

ma (It.) but.

M.A.F. Ministry of Agriculture and Fisheries.

Mafia (It.) secret terrorist organisation originating in Sicily (members are called **mafiosi**).

mag. magazine.

magnum opus (L.) chief work of a creative artist.

Maj. Major.

Mal. Malachi (O.T.)

mal de mer (F.) sea-sickness.

malentendu (F.) a misunderstanding.

mañana (Sp.) 'tomorrow,' a mood which prompts one to leave everything until to-morrow.

Manch. Manchester.

Manche (F.) The English Channel.

Mancun. of Manchester (L. *Mancuniensis*).

Manit. Manitoba.

Mar. March.

March. Marchioness.

Mardi Gras (F.) Shrove Tuesday.

mariage de convenance (F.) marriage from financial motives.

Marq. Marquess.

Marsala all'uovo (It.) sweet Sicilian wine, of a sherry type, mixed with egg.

Mass. Massachussets.

maté (F.) a Brazilian variety of tea.

Matt. Matthew (N.T.)

mauvaise honte (F.) false modesty.

mazurka (Pol.) Traditional Polish dance, developed in the nineteenth century into a virtuoso composition, esp. for piano.

M.B. Bachelor of Medicine (L. *Medicinae Baccalaureus*).

M.B.E. Member of the Order of the British Empire.

MC (*international registration*) Monaco.

M.C. Master of Ceremonies; Military Cross; Member of Congress.

M.C.C. Marylebone Cricket Club.

M.D. Doctor of Medicine (L. *Medicinae Doctor*); mentally deficient.

Md. Maryland.

M.E. Middle English; Mechanical Engineer; Mining Engineer.

Me. Maine.

mea culpa (L.) by my fault.

Medit. Mediterranean.

me judice (L.) according to my judgment.

mélange (F.) mixture, medley.

mem. remember (L. *memento*).

memento mori (L.) remember death.

memo. memorandum.

meno (It.) less.

M.Eng. Master of Engineering.

mens sana in corpore sano (L.) 'a sound mind in a sound body.'

mésalliance (F.) marriage with someone of lower status.

messa (It.) Mass.

Messrs. the plural of **Mr.** used before the name of a business firm or in a list referring to the names of several men. (see Dictionary)

Met. Metropolitan; meteorological

meths. methylated spirits.

Meth. Methodist.

métier (F.) trade, profession.

Métro (F.) Paris Underground Railway (F. *Chemin de Fer Metropolitain*).

MEX (*international registration*) Mexico.

Mex. Mexico.

mezza voce (*mus.*) 'half voice,' i.e. singing or playing at half power.

mf. (*mus.*) moderately loud (It. *mezzo forte*).

mfd. manufactured.

mfg. manufacturing.

mfr. manufacturer.

Mg magnesium.

mg. milligramme.

Mgr. Monsignor; Monseigneur.

M.I.5 Military Intelligence Department 5.

Middx Middlesex.

milieu (F.) sphere, medium.

mille (F.) a thousand; a mile.

Min. Minister; Ministry.

min. minute.

Minn. Minnesota.

mirabile dictu (L.) wonderful to relate.

misc. miscellaneous.

mise en scène (F.) scenic setting.

Miss. Mississippi.

Missa (L.) Mass.

mk. Mark (German currency).

mkt. market.

ml. millilitre.

Mlle(s). Mademoiselle (*pl.* Mesdemoiselles).

MM Messieurs; Majesties; 2,000.

mm. millimetre.

Mme(s). Madame (*pl.* Mesdames).

Mn manganese.

M.O. Medical Officer; Money Order; mass observation.

Mo. Missouri.

Mod. Modern.

modiste (F.) milliner.

Mods. Moderations (Oxford University).

modus operandi (L.) manner of working.

M.O.H. Ministry of Health; Medical Officer of Health.

M.O.I. Ministry of Information.

M.O.L. Ministry of Labour.

molto (It.) very, much.

Mon Monmouthshire.

Mon. Monday.

monde (F.) 'world', people, society.

Mont. Montana.

M.O.S. Ministry of Supply.

M.O.T. Ministry of Transport.

mot juste (F.) the absolutely right word.

M.P. Member of Parliament; Military Police; Metropolitan Police.

m.p. melting point.

mp (*mus.*) moderately soft (It. *mezzo piano*).

m.p.g. miles per gallon.

m.p.h. miles per hour.

Mr. Mister.

Mrs. Mistress.

MS (*international registration*) Mauritius.

MS(S). manuscript(s).

M.Sc. Master of Science.

m.s.l. mean sea-level.

M.S.M. Meritorious Service Medal.

mt. mountain.

M.T.B. Motor Torpedo Boat.

Municipio (It.) Town Hall.

mus. *music*; musical; musician; museum.

Mus.B. *or* **Mus.Bac., Mus.D.** *or* **Mus.Doc., Mus.M.** Bachelor of Music (L. *Musicae Baccalaureus*), Doctor of Music (L. *Musicae Doctor*); Master of Music (L. *Musicae Magister*).

MW (*international registration*) Malawi.

M.W. Most Worshipful; Most Worthy.

M.W.B. Ministry of Works and Buildings; Metropolitan Water Board.

N

N nitrogen; (*international registration*) Norway.

N. North; Norse; normal; (with other initials) New, National.

n. name; noun; neuter; noon; nephew; born (L. *natus*).

NA (*international registration*) Netherlands Antilles.

Na sodium (L. *natrium*).

n.a., n/a (*banking*) no account.

N.A.A.F.I. Navy, Army and Air Force Institutes.

N.A.B.C. National Association of Boys' Clubs.

N.A.F.T.A. North Atlantic Free Trade Area.

N.A.G.C. National Association of Girls' Clubs.

Nah. Nahum (O.T.).

N.A.L.G.O. National Association of Local Government Officers.

Nat. National; Nationalist; Nathaniel; Natal (S. Africa); Natural.

N.A.T.O. North Atlantic Treaty Organisation.

naut. nautical.

nav. naval; navigation.

N.B. note well (L. *nota bene*); New Brunswick; North British.

Nb niobium.

n.b. no ball (in cricket).

N.B.C. National Broadcasting Company (U.S.A.).

N.C. North Carolina.

N.C.B. National Coal Board.

N.C.C.L. National Council for Civil Liberties.

N.C.O. Non-commissioned officer.

Nd neodymium.

n.d. no date, not dated.

N. Dak. North Dakota.

N.E. New England; North-East(ern); New Edition.

Ne neon.

Neb., Nebr. Nebraska.

N.E.D. New English Dictionary.

née (F.) 'born', used (especially in birth announcements) to indicate a woman's maiden name.

neg. negative.

Neh. Nehemiah (O.T.).

nem. con. 'no one contradicting,' unanimously agreed (L. *nemine contradicente*).

nem. diss. 'no one dissenting' (L. *nemine dissentiente*).

nemo me impune lacessit (L.) 'no one shall attack me with impunity' (motto of Scotland and the Order of the Thistle).

ne plus ultra (L.) 'nothing more beyond', i.e. the uttermost point, the ultimate.

n'est-ce pas? (F.) isn't that so?

Neth. Netherlands.

neut. neuter; neutral.

Nev. Nevada.

nez retroussé (F.) turned-up nose.

N.F. Newfoundland; Norman French.

N.F.S. National Fire Service.

N.F.U. National Farmers' Union.

N.H. New Hampshire.

n.h.p. nominal horse power.

N.I. Northern Ireland.

Ni nickel.

NIC (*international registration*) Nicaragua.

NIG (*international registration*) Niger.

nil admirari (L.) 'to admire nothing', i.e. to be superior.

nil desperandum (L.) never despair.

n'importe (F.) it doesn't matter, never mind.

N.J. New Jersey.

NL (*international registration*) Netherlands.

n.l. 'it is not allowed' (L. *non licet*).

N.L.I. National Lifeboat Institution.

N.M., N.Mex. New Mexico.

N.N.E.(W.) North-North-East (West).

N.O. New Orleans; Natural Order (in botany).

No., Nos. number, numbers (L. *numero*).

n.o. (*cricket*) not out.

noblesse oblige (F.) rank imposes obligations.

nolens volens (L.) whether he will or not, willy-nilly.

noli me tangere (L.) 'don't touch me.'

nom. nominative.

nom de guerre (F.) an assumed name (likewise **nom de plume**).

nom de théâtre (F.) stage name.

Noncon. Nonconformist.

non compos mentis (L.) insane.

non licet see **n.l.**

non sequitur (L.) (**non seq.**) 'it does not follow', i.e. it is an illogical conclusion.

Northants Northamptonshire.

Norvic. of Norwich (L. *Norvicensis*).

Norw. Norwegian.

nota bene see **N.B.**

Notts Nottinghamshire.

nouveau riche (F.) 'one newly enriched,' a social upstart.

Nov. November.

n.p. new paragraph.

N.P.O. New Philharmonia Orchestra.

N.R. North Riding (of Yorkshire).

nr. near.

N.R.A. National Rifle Association.

N.S. Nova Scotia; New Style (of dates).

n.s. not specified; insufficient.

N.S.P.C.C. National Society for the Prevention of Cruelty to Children.

N.S.W. New South Wales (Australia).

N.T. New Testament; National Trust; Northern Territory (of Australia).

n.u. name unknown.

nuance (F.) subtle change in tone of voice, instrument etc. for expressive purposes.

N.U.G.M.W. National Union of General and Municipal Workers.

N.U.J. National Union of Journalists.

nulli secundus (L.) second to none.

Num., Numb. Numbers (O.T.).

Nunc Dimittis (L.) 'now lettest thou depart' (the first words of the Latin version of the canticle in St. Luke, c.2, vv. 31-5).

N.U.R. National Union of Railwaymen.

N.U.S. National Union of Seamen; National Union of Students.

N.U.T. National Union of Teachers.

N.V. New Version.

N.W. North-West(ern).

N.W.T. North-West Territories (Canada).

N.Y. New York.

NZ (*international registration*) New Zealand.

N.Z. New Zealand.

O

O oxygen.

O. Ohio; (with other initials) Officer, Old, Order.

O.A. Officier d'Académie.

O.A.S. Organisation Armée Secrète; On Active Service.

Ob., Obad. Obadiah (O.T.).

ob. he/she died (L. *obiit*).

obbligato (*mus.*) An accompaniment which plays almost as prominent a part as the main performer; often used of a solo instrument accompanying the voice (lit. 'essential').

O.B.E. Order of the British Empire.

obiter dictum (L.) (*pl.* **obiter dicta**) 'something said by the way', i.e. a passing observation.

obj. object; objective.

obs. obsolete; observation.

O.C. Officer Commanding.

o/c. overcharge.

Oct. October.

oct., 8vo. octavo.

O.E. Old English.

O.E.C.D. Organisation for Economic Co-operation and Development.

O.E.D. Oxford English Dictionary.

œuvre (F.) a literary or artistic work.

O.F., O.Fr. Old French.

off. official.

O.H.G. Old High German.

O.H.M.S. On His/Her Majesty's Service.

O.K. all correct.

Okla. Oklahoma.

O.M. Order of Merit.

omnia vincit amor (L.) 'love conquers all things.'

O.N. Old Norse.

on dit (F.) 'they say,' i.e. a rumour.

Ont. Ontario.

O.P. (*stage*) opposite prompter; observation post.

o.p. out of print; over-proof (of spirit).

op. a literary, musical or artistic work (L. *opus*, *pl. opera*).

op. cit. in the work quoted (L. *opere citato*).

opp. opposite; plural of **op.**

opt. optative.

opus see **op.**

ora et labora (L.) 'pray and work.'

ora pro nobis (L.) 'pray for us.'

ord. ordained; order, ordinary, ordinance.

Ore., Oreg. Oregon.

O.S. Old Saxon; Ordnance Survey; ordinary seaman; (*tailoring*) outsize; old style.

Os osmium.

O.S.A., O.S.B., O.S.D., O.S.F Order of St. Augustine, St. Benedict, St. Dominic, St. Francis.

ostinato (*mus.*) persistent bass rhythm.

O.T. Old Testament.

O tempora! O mores! (L.) 'O the times! O the manners'!, i.e. How depraved are the times we live in!

otium cum dignitate (L.) dignified retirement.

O.U.P. Oxford University Press.

outré(e) (F.) extravagant, eccentric.

Oxfam Oxford Committee for Famine Relief.

Oxon Oxford; Oxfordshire; of Oxford (L. *Oxoniensis*).

oz. ounce(s).

P

P phosphorus; (*international registration*) Portugal, Azores, Cape Verde Is., Madeira, Mozambique, Portuguese Guinea, Portuguese Timor, Portuguese W. Africa (Angola), São João Baptista de Ajuda, São Tomé, Principe Is.

P. Pawn; Prince; (with other initials) President, Public.

p. page; participle; (*linear measure*) perch; pint; (*mus.*) soft (It. *piano*).

PA (*international registration*) Panama.

P.A. Press Association; Publishers' Association.

p.a. per annum, yearly.

Pa protoactinium.

Pa. Pennsylvania.

pa. past.

P.A.A. Pan American Airways.

pace (L.) by leave of.

padre (It.) father.

PAK (*international registration*) Pakistan.

Pal. Palestine.

panache (F.) a plume of feathers used as a headress; a swaggering manner.

panem et circenses (L.) 'bread and circuses,' (the demand of the populace for food and entertainment during the time of the later Roman emperors).

P. & O. Peninsular and Oriental (Steamship Co.).

par. paragraph; parallel; parish.

par avion (F.) by air mail.

par excellence (F.) pre-eminently.

pari passu (L.) 'with equal pace,' i.e. in the same proportion; likewise.

parl't. parliament.

parti (F.) a marriage-match; a political party; a decision.

partita see **suite.**

pass. passive.

passacaglia see **chaconne.**

passé(e) (F.) past the prime of life; out of date.

passim (L.) everywhere; all through; here and there.

Pater Noster (L.) Our Father.

pâté (F.) paste, pie (**pâté de foie gras** savoury meat paste made from fat goose liver).

pâtisserie (F.) pastry; confectionery; a pastry-cook's shop.

pavane (*mus.*) stately dance in double time, perhaps originating in Padua.

pax vobiscum (L.) 'peace be with you.'

P.A.Y.E. Pay As You Earn (Income Tax).

Pb lead (L. *plumbum*).

P.C. police constable; parish council; Privy Council; Privy Councillor.

p.c. per cent; post card.

Pd palladium.

pd. paid.

PE (*international registration*) Peru.

peccavi (L.) 'I have sinned.'

Pembs Pembrokeshire.

P.E.N. International Association of Poets, Playwrights, Essayists, Editors and Novelists.

penchant (F.) inclination, liking for.

Penn., Penna. Pennsylvania.

pension (F.) board and lodging; a guest house.

per aerea (It.) by air mail.

per annum (L.) (**per an., p.a.**) yearly.

per ardua ad astra (L.) 'through difficulties to the stars' (R.A.F. motto).

per capita (L.) 'by heads', i.e. individually.

per diem (L.) daily.

perf. perfect.

perp. perpendicular.

per pro., p.p. by proxy, by the agency of (L. *per procurationem*).

pers. person.

per se (L.) by itself, of itself.

persiflage (F.) idle banter, light mockery.

persona (**non**) **grata** (L.) (un)acceptable person.

Pet. Peter (N.T.).

Petriburg. of Peterborough (L. *Petriburgensis*).

P.F. Procurator Fiscal.

pf. (*mus.*) soft becoming loud (It. *piano forte*).

pfd. preferred.

Ph.B., Ph.D. Bachelor, Doctor of Philosophy.

Phil. Philippians (N.T.).

PI (*international registration*) Philippine Islands.

piazza (It.) an open square, usually with places to sit.

P.I.B. Prices and Incomes Board.

pièce de resistance (F.) principal dish of the meal; a climax.

pied-à-terre (F.) occasional lodging.

pinx. he/she painted it (L. *pinxit*).

pis-aller (F.) the last resource.

più (It.) more.

pizzicato (*mus.*) with plucked strings

PL (*international registration*) Poland

P.L. Poet Laureate.

pl. *plural*; plate (illustration); place (in an address).

P.L.A. Port of London Authority.

planchette (F.) heart-shaped board mounted on a pencil point through which spiritualists' messages are received.

plat du jour (F.) a special dish on the menu for the day.

plebs (L.) in ancient Rome, the common people as distinct from the nobility.

plein air (F.) the open air.

P.M. Prime Minister; Postmaster; Provost Marshal.

p.m. afternoon (L. *post meridiem*); after death (L. *post mortem*).

P.M.G. Postmaster General.

P.N.E.U. Parents' National Educational Union.

P.O. Petty Officer; Post Office; Postal Order.

po', poco (It.) little, few.

P.O.D. paid on delivery.

Pol. Polish

polka (Pol.) energetic Bohemian dance very popular in 19th century Europe.

pomme de terre (F.) 'apple of the earth,' i.e. a potato.

pop. population.

Port. Portugal; *Portuguese*.

P.O.S.B. Post Office Savings Bank.

poseur (F.) (*fem.* **poseuse**) an affected person; a show-off.

poss. possessive; possible.

poste restante (F.) department of a Post Office where travellers' letters are kept until called for.

postmortem (L.) diagnosis carried out on a corpse to ascertain the reasons for death; an autopsy.

potage (F.) soup.

pot au feu (F.) thin meat-broth.

pot-pourri (F.) rose leaves and spices kept in a pot for their scent; a string of popular tunes arranged for one instrument or orchestra.

pourboire (F.) a tip.

P.O.W. Prisoner of War; Prince of Wales.

P.P. Parcel Post; Parish Priest; Past President; Post Paid.

p.p. see **per pro.**

pp. pages; (*mus.*) very softly (It. *pianissimo*).

P.P.C. to take leave (F. *pour prendre congé*).

ppp. (*mus.*) very very softly.

P.P.S. an additional postscript (L. *post postscriptum*).

Pr. Prince; Priest.

pr. pair; present; price; pronoun.

P.R.A. President of the Royal Academy.

précis (F.) an abstract or summary.

pref. preface; preference; preferred; prefix.

Pres. Presbyterian; President.

pres. present.

presto (It.) fast.

prima donna (It.) 'first lady,' i.e. the most prominent female singer in the cast of an opera.

prima facie (L.) at a first view; on the face of it.

primus inter pares (L.) 'the first among equals'.

prix (F.) prize.

P.R.O. Public Relations Officer.

pro bono publico (L.) 'for the public good.'

Prof. Professor.

pro forma (L.) 'for form's sake.'

pron. pronoun; pronunciation.

pronto (It.) ready.

pro patria (L.) for the sake of one's country.

pro rata (L.) in proportion.

Prot. Protestant.

protegé(e) (F.) one under the care and protection of another.

pro tempore (L.) (**pro tem.**) for the time being.

Prov. Proverbs (O.T.); Province; Provost.

prox. next; of the next month (L. *proximo*).

prox. acc. 'he came next,' i.e. the runner-up (L. *proxime accessit*).

P.R.S. President of the Royal Society.

P.S. postscript; Privy Seal; (*stage*) prompt side; paddle steamer.

Ps. Psalm(s) (O.T.).

P.T. Physical Training.

Pt platinum.

Pt. Point; Port.

pt. part; payment; pint(s).

Pte. Private (rank).

PTM (*international registration*) Malaysia.

P.T.O. Please turn over.

purée (F.) vegetables, meat, fruit etc. reduced to a smooth pulp.

pur sang (F.) 'pure blood', i.e. through and through, genuine.

P.W.D. Public Works Department.

pxt. see **pinxit.**

PY (*international registration*) Paraguay.

Q

Q. Queen; Question; quart(s); Quarter-master.

q. query; quintal; quire(s).

Q.B. Queen's Bench.

Q.C. Queen's Counsel; Queen's College.

Q.E. The Queen Elizabeth (ship).

q.e. which is (L. *quod est*).

Q.E.D., Q.E.F., Q.E.I. 'which was to be proved, done, found' (L. *quod erat demonstrandum, faciendum, inveniendum*).

Q.F. quick-firing.

Q.M. The Queen Mary (ship.)

Q.M., Qmr. Quartermaster.

qr. quarter(s); quire(s).

Q.S. Quarter Sessions; Queen's Scholar.

qt. quart(s).

qto., 4to. quarto.

qu. query; question; as if (L. *quasi*).

qua (L.) in the capacity of.

quadrille (F.) square dance in five sections.

quantum sufficit (L.) (**quant suff.**) 'as much as suffices.'

Quattrocento (It.) the 15th century, especially with reference to Italian art and music.

Que. Quebec.

quid pro quo (L.) equivalent; something done in return.

quin. quintuplet.

quis custodiet ipsos custodes? (L.) 'who will guard the guards?'

qui vive? (F.) who goes there?

quot homines tot sententiae (L.) 'as many opinions as there are men.'

quo vadis? (L.) 'where are you going?'

q.v. which see (L. *quod vide*).

qy. query.

R

R (*international registration*) Rumania.

R. King, Queen (L. *Rex, Regina*); Réaumur (thermometer); Robert; River; take (L. *Recipe*); (with other initials) Rail(way), Royal.

r. right; rises; rood; rupee; (*cricket*) runs.

RA (*international registration*) Argentina.

R.A. Royal Academy; Royal Artillery; Rear Admiral (or **R.Adm.**).

Ra radium.

R.A.A. Royal Academy of Arts.

R.A.C. Royal Automobile Club; Royal Armoured Corps; Royal Agricultural College.

raconteur (F.) a good story-teller (*fem.* **raconteuse**).

Rad. Radical.

rad. root (in mathematics) (L. *radix*).

R.A.F. Royal Air Force; Royal Aircraft Factory.

R.A.F.V.R. Royal Air Force Volunteer Reserve.

ragoût (F.) rich meat stew.

raison d'être (F.) reason for existence.

rall. (*mus.*) gradually becoming slower (It. *rallentando*).

R.A.M. Royal Academy of Music.

R.A.M.C. Royal Army Medical Corps.

R.A.O.C. Royal Army Ordnance Corps.

rapprochement (F.) the re-establishment of friendly relations between two countries or people.

R.A.S. Royal Agricultural Society; Royal Astronomical Society; Royal Asiatic Society.

R.A.S.C. Royal Army Service Corps.

R.A.T.O. Rocket-Assisted take-off (or **RATO**).

R.A.V.C. Royal Army Veterinary Corps.

R.B. Rifle Brigade.

Rb rubidium.

R.B.A., R.B.S. Royal Society of British Artists, Sculptors.

RC (*international registration*) Formosa (Tai-Wan).

R.C. Roman Catholic; Red Cross.

r.c. right centre.

RCA (*international registration*) Central African Republic.

439

R.C.A. Royal College of Art; Royal Cambrian Academy; Railway Clerks' Association.

RCB (*international registration*) Republic of Congo.

RCH (*international registration*) Chile.

R.C.M. Royal College of Music.

R.C.M.P. Royal Canadian Mounted Police.

R.C.P. Royal College of Physicians; Royal College of Preceptors.

rcpt. receipt.

R.C.S. Royal College of Surgeons; Royal College of Science.

R.D. Royal Dragoons; (*cheque*) refer to drawer (or **R/D**).

Rd. Road.

R.D.C. Rural District Council.

R.D.I. Royal Designer for Industry.

R.D.Y. Royal Dockyard.

R.E. Royal Engineers; Royal Exchange; Right Excellent.

Re rhenium.

re (L.) with regard to.

Realpolitik (G.) theory that a country's foreign policy is entirely dictated by her material interests.

Rec. Recorder.

rec. recipe.

réchauffé(e) (F.) warmed-up dish; stale.

recherché(e) (F.) 'sought-after,' exquisite.

recit. (*mus.*) recitative, solo vocal singing without melody, used in opera for dialogue or narration.

recpt. receipt.

Rect. Rector, Rectory.

rect. rectangle; rectified.

rédacteur (F.) editor.

reductio ad absurdum (L.) 'reducing (the position) to an absurdity'.

ref. referee; reference.

refd. referred.

refl., reflex. reflexive.

Reg. Queen (L. *Regina*); Reginald; Registrar.

reg. region(al); regulation; regular.

regd. registered.

Reg. Prof. Regius Professor.

Regt. Regiment; Regent.

Reichstag (G.) Parliament.

rel. related; relative; religion.

reliquae (L.) relics.

R.E.M.E. Royal Electrical and Mechanical Engineers.

Rep. Republic; Republican; Representative; Repertory; Reporter.

rep. report; representing; reprimand.

répétiteur (F.) a musical coach, esp. in an opera house to teach singers their parts.

repr. reprinted.

repro. reproduction.

requiem (L.) a Mass held for the soul of a dead person (lit. 'rest').

requiescat in pace (L.) 'may he/she rest in peace.'

res. resigned; resident; residence.

resp. respondent; respectively.

respice finem (L.) 'look to the end,' i.e. remember you are mortal.

resumé (F.) a summary.

resurgam (L.) 'I shall rise again.'

ret(d). retired; returned; retained.

Rev. Revelation (N.T.); Reverend; Revised; Revenue; Review.

revenons à nos moutons (F.) 'let us return to our sheep,' i.e. to return to the subject.

R.F. Royal Fusiliers; French Republic (F. *République Française*).

r.f. radio-frequency.

R.F.C. Rugby Football Club; Royal Flying Corps (now **R.A.F.**).

R.G.S. Royal Geographical Society.

RH (*international registration*) Haiti.

R.H. Royal Highness; Royal Highlanders (Black Watch).

r.h. right hand.

R.H.A. Royal Horse Artillery; Royal Hibernian Academy.

R.H.S. Royal Horticultural Society; Royal Humane Society.

442

RI (*international registration*) Indonesia.

R.I. Rhode Island; Royal Institute (of Painters in Watercolours); Royal Institution.

R.I.A. Royal Irish Academy.

R.I.B.A. Royal Institue of British Architects.

R.I.C.S. Royal Institute of Chartered Surveyors.

RIM (*international registration*) Islamic Republic of Mauritania.

R.I.P. see **requiescat in pace.**

risorgimento (It.) the period (1830-70) when Italy struggled for national unity.

risqué (F.) offending against propriety.

R.L. Rugby League.

R.L.O. Returned Letter Office.

Rly. Railway.

RM (*international registration*) Malagasy Republic.

R.M. Royal Marines; Royal Mail; Resident Magistrate.

rm. ream.

RMM (*international registration*) Mali.

R.M.P. Royal Military Police.

R.M.S. Royal Mail Steamer; Royal Society of Miniature Painters; root mean square (in electricity).

R.N. Royal Navy.

Rn radon.

R.N.L.I. Royal National Lifeboat Institution.

RNR (*international registration*) Zambia.

R.N.(V.)R. Royal Naval (Volunteer) Reserve.

R.O. Receiving Office(r); Returning Officer; Routine Order(s).

ro. right-hand page (L. *recto*).

R.O.C. Royal Observer Corps.

R.O.F. Royal Ordnance Factory.

Roffen. of Rochester (L. *Roffensis*).

Rom. Romans (N.T.); Roman.

rom. roman typeface.

roman (F.) a novel.

R.P. Received Pronunciation; reply paid.

r.p.m. revolutions per minute.

r.p.s. revolutions per second.

R.Q.M.S. Regimental Quartermaster-Sergeant.

R.S. Royal Society; Royal Scots (Regiment).

r.s. right side.

R.S.A. Royal Scottish Academy; Royal Society of Arts.

RSM (*international registration*) San Marino.

R.S.M. Regimental Sergeant-Major; Royal Society of Medicine; Royal School of Mines.

R.S.P.B., R.S.P.C.A. Royal Society for the Protection of Birds, for the Prevention of Cruelty to Animals.

RSR (*international registration*) Southern Rhodesia.

R.S.S. Fellow of the Royal Society (L. *Regiae Societatis Sodalis*).

R.S.V.P. Please reply (F. *Répondez s'il vous plaît*).

R.T.C. Royal Tank Corps.

Rt. Hon. Right Honourable.

RU (*international registration*) Burundi.

R.U. Rugby Union.

Ru ruthenium.

rubato (*mus.*) lingering on and hurrying through the notes of a phrase whilst maintaining the overall tempo.

rus in urbe (L.) 'the country in the city.'

R.V. Revised Version.

RWA (*international registration*) Rep. of Rwanda and Republic of Burundi.

R.W. Right Worthy; Right Worshipful.

R.W.S. Royal Society of Painters in Water Colours.

Ry. Railway.

R.Y.A. Royal Yachting Association.

R.Y.S. Royal Yacht Squadron.

S

S sulphur; (*international registration*) Sweden.

S. South; Saint; Sabbath; Sunday; soprano; (with other initials) Society, Socialist, Scottish.

s. second; shilling(s); son; singular; substantive; solubility.

S.A. South Africa; South America; South Australia; Salvation Army; Storm Troops (G. *Sturm-Abteilung*); sex appeal.

saignant (F.) underdone (of cooked meat).

Salop Shropshire.

Salve! (L.) Hail!

Sam. Samuel.

sang froid (F.) 'cold blood,' i.e. imperturbable calmness.

Sans. Sanskrit.

sans culotte (F.) extreme Republican; Jacobin.

sans pareil (F.) 'without equal.'

sans peur et sans reproche (F.) 'fearless and blameless.'

sans serif (F.) Term used in printing to denote type without horizontal adornments, e.g. b,d,l,t.

sans souci (F.) 'without care,' heedless.

Sask. Saskatchewan.

Sassennach (Gael. Sasunnach, a Saxon) Englishman, formerly non-Highlander.

Sat. Saturday.

Sauerkraut (G.) cabbage chopped and fermented.

sauté (F.) tossed in butter.

sauve qui peut (F.) 'save himself who can,' i.e. everyone for himself.

savant (F.) man of academic distinction.

savoir-faire (F.) 'to know how to do,' i.e. gumption, common sense.

Sb antimony (L. *stibium*).

S.C. South Carolina; Supreme Court; Staff College; Special Constable/Constabulary; Statutory Committee.

s.c., s.caps., sm. caps. small capitals.

Sc scandium.

Sc. Science.

sc. he/she carved/engraved it (L. *sculpsit*); scene; scruple (weight); namely (L. *scilicet*).

Sc.B. Bachelor of Science. (L. *Scientiae Baccalaureus*).

Sc.D. Doctor of Science (L. *Scientiae Doctor*).

Sch. School.

Schadenfreude (G.) malicious joy.

scherzo (*mus.*) 'a joke,' musical term for the lightest movement (usually in triple time) of a sonata or symphony.

Scot. N(at). Scottish Nationalist.

sculp, sculps., sculpt. see **sc.**

SD (*international registration*) Swaziland.

s.d. indefinitely, without a day being set (L. *sine die*).

S. Dak. South Dakota.

S.D.N. League of Nations (F. *Société des Nations*).

S.D.P. Social Democrat Party (in Germany).

S.E. South-East.

S.E. Stock Exchange.

Se selenium.

séance (F.) an assembly, especially of spiritualists for consulting spirits and communicating with spirit world; sitting of parliament.

S.E.A.T.O. South-East Asia Treaty Organisation.

Sec. Secretary; Section; Secondary.

sec. second; secant.

sec. leg. 'according to law' (L. *secundum legem*).

sec. reg. 'according to rule' (L. *secundum regulam*).

seguidilla (Sp.) old Spanish dance with vocal passages.

Selw. Selwyn College, Cambridge.

Sem. Seminary; Semitic.

semper fidelis (L.) 'always faithful.'

semper idem (L.) 'always the same.'

Sen. Senate; Senator.

Sep., Sept. September, Septuagint.

sep. separate; sepal.

seq., seqq. the following (L. *sequens, sequentia*).

ser. series.

seriatim (L.) serially.

Sess. Session.

SF (*international registration*) Finland; Science Fiction.

S.F. Sinn Fein (Irish for 'we ourselves').

s.f. towards the end (L. *sub finem*).

sf(z). (*mus.*) with sudden emphasis (It. *sforzando*).

S.G. Solicitor-General.

s.g. specific gravity.

sgd. signed.

SGP (*international registration*) Singapore.

Sgt. Sergeant.

S.H.A.P.E. Supreme Headquarters of the Allied Powers in Europe.

S.I. Staten Island.

Si silicon.

sic. Used to draw attention to a quoted mistake or arguable conclusion (Latin for 'thus').

sic itur ad astra (L.) 'such is the way to the stars,' i.e. to fame or immortality.

sic transit gloria mundi (L.) 'so passes the glory of the world.'

siècle d'or (F.) 'the century of gold,' i.e. France in the 17th century.

sin. (*maths*) sine.

sine die see **s.d.**

sine prole see **s.p.**

sine qua non (L.) an indispensable condition.

sing. singular.

S.J. Society of Jesus, i.e. the Jesuits.

S.M. Senior Magistrate; Sergeant-Major; Society of Mary.

Sm samarium.

SME (*international registration*) Surinam.

SN (*international registration*) Senegal.

Sn tin (L. *stannum*).

S.N.P. Scottish Nationalist Party.

s.o. seller's option.

soi-disant (F.) self-styled, supposed.

soigné(e) (F.) well-groomed; self-assured in matters of taste.

Sol. solicitor.

sol. solution.

sop. soprano.

S.O.S. signal of distress (in Morse, three dots followed by three dashes followed by three dots).

sotto voce (*mus.*) 'under the voice,' i.e. sung or played extremely softly.

soupçon (F.) 'a suspicion,' i.e. a very small amount of something.

sov. sovereign.

Sp. Spain; Spanish.

s.p. without issue (L. *sine prole*).

S.P.C.C. Society for the Prevention of Cruelty to Children.

S.P.C.K. Society for Promoting Christian Knowledge.

spec. special; specification; speculation.

sp. gr. specific gravity.

S.P.Q.R. Senate and People of Rome (L. *Senatus Populusque Romanus*).

spremuta (It.) Italian iced fruit drink.

sq. (the) following (L. *sequens*); square.

sqn. squadron.

Sr strontium.

Sr. Senior; Sir.

S.R.N. State Registered Nurse.

S.R.O. Statutory Rules and Orders.

S.S. Steamship; Sunday School.

SS. Saints.

S.S.E.(W.) South-South-East (West).

St. Saint; Strait; Street.

Staffs Staffordshire.

Stat. Statute.

status quo (L.) 'the state in which,' i.e. the pre-existing state of affairs. (The full phrase is *status quo ante bellum* 'the state of things before the war').

S.T.B., S.T.D. Bachelor, Doctor of (Sacred) Thelogoy (L. *Sacrae Theologiae Baccalaureus, Doctor*).

stet (L.) An instruction, usually by a proof-corrector to a printer, to ignore his correction of the text (Latin for 'Let it stand').

stg. sterling.

stn. station.

Sturm und Drang (G.) storm and stress.

SU (*international registration*) U.S.S.R.

suaviter in modo, fortiter in re (L.) 'gentle in manner, strong in deed,' i.e. an iron hand in a velvet glove.

451

sub judice (L.) 'under judgement.'

subpoena (L.) 'under a penalty,' a legal summons to appear as a witness.

sub rosa (L.) 'under the rose,' i.e. secretly.

subst. substantive; substitute.

succès de scandale (F.) success (of a person, novel, play etc.) due to notoriety or scandalous character.

SUD (*international registration*) Sudan.

suf., suff. suffix.

sui generis (L.) 'of its own kind,' i.e. unique (ly).

suite (F.) (*mus.*) a composition of 4 or 5 movements based on dance rhythms; the rooms comprising a flat, or in a hotel; matching furniture for one room in a house.

Sun. Sunday.

sup. superfine; superior; superlative; supine; above (L. *supra*); supreme.

supp. supplement.

Supt. Superintendent.

Surg. Surgeon; Surgery.

sursum corda (L.) lift up your hearts (to God).

surv. surveyor.

SWA (*international registration*) South-West Africa.

SY (*international registration*) Seychelle Is.

S.Y. Steam Yacht.

syn. synonym; synonymous.

SYR (*international registration*) Syria.

T

T (*international registration*) Thailand.

T. tenor; temperature; territory; Tuesday; Turkish; Testament.

t. time; ton; town; in the time of (L. *tempore*).

Ta tantalum.

T.A. Telegraphic Address; Territorial Army; Typographical Association.

table d'hôte (F.) Meal of several courses at a fixed price.

tan. tangent.

tant mieux (F.) so much the better.

tant pis (F.) so much the worse.

tarantella (It.) S. Italian dance of increasing speed in double time.

T.A.S.S. Official News Agency of the U.S.S.R.

Tb terbium.

T.B. Tuberculosis; Torpedo-Boat.

T.C. Town Councillor.

T.C.P.B. Town and Country Planning Bill.

T.C.D. Trinity College, Dublin.

T.D.R. Treasury Deposit Receipts.

Te tellurium.

tel. telegram; telegraph; telephone.

temp. temperature; tempo; temporary; in the time of (L. *tempore*).

tempus fugit (L.) 'time flies.'

Tenn. Tennessee.

term. terminology; termination; terminus.

Ter(r). Terrace; Territory.

terra firma (L.) 'solid earth,' i.e. dry land.

terra incognita (L.) 'unknown country.'

tertium quid (L.) 'a third something,' i.e. a compromise between two opposing principles.

Test. Testament; testator.

tête-à-tête (F.) confidential talk between two people.

Tex. Texas.

text. rec. the received or accepted text (L. *textus receptus*).

tfer. transfer.

TG (*international registration*) Togo.

T.G.W.U. Transport and General Workers' Union.

Th., Thurs. Thursday.

Th.D. Doctor of Theology.

thé dansant (F.) tea with dancing.

Thess. Thessalonians (N.T.).

Thos. Thomas.

T.H.W.M. Trinity High Water Mark.

Ti titanium.

tilde (Sp.) wavy mark over Spanish n, as in Señora.

Tim. Timothy (N.T.).

timbre (F.) tone-quality of a musical instrument or voice.

Tit. Titus (N.T.).

Tl thallium.

T.L.R. Times Law Reports.

Tm thulium.

T.M. trade mark; true mean.

TN (*international registration*) Tunisia.

tn. ton.

T.N.T. trinitrotoluene.

T.O. Telegraph/Telephone Office; Transport Officer.

toccata (It.) rapid piece of music for harpsichord or piano.

Toc H Talbot House.

tonn. tonnage.

tour de force (F.) a feat of strength or skill; remarkable achievement.

tournedos (F.) small round fillets of beef served as an entrée.

tout ensemble (F.) 'everything together', i.e. the general effect.

T.P.I. Town Planning Institute.

TR (*international registration*) Turkey.

Tr. Treasurer; Trustee.

trans. transaction; translation; translated; transitive.

trattoria (It.) restaurant.

T.R.H. Their Royal Highnesses.

trouvaille (F.) a windfall.

TT (*international registration*) Trinidad and Tobago.

T.T. total abstainer (teetotal); Tuberculin Tested.

Tu., Tues. Tuesday.

T.U. Trade Union; Transmission Unit.

T.U.C. Trades Union Congress.

tu quoque! (L.) 'You also,' i.e. people in glass houses shouldn't throw stones.

tutoyer (F.) to call someone by the 2nd person singular 'tu,' i.e. to be on intimate terms.

typog. typography; typographical.

U

U uranium; (*international registration*) Uruguay

U. University; (with other initials) United, Upper, Union.

U.A.R. United Arab Republic.

U.C. University College; Upper Canada.

u.c. upper case (in printing).

U.D.I. Unilateral Declaration of Independence.

U.F.O. Unidentified Flying Object.

u.i. as below (L. *ut infra*).

U.K. United Kingdom.

ult. in the preceding month (L. *ultimus* 'last').

ultima Thule (L.) 'the last Thule,' i.e. the final limit, the utmost point.

U.N.(O.) United Nations (Organisation).

U.N.A. United Nations Association.

una voce (L.) 'with one voice,' i.e. in complete agreement.

U.N.C.F.A., U.N.C.I.O., U.N.C.T.A.D. United Nations Conference on Food and Agriculture, International Organisation, Trade and Development.

U.N.E.S.C.O. United Nations Educational, Scientific and Cultural Organization.

U.N.I.C.E.F. United Nations International Children's Emergency Fund.

Univ. University College, Oxford; University.

U.N.R.R.A. United Nations Relief and Rehabilitation Organisation.

U.N.S.C. United Nations Security Council.

U. of S.A. Union of South Africa.

u.p. under-proof.

Uru. Uruguay.

USA (*international registration*) United States of America.

U.S.A. United States of America.

U.S.N. United States Navy.

U.S.S.C. United States Steel Corporation.

U.S.S.R. Union of Soviet Socialist Republics.

U.S.S.S. United States Steamship.

Ut. Utah.

ut inf. as below (L. *ut infra*).

ut sup. as above (L. *ut supra*).

V

V vanadium; (*international registration*) Vatican City.

V. volts.

v. against (L. *versus*); see (L. *vide*); verb; verse; in place of (L. *vice*); volume.

V.A. Vice-Admiral.

Va. Virginia.

vade in pace (L.) 'go in peace.'

vade mecum (L.) 'go with me,' i.e. a constant companion, usually said of a book.

vale! (L.) farewell!

valet de chambre (F.) a gentleman's personal manservant.

vaudeville (F.) theatrical piece with light or satirical songs; a variety show.

vb. verb.

V.C. Vice-Chairman; Vice-Chancellor; Vice-Consul; Victoria Cross.

V.D. venereal disease.

V.D.H. valvular disease of the heart.

Ven. Venerable.

veni, vidi, vici (L.) 'I came, I saw, I conquered' (said by Julius Casear when announcing to the Senate his victory over Pharnace II).

ventre à terre (F.) 'belly to the ground,' i.e. at high speed.

verb. (sat.) sap. 'a word to the wise (is enough)' (L. *verbum (satis) sapienti*).

verbatim et literatim (L.) 'word for word and letter for letter.'

Verboten (G.) forbidden.

versus (L.) against.

V.G. Vicar-General; very good.

V.H.F. Very High Frequency.

via (L.) by way of.

via media (L.) 'the middle way.'

Vic. Vicar; Queen Victoria.

vice (L.) in place of.

vice versa (L.) the other way round.

vide (L.) see.

videlicet (L.) namely (often **viz.**).

vin blanc (F.) white wine.

vin de marque (F.) vintage wine.

vin du pays (F.) local wine.

vin ordinaire (F.) cheap everyday wine.

vin rouge (F.) red wine.

V.I.P. Very Important Person.

virginibus puerisque (L.) 'for girls and boys.'

virtute officii (L.) by virtue of office.

vis à vis (F.) facing, opposite.

vis inertiae (F.) 'the power of inertia.'

vita brevis, ars longa (L.) 'life is short, but art lives longer.'

Viva! (It.) Long live!

viva voce (L.) 'by the living voice,' i.e. orally.

viz. namely (L. *videlicet*).

vl. (*mus.*) violin.

VN (*international registration*) Vietnam.

vo. on the left-hand page (L. *verso*).

voc. vocative.

vocab. vocabulary.

voilà tout (F.) that's all.

vol. volume.

vol-au-vent (F.) a case of light, flaky pastry with a savoury filling.

volente Deo (L.) God willing.

volte-face (F.) a sudden and unexpected change of opinion or plans.

vox et praeterea nihil (L.) 'a voice and nothing more.'

vox populi, vox Dei (L.) 'the voice of the people is the voice of God.'

V.R. Queen Victoria (L. *Victoria Regina*).

V.S. Veterinary Surgeon.

v.s. see above (L. *vide supra*); (*mus.*) turn over quickly (It. *volta subito*)

vs. against (L. *versus*).

Vt. Vermont.

v.t. transitive verb.

vv. verses.

W

W tungsten (L. *wolframium*).

W. West; Western; Women's; Welsh; electrical energy.

w. wicket; wife; with.

W.A. West Africa; West Australia.

W.A.A.C., W.A.A.F., W.A.F.S. Women's Auxiliary Army Corps, Air Force, Fire Service.

WAG (*international registration*) Gambia.

wagon-lit (F.) a sleeping-carriage.

WAL (*international registration*) Sierra Leone.

WAN (*international registration*) Nigeria.

Wanderjahre (G.) unsettled, roving years before settling down.

Wash. Washington.

W.C. West Central; water closet; Wesleyan Chapel.

W.Comm. Wing-Commander.

WD (*international registration*) Dominica.

W.D. War Department.

W.E.A. Workers' Educational Association.

Wed. Wednesday.

Wehrmacht (G.) the armed forces.

Wein, Weib und Gesang (G.) Wine, Women and Song.

Weltschmerz (G.) world-weariness.

w.f. wrong fount (in printing).

W.F.T.U. World Federation of Trade Unions.

WG (*international registration*) Grenada.

wgt. weight.

whf. wharf.

W.H.O. World Health Organisation.

W.I. West Indies.

Wiener Schnitzel (G.) 'Vienna cutlet,' i.e. veal cutlet dressed in egg and breadcrumbs.

Wilts Wiltshire.

Wis. Wisconsin.

wk. week.

WL (*international registration*) St. Lucia.

W/L wave-length.

W.L.A. Women's Land Army.

Wm. William.

W.N.W. West-North-West.

W.O. War Office; Warrant Officer.

w.o. walk-over.

Wor., Wp., Wpful. Worshipful.

Worcs Worcestershire.

W.R. West Riding (of Yorkshire).

Wr., Wlr. Walter.

W.R.A.C., W.R.A.F., W.R.N.R., W.R.N.V.R., W.R.N.S. Women's Royal Army Corps, Air Force, Naval Reserve, Naval Volunteer Reserve, Naval Service.

WS (*international registration*) Western Samoa.

W.S. Weather Ship.

W/T. wireless telegraphy.

wt. weight.

W.T.U.C. World Trades Union Conference.

WV (*international registration*) St. Vincent.

W.Va. West Virginia.
W.V.S. Women's Voluntary Services.
Wyo. Wyoming.
W.Y.R. West Yorkshire Regiment.

X

X ten.
x.d., xd., x.div. ex dividend.
Xe xenon.

Y

Y yttrium.
Yb ytterbium.
yd. yard(s).
Y.H.A. Youth Hostels Association.
Y.L.I. Yorkshire Light Infantry.
Y.M.C.A. Young Men's Christian Association.
yr. year; younger; your.
YU (*international registration*) Yugoslavia.
YV (*international registration*) Venezuela.
Y.W.C.A. Young Women's Christian Association.

Z

ZA (*international registration*) South Africa.
zapateado (Sp.) Spanish clog-dance with fierce rhythm.
Z.C. Zionist Congress.
Zech. Zechariah (O.T.).

Zeitgeist (G.) the spirit of the times.
z.f. zero frequency.
Zn zinc.
zoo. zoology.
Zr zirconium.
Z.S. Zoological Society.

4. WORDS WITH A STORY

by A. H. Irvine, M.A., Officier d'Académie

abacus. The *abacus* in Ancient Greece was originally a square slab [Gk. *abax*, a slab] covered with a thin layer of sand in which figures could be traced for counting purposes and then erased; later, strings of little stones or pebbles [Lat. *calculus*, a pebble] were used for this purpose. The modern *abacus*, used by infant teachers and extensively in the East as an essential business aid, is an instrument in the form of a frame with parallel wires on which arithmetical calculations are made with sliding balls or beads.

above-board. This word, meaning 'open', 'openly', 'honest' was, strange to say, born of a fear of dishonesty. In gaming, cards had to be shuffled over (not under) the board or table to prevent any possibility of their being 'stacked'.

adder. The influence of the spoken language on the written word is seen in *adder*, *apron*, *orange*, all of which, beginning originally with *n*, have lost this sound through its being confused with the *n* of the indefinite article *an*. Since *adder* comes from O.E. *naedre* we ought to say *a nadder*. Similarly *apron*, coming from M.E. *napron* should give us *a napron* (a spelling found

465

in Spenser) and not *an apron*. The *n*, however, has been preserved in the related words *nap* (of cloth), *napery* and *napkin*. When the street urchin talks of *a norange*, he is etymologically correct because *orange* comes from Spanish *naranja*. To return to *adder*, it is interesting to know that the phrase 'as mad as a hatter' ought to be 'as mad as *an adder*'.

anagram. *Anagrammatism* is the art of transposing the letters of a word or phrase to form a new word or phrase. Derived from Gk. *ana-*, backwards, and *gramma*, a letter, an anagram in its simplest form is made by writing a word backwards, e.g. 'evil' for 'live', 'emit' for 'time'. Further transposition of the letters produces 'vile' and 'mite'. Such word-puzzles are of very ancient origin, having been invented by Lycophron, a Greek poet, in A.D. 280. Anagrams can often be most skilfully constructed so as to produce, in the re-arrangement of the letters, a statement appropriate to the original.

arena. Lat. *harena* means 'sand', or 'a sandy place', and so *arena* came to denote the sand-strewn central space of the Roman amphitheatre in which the gladiators fought. The sand was used to soak up the blood. The word is now used for 'any scene of contest'.

Atlas. In Greek mythology, *Atlas* was a Titan who, for rebelling against Zeus, was condemned to stand near the garden of the Hesperides (in N. Africa) and to support the universe on his shoulders. Mercator, the 16th century geographer, used a picture of the 'world-bearing' *Atlas* as a frontispiece to a collection of maps, and so originated the use of the word as the name for a book of maps.

The plural of *Atlas* (in Greek) is *Atlantes* and in architecture this name is given to male figures in stone used instead of columns to support the entablature of a building; female figures so used are called 'caryatides'.

attic. *Attica*, a district of ancient Greece, gave its name to the *Attic* order of architecture (cf. Ionic, Doric, etc.). One special feature of this style was a small decorative row of square pillars on the uppermost storeys of buildings. Eventually the word *attic* was used to denote the top storey of any tall building.

ballot [It. *ballota*, a diminutive of *balla*, a ball] means 'a method of secret voting'. It is so called because in early times voting was by the use of white or black balls secretly put into a receptacle. White was a vote 'for', black 'against'. This practice still obtains in certain clubs, societies, Masonic Lodges, etc., and has given us the word 'to blackball', i.e. 'to reject (for membership)'.

The present British method of voting in Parliamentary elections—by the use of official slips of paper put into a *ballot*-box—was first used in 1870.

bedlam. In the 16th century, the priory of St. Mary of Bethlehem in Bishopsgate, London, was converted into a lunatic asylum. No doubt people used some such expression as 'a real Bethlehem' as a synonym for the pandemonium and uproar associated in their minds with a madhouse. Slovenly pronunciation soon corrupted the word 'Bethlehem' into *bedlam*.

bitter. This word a s used in the phrase 'to the *bitter* end' is not the same *bitter* as the epithet for 'beer.' On board ship, the *bitts* are the two posts round which ropes, cables, etc., are secured, and a *bitter* is a turn of the cable round them. The phrase, therefore, means, in its nautical sense 'to the last piece of rope'. Used figuratively, it signifies 'to the last extremity'; 'to the death'.

blazer, meaning a light jacket, usually of wool, for wear at tennis, cricket, boating or other sports, is derived by most dictionaries because of its bright colours from O.E. *blæse*, a flame, torch, or fire. It is said that the name was originally applied (in 1889) to the red flannel jackets worn by the crew of the Lady Margaret Boat Club of St. John's College, Cambridge.

There is, however, another theory which gives the credit of the invention of the garment to Captain J. W. Washington, R.N. in 1845. In those days there was no uniform for ratings of the Royal Navy and so a ship's captain just dressed his own boat's crew in any rig-out he fancied. Captain Washington, who commanded H.M.S. *BLAZER*, put his crew into blue and white striped jackets and it was not very long till other ships, in derision, nicknamed these coats *blazers*.

boycott. This method of coercion by conspiracy whereby all dealings cease with an undesirable person, group of people, or commercial concern, perpetuates the name of Captain Charles *Boycott* (1832–97). *Boycott*, an Irish landowner's agent in Co. Mayo, was its first victim in 1880. By asking extortionate rents and by the consequent number of evictions, he incurred the hostility of the Irish Land League which forbade the population to work on his land or to have any dealings, social or commercial, with him. To *boycott* has been introduced into several foreign languages, e.g. Fr. *boycotter*; German *boykottieren*; It. *boicottare*.

bullion is the name for refined gold or silver in the mass as distinguished from gold or silver coins, though the latter may be included in the term when for import or export. The word once meant a melting-house or mint, and its first recorded mention is in 1451. Stores of *bullion*, both gold and silver, are kept at the Bank of England and the Royal Mint. It is probably derived from Late Lat. *bullio*='the swelling of boiling water', coming to us through Fr. *bouilli*, boiled, and *bouillon*, a bubble, broth or soup. *Bullion* is, therefore, the result of the boiling or melting process in the Mint, to produce, so to speak, gold or silver 'soup', thereafter to be stored in solid form as bars or ingots of these metals.

calculate. When the early arithmeticians did their additions and subtractions on the 'abacus' (q.v.) they used as counters, pebbles or stones [Lat. *calculus*, a stone]; they were, in fact, *calculating* by means of stones. We have retained in English the Latin word *calculus* as a medical term in its original sense of 'stone', e.g. 'a renal *calculus*' is 'a stone in the kidney'; also a higher branch of mathematics, we find it in the 'differential *calculus*' and the 'integral *calculus*'.

calendar is derived from Lat. *kalendarium* which in turn comes from *kalendae*, the name the Romans gave to the first day of each month. The *kalendae* (*calends* or *kalends* in English) [from the old Latin verb *kalare* meaning 'to make announcements on religious matters'] were so called because they were solemnly proclaimed by the Pontifex Maximus, the chief priest, who also announced the order of the days of the month, the feast days, and the days on which no business could be done. On the *calends*, too, interest fell due and all accounts had to be paid. Horace had this well in mind when he called them the *tristes Kalendae*, i.e. the 'sad *calends*'. Our modern banking and business systems have retained the idea of the first of the month as a settling-day. Since the *Kalendae* were associated with interest, debts, etc., the *Kalendarium* became the word for 'an account-book'.

The Greeks, on the other hand, had no *calends* in their *calendar* so the phrase 'At the Greek *calends*' was the equivalent of 'never'; e.g. 'To be paid at the Greek *calends*' meant 'Never to be paid'.

candidate. The Latin for 'white' is *candidus*, and in Roman times, one who sought election to any office or appointment appeared wearing a white toga to symbolize his unblemished character, sincerity and honesty. He was called a *candidatus* [Lat.=robed in white], in English, a *candidate*. The adjective *candid*, meaning 'fair', 'frank', 'ingenuous', 'honest' is from the same root. An associate word is *candour*, meaning 'sincerity', 'frankness', 'justice', which comes from Lat. *candor*, whiteness, and is from the verb *candere*, to shine.

cheque. This is the modern spelling of the earlier form *check* (still used in the U.S.A.) which is the same word as *check* meaning 'a control, verification, stop, etc'. A bank *check* was originally a carbon copy of a transaction which could be used to verify or *check* the customer's account. By similarity of sound it became associated with *exchequer* from which it derived the spelling *cheque*.

companion. Just as a 'comrade' (q.v.) is a 'room-sharer', so a *companion* is a 'bread-sharer'. It is from Lat. *cum*, with, and *panis*, bread, by way of O.Fr. *compaignon*, and so derivatively means 'one with whom one can break bread'; hence, 'an intimate friend'.

The 'nautical' *companion* is very indirectly connected with this. It is derived from O.Fr. *compagne*, a ship's pantry [Lat. *panis*, bread] and It. *compagna*, a storeroom, but may perhaps be connected with Dutch *kampanje*, a cabin. A *companion* is a shelter over a stairway leading to the cabin. It appears, too, in the compounds '*companion*-ladder', the ladder by which officers pass from the quarter-deck to the main deck or to the cabins, and '*companion*-way', the steps or stairway leading from the deck to the saloon or cabins.

comrade, 'a close companion', 'an intimate friend', comes from Lat. *camera*, a room, by way of Fr. *camarade* and Sp. *camarada*. It meant originally a 'room-full' but acquired the sense of a close friend with whom one could share a room. He was a 'room-mate' or 'chamber-mate'. It is probable that in the 17th century a colloquial abbreviation of this latter word to *cham* resolved itself, in course of time, to *chum* which since the days of Dickens has been a popular synonym for a 'pal'.

cutler, cutlet. The shopkeeper who sells knives, forks, spoons, etc., is called a *cutler*, but not because some of his wares happen to *cut*. Etymologically it comes from O.Fr. *coutel*, a knife, through Mod.Fr. *coutelier*, a *cutler*.

A *cutlet* is not even remotely connected with *cutting*. Derivatively it is not a little bit of meat *cut* off. The word, like so many cookery terms, is of French origin and comes from *côtelette*, a diminutive of *côte*, a rib [Lat. *costa*, the side]. A *cutlet* is, therefore, a little rib; hence, a little bit of meat off the rib.

decibel. A *decibel*, the smallest variation in sound that the human ear can detect, is one tenth [Lat. *decem*, ten] of a *bel*. A *bel* is a measure for comparing intensity of noises and of current in all types of electrical communication circuits. The word was coined in honour of Alexander Graham *Bell* (1847–1922), the Scots-born inventor of the telephone.

decimate comes from Lat. *decimus*, tenth, and *decimare*, to decimate. In ancient Rome, it was the practice to select by lot, and punish with death, every tenth man of a company of soldiers guilty of mutiny, cowardice, or other serious crime. The term has lost its original meaning and is now used loosely in the sense of 'to destroy a very large, but unspecified, number of people by disease, fire, flood, etc'. At times, it is even regarded, though improperly, as a synonym for 'to wipe out completely', 'to annihilate'.

decoy is from Dutch *de*, the, and *kooi*, cage. It may be, however, that *de* is a loose pronunciation of 'duck', in which case *decoy* would mean *duckcoy*. In fowling, a *decoy* is any device for leading wild birds into a trap or within gun-shot range. It can take the form of an artificial contrivance, e.g. an imitation duck floating on the water, or a live, tame duck trained to 'call' to the wild ones. In the saltings of the Wash in England, an artificial model of a goose is set to stand in the mud. The fenmen call it a *coy*, not a *decoy*. Figuratively, the word is used of persons, especially a card-sharper's confederate, employed to lure an innocent victim into the trap set for him.

denizen. The word is no etymological relation of 'den' but comes from O.Fr. *deinzein*, meaning 'one living within a city', the first part being from O.Fr. *deinz*=Mod.Fr. *dans*, in, within. It was the opposite of *forein*, meaning 'one living outside a city', from O.Fr., and Lat. *foris*, out-of-doors, outside, abroad. From this comes the word 'foreigner'.

Denizen gradually extended its connotation to mean an 'inhabitant' in the most general sense, whether human being or animal, as in the phrase 'the *denizens* of the deep'. It does, however, retain its original meaning of 'citizen' when used in royal letters patent to denote a foreigner who has acquired citizenship of this country by naturalization. In medieval language, he ceases to be a *forein* and becomes a *deinzein*.

diploma. The modern diploma, bearing the written record of the conferment of a degree, honour, privilege, etc., is an unfolded sheet of parchment, vellum, or paper. The Greek *diploma* [*diploun*, to double] was a document folded once and, therefore, divided into two parts.

etiquette has been defined as 'the conventional

code of good manners which governs behaviour in social life'. It is the etymological twin of 'ticket', is allied to German *strecken*, to stick or to pin, and comes to us by way of O.Fr. *estiquete*.

Originally the *etiquette* (or 'ticket') was a notice pinned to a post outside a castle or palace on which were detailed the orders of the day, ceremonial duties, etc. Hence, to observe the terms of the *etiquette* was to conform to the social conventions prescribed by authority.

exchequer. Very appropriately *exchequer* comes from O.Fr. *eschequier*, meaning 'a chessboard', for it was on such a table marked out in squares that, in the Middle Ages, the predecessor of our Chancellor of the Exchequer, worked out, with the help of coloured counters, the details of the country's finances. Seated round this *checkered* board he and his assistants, to whom as a group the name *The Exchequer* was given, could *check* the figures and square the accounts of the royal revenue.

gin. (a) *Gin*, the alcoholic liquor, is distilled from grain (usually rye) and flavoured with 'juniper' berries. *Gin* is a contraction of *geneva* which has no connection with the Swiss town but is a corruption of the Fr. *genièvre*=a juniper-tree, which, in turn, comes from Lat.

476

juniperus also meaning 'a juniper-tree'. *Gin*, therefore, gets its name from 'juniper', the flavouring put into it.

(b) *Gin*, meaning 'a snare' or 'trap', is a contraction of *engine* in its sense of 'a device'.

gourmand, gourmet. Both words, derived from Lat. *gula*, the throat, have come direct to us from French and have remained unchanged in pronunciation as well as in spelling. They are often erroneously regarded as synonyms but the distinction is very clear. A *gourmand* is a glutton, a ravenous eater, whereas a *gourmet* is a lover of good food, especially of delicately prepared dishes, and a connoisseur of wines. A *gourmand* is a good trencherman who wants quantity while the *gourmet* is an epicure who expects quality.

greyhound. *Grey* here had nothing to do with colour but is O.N. for 'a dog' or O.E. 'a bitch'. The owner of a *greyhound* has therefore, so to speak, two dogs!

guerilla, guerrilla. The latter spelling is derivatively the correct one as *guerrilla* [a diminutive of Sp. *guerra*]='a little war', or 'petty warfare'. It was first used in the North of Spain during the Peninsular War (1808–1814) to denote an irregular way of carrying on war ('a little war') against an enemy by armed bands acting independently of the principal combatants. The term is now used mainly adjectivally, e.g. 'guerrilla bands', 'guerrilla headquarters', and even pleonastically in 'guerrilla warfare'. It is sometimes used as a noun, e.g. the guerrillas meaning 'irregular armed bands'.

halcyon. The Greek name for the *halcyon* or kingfisher was *alkyon* [*hals*, the sea; *kyon*, brooding]. The ancients believed that this bird built a nest that floated on the sea and sat on the eggs for the seven days before and after the winter solstice, i.e. about the 21st December. During the period the eggs were hatching, the waters remained calm and so mariners could put to sea without fear of storms. Hence, the expression 'halcyon days' came to mean, figuratively, a period of security, peace and prosperity.

haversack. See KNAPSACK.

humble-pie has etymologically no connection with the 'humble' of 'humility' but is a distortion of *umble-pie*, i.e. a pie made from the 'umbles' or 'numbles' (the entrails) of a deer. While the lord of the manor and his household were served at the high table with the choice parts of the animal, the menials at the lower end had 'to eat umbles-pie'. Hence the expression *to eat humble-pie* came to mean figuratively: 'to suffer humiliation'; 'to submit tamely to'; 'to apologize abjectly'.

idiot [Lat. *idiota*, an uneducated person, and Gk. *idiotes*, a private person] carried in ancient times no taint of idiocy or imbecility. It meant simply a private person who held no public office or had no professional knowledge. Since, however, only educated persons were eligible for public appointments, the word came gradually to denote one who was unfitted for these posts because of lack of education. Later, such unfitness was associated with mental, not educational deficiency and so *idiot* came to mean: 'a simpleton'; 'an imbecile'. Even in 17th century English the word was commonly used in the Greek sense of 'a private person holding no public office'.

imbecile (Lat. *imbecillis*, weak, frail, or helpless, and *baculus*, a stick] meant originally 'destitute of strength of body', i.e. physically but not mentally weak. Derivatively it implied 'helpless without the aid of a stick'. Later it referred to weakness whether in body or in mind. Then it came to be used only in its modern sense of:

'feeble-minded'; 'incapable of managing one's own affairs because of low mentality'.

janitor. Lat. *janua*, a door, is the origin of *janitor* which formerly meant 'a doorkeeper', 'a porter'. Later the meaning was extended to include 'a caretaker', especially of public buildings, universities, schools, etc. See JANUARY.

January. *Janus*, the Roman god of gates and doors, *janitor*, the doorkeeper (q.v.) and *January*, as the doorway of the year are all connected with Lat. *janua*, a door.

The ancient deity to whom the Romans dedicated the month of *January* was not only the guardian of gates and doors, but also, of beginnings especially in divisions of time. Hence, 'first' was sacred to him, e.g. the 'first' hour of the day, the 'first' day of the month (the Calends) and the 'first' month of the year. As he had been endowed with the gift of seeing both the past and the future, he was represented as having two faces, one in front and one behind. On the 'first' day of the 'first' month he was able, therefore, to view the old year and look into the new. The doors of his temple in the Forum at Rome were closed in times of peace which, during the Republic, happened only nine times in a thousand years.

knapsack [Dutch *knapzak* from *knappen*, to eat,
and *zak*, a bag] was originally the food-bag for
holding provisions (for humans) whereas the
haversack [German *Hafer*, oats] was the oats-bag
for carrying food (for horses).

We find a variant of *knapsack*, in *snapsack*, once
used dialectically but now obsolete, where
'snap' meant 'to bite, eat, or crunch' as in
'ginger-snap', a crisp kind of gingerbread
biscuit.

larder. See PANTRY.

libel is defamation of a person's character by
the written word, whereas *slander* is by the
spoken word. It comes from *libellus*, a diminutive of Lat. *liber* and means, therefore, 'a
little book'; 'a booklet'. It was common
practice in England, as early as the 17th
century, to publish booklets or pamphlets full
of sarcastic and scurrilous attacks on the
character of individuals. Later, *libellus* was
used to describe, not the booklet, but the
contents. Hence the word *libel*.

lumber-room. The *lumber-room* was originally
the *Lombard* room, i.e. the place in which the

Lombard pawnbrokers stored the goods of every description accepted by them as pledges for loans. Hence, later, the term *lumber* was used to describe old or discarded household articles, and the apartment of the house, often the attic, in which they were stored became known as the *lumber-room.*

meticulous. The original, and now obsolete, meaning of *meticulous* was 'fearful' or 'timid', being derived from Lat. *metus*, fear. A *meticulous* person was, therefore, one who, 'fearful' of making mistakes, examined with excessive care every little detail. Hence, 'over-careful'; 'scrupulously exact'.

mint. See MONEY.

money. One of the epithets of the Roman goddess Juno was *Moneta* [Lat. *monere*, to warn], so called because she was the 'Admonisher'. Part of the goddess's temple was chosen as a place for the minting of Roman coins and so became the *moneta* (or mint) of Rome. During the Gallic Wars the Romans introduced their coinage (*moneta*) into France to which the name *moneie* was given in O.Fr., passing into English as *money*. Both words, *money* and 'mint' (the place where it is coined), come from *moneta*.

mortgage. This is the legal term for the conveyance of property to another person in security of a loan. Though the word is compounded of Lat. *mors, mortis,* death, and Fr. *gage,* a pledge, its modern definition does not connect it in any way with *death.* Originally, however, it was born of the practice of a hard-up heir to an estate borrowing money on the security of his succession, and *pledging* to repay the loan on the *death* of his father. This *death-pledge* became the *mort-gage,* i.e. the *mortgage.*

navvy is a contraction (though with two *v*'s) of *navigator* in an old, but now obsolete, sense of a labourer employed in excavating canals, inland waterways, etc. Since these were to be used for (inland) *navigation,* the word *navigator* became associated with such work; and later, with earth-work in general. By writing the word with two *v*'s, confusion with 'navy' was avoided, and in pronunciation, the 'ah' sound was preserved.

neighbour. In rural England in olden days the name for a *neighbour* was *nigh boor,* i.e. a 'near-at-hand farmer' from O.E. *neahgebur* [*neah,* near or nigh, and *gebur,* a farmer; a dweller]. *Boor,* an early word for a peasant or farmer (cf. German *Bauer,* a peasant) has degenerated in

483

meaning though it survives in its original sense in the S. African word *Boer*, the name given to the first Dutch colonists, who were farmers.

pantry. While the modern housewife may keep pots and pans in her *pantry*, such was not the original purpose of that storeroom. From Lat. *panis*, bread, and Fr. *pain*, i t was the place where bread was kept. Similarly, the *pannier*, one of a pair of baskets carried on each side of a pack-animal, was used for carrying bread and provisions.

The *pantry*'s companion-word, *larder*, was originally a storeroom for bacon [O.Fr. *lardier*, a bacon-tub, and Mod.Fr. *lard*, bacon].

pecuniary comes from Lat. *pecunia*, which was a derivative of *pecus*, meaning 'cattle'. This is explained by the fact that in early times money or property was calculated in terms of heads of cattle which were used as a medium of exchange or barter, to be replaced in time by the coinage of later days.

pedigree. The resemblance to 'a crane's foot' of the branches of a family tree depicting genealogical descent originated in O.Fr. the phrase *pie(d) de grue* which became in 15th century English *pedegru* or *pedegrew*, giving the modern spelling *pedigree*. An alternative old spelling *petigrew* is the origin of the family named *Pettigrew*.

pen, pencil. *Pen* takes us back to the days of quills before steel nibs were invented, for it comes, through O.Fr. *penne*, from Lat. *penna*, a feather (the source of the quill). The other writing instrument, the *pencil*, had no connection with *pen* but is from O.Fr. *pincel* [Mod.Fr. *pinceau*], a painter's brush. *Pincel* was derived from Lat. *penicillus*, a brush, from *peniculus* a little tail, which was a diminutive of *penis*, a tail.

puny, meaning 'feeble' comes from O.Fr. *puis né*, i.e. 'later born' from Lat. *post natus*. It was assumed that the later born child was physically weaker than the earlier one(s) and was therefore frail.

quorum. The Latin word *quorum*, meaning 'of whom' was the first word of the written commission appointing Justices of the Peace. The document said "*quorum unum esse volumus*" (of whom we wish you to be one). Originally each J.P. was a *quorum* but later it was used for the whole body of J.P.s required to constitute a legal court. Then it came to have its present meaning of 'the number of members of a body, society, committee, etc. that must be present before business can be legally transacted'.

rigmarole, meaning 'a series of incoherent and foolish statements', 'a nonsensical string of words', is a corruption of *ragman roll*. This was an official register or roll of the names of the Scottish nobles and gentry who paid homage to Edward I of England during his passage through Scotland in 1296. The word *ragman* is of uncertain origin, but it is thought to have meant in the 13th century 'a document with many names and seals', as on a parchment scroll or papal bull. Another theory names it after *Ragimunde*, a papal legate, who had earlier in the century been sent to Scotland by the Pope to draw up a register of the Scottish Clergy.

rival and **river** are associate words, because *rivals* were originally dwellers on opposite sides of a *river*. The competing claims of both sides to water-rights, fishing-rights, etc., beginning as *rivalry*, often ended up in open conflict, especially if the *river* was the boundary between two countries, e.g. the Rhine (France and Germany) or the Tweed (England and Scotland).

rote. The source of *rote* in the phrase 'to learn by *rote*' is uncertain. Probably it comes from O.Fr. *rote*, a track [Mod.Fr. *route*] implying that the mechanical repetition of words, etc. as an aid to memorization, is a process of going

over and over again the same *route*. Lat. *rota*,
a wheel, is a conjectural derivation, introducing
the idea of going round and round, but returning always to the starting-point.

salary. It is surprising to learn that *salary* comes
from Lat. *sal*, salt, and *salarium*, a salt-allow-
ance. In ancient times, when salt was a
precious commodity, especially for preserving
meat, the Romans included it as part of the
soldiers' daily rations. This salt allowance was
called *salarium*, and even after payment in
money took the place of the salt ration, the
word was used (later as *salary*) to mean 'wages'.
Our phrase 'He is worth his salt' meaning 'He
is efficient; worth his wages or keep' is a
reminder of those days.

scot-free. The word *scot* in this phrase has no
connection with a native of Scotland. It comes
from O.N. *skot*, a tax, and was formerly a tax,
contribution, or fine, graduated according to
an individual's ability to pay. If exempted
from such a tax, a person got off *scot-free*. In
time it acquired the present-day figurative
meaning of 'unhurt' or 'safe'. *Scot* also appears
in the phrase *scot and lot*, in which *scot* is the tax
and 'lot', the amount allotted. These taxes
were parochial assessments formerly payable

by householders in certain constituencies entitling them to a parliamentary vote.

slave. The word has radically changed in meaning since the days when the *Slavonians*, a tribe of S.E. Europe, regarded themselves as a 'noble and glorious' race, for that was what *slav* signified in their language. Their land, however, was overrun by the Romans and the people were carried off to Rome, there to be held in bondage and to hear their names—*Slavi* or *Sclavi*—used by their conquerors as equivalent for 'servants'. They had become *slaves*.

taffrail. The common definition of *taffrail* as the 'hand-rail round a ship's stern' arose from confusion with *rail*. Its more correct form is *tafferel* from Dutch *tafereel*, a diminutive of *tafel*, meaning 'a picture' and from Lat. *tabula*, a board. It was originally in wooden ships, the flat part of the poop which was generally ornamented with carvings, pictures, or panels, and bore the ship's name and emblems. (The French word for *taffrail* is *tableau*, i.e. 'picture'.)

trophy comes via Fr. *trophée* from Lat. *tropaeum* and Gk. *tropaion*, all of which are derived from Gk. *trope*, a turn or turning back. A *trophy* was originally a memorial erected on the battlefield in commemoration of the 'turning back' (*trope*) or defeat of the enemy. It was formed by collecting in a huge pile the armour and standards of the vanquished. Sometimes, however, these were brought home to cities, e.g. to Rome, for display as evidence of victory or conquest. In course of time it came to denote anything taken from an enemy and preserved as a symbol of victory. From this it later acquired its modern meaning—'a memento of success or glory, in any field', e.g. stags' antlers displayed on a wall are *trophies* of the chase.

turkey. This bird was erroneously believed to have come from Turkey whereas it was an American fowl, of the pheasant family, imported into Europe in the 16th century. In those days, when people had little geographical knowledge, it was usual for them to make the East in general, and China, India, or Turkey in particular, the birthplace of any exotic import. So the new bird was called the *turkey* while the French named it *la poule d'Inde* (the Indian hen) later to be contracted to *dinde* and provided with a masculine form *dindon*.

university. The word is derived from Lat. *universitas* meaning 'all together', 'a society', 'a corporation' and *universus*, universal. It was so called because in the Middle Ages it was an educational institution organized for teaching the *universitas literarum*, i.e. the whole range of academic subjects, arts, theology, law, etc.

veto. The number of Latin words used in their original form in everyday English is very large and this is a common one. In Latin it means 'I forbid' and was the formula used by the Roman tribunes—who were the representatives of the common people—when they wished to dissent from a decree of the Senate.

villa, villain. It is fitting to treat *villa* and *villain* together since, in feudal times, they were closely connected. The Roman *villa* was a country-house and when the word came into our language in the 12th century, it was used to denote a farmhouse and its annexed buildings; later it came to mean a mansion-house or manor. The *villain* (the *villanus*) was a serf or agricultural labourer working for the owner of the *villa* and there was no implication of evil or wickedness attached to the word. Like several other 'land' words, however, e.g. 'boor' and 'churl', it deteriorated in meaning though even in Shakespeare's time it occurs in his plays in the sense of 'serf', 'bondsman', or 'servant'. It gradually degenerated to become the equivalent of an 'evil-doer'.

windfall. The accepted meaning of *windfall* (not in the metaphorical sense) is 'anything which falls down from a tree, e.g. fruit'. But originally it could also mean the tree itself, and as only the overlord had the right to cut down growing trees, fallen timber brought down by wind or storm was particularly welcome. From the fallen 'tree', therefore, and not from the fallen 'fruit', comes the metaphorical use of *windfall* as 'an unexpected gift', 'a legacy'.

yards. There are two *yards* quite unrelated to each other: (a) the measure of length, and (b) an enclosure. The *yard* of measure comes from O.E. *gerd*, a root or small stick and was originally the general word for a rod or wand. It is still used, though pleonastically, in this sense in the combination *yardstick* meaning 'a stick three feet long', or figuratively as 'a formula or standard of measurement accepted as a basis for statistical comparison'.

Again a *yard* on board a sailing-ship is a spar (i.e. a rod or stick) for supporting a sail. Nautical *yards*, therefore, are not measures of length, but 'sticks'. *Yard* as an enclosure comes from O.E. *geard*, a fence or enclosure, and etymologically belongs to the garden family. In American English the garden round a house is still called the *yard*. In the sense of an enclosed place near a building, it is used in such combinations as 'farm*yard*', 'stack*yard*', 'court*yard*', 'grave*yard*', etc.